TROUT
TACKLE
Part One

OTHER BOOKS BY ERNEST SCHWIEBERT

Matching the Hatch
Salmon of the World
Remembrances of Rivers Past
Nymphs
Trout
Death of a Riverkeeper

"Ernest Schwiebert's *Trout* is a masterpiece, the most useful and inclusive study ever written on a timeless subject noted for classical and scholarly works. Worldwide in scope, brilliantly researched, beautifully written, illustrated by the author with hundreds of drawings and color paintings, Schwiebert's *Trout* is destined to remain *the* great reference work for generations of trout fishermen to come."—A. J. McClane

"A stupendous achievement . . . unparalleled and unapproached by any writer."—Arnold Gingrich

"For several weeks I have been sampling and savoring it the way one samples and savors the contents of the pastry cart at a great French restaurant. One cannot consume every calorific delicacy at a single sitting. One cannot digest the contents of Ernest Schwiebert's 1,745-page masterpiece in a month of sittings. I suspect, indeed, that every fact known to man about trout and trout fishing can be found therein. . . . Ernest Schwiebert's *Trout* will remain a classic so long as a single trout survives in the last clear-running stream."—Les Line

"Cold numbers aside, *Trout* is a prodigious landmark in the literature of angling. It is more than a book about fishing. It is *the* book about fishing for *trout,* which means it is about insects and rocks, about rivers and fine bamboo. It is about good fellowship, sturdy adventures, and a hundred other experiences that make time worth wasting. It is about how life evolves, sustains, and ends—and it is about how life may be craftsman-copied through delicate creations of marabou, mallard, and hare. *Trout* does not mark the arrival of Ernest Schwiebert; it seals his place in the fisherman's pantheon. It retires his fly rod. For it is hard to imagine a more rigorous and loving examination of why something happens—or doesn't—when a man throws a calculation of feathers at a fish."—Lee Eisenberg

"Certain to stand as a landmark book in the history of angling literature, *Trout* is Schwiebert's crowning achievement and firmly establishes his place in the firmament of the immortals of angling."—William Kaufmann

Ernest Schwiebert has travelled the trout fishing world with his flies and paint boxes and tackle for nearly forty years. Fishing and collecting fly hatches evolved into his first book, *Matching the Hatch,* in 1955. It has been printed and reprinted more than a dozen times. His portfolio of 30 paintings titled *Salmon of the World* was published in a limited edition of 750 sets in 1970. His collection of streamside stories, *Remembrances of Rivers Past,* was published in 1972, and his major book on stream entomology, *Nymphs,* was published in 1973. Schwiebert's magnum opus is his two-volume *Trout,* from which this work is drawn. Published in 1978, fifteen years in its planning, writing, and preparation of extensive illustrations, *Trout* is nearly 1,800 pages in length, including fifteen color plates of flies and trout species and more than 1,000 black-and-white drawings and diagrams. Its first edition was sold out shortly after publication, and a second edition is planned for Fall 1984. Schwiebert's most recent book is *Death of a Riverkeeper,* which appeared in 1980. Like his earlier *Remembrances of Rivers Past,* it is a gathering of fishing stories from several countries.

Ernest Schwiebert (pronounced Schwee-bert) is an architect and planner who has played a major role in several famous projects around the world. He holds degrees from Ohio State and Princeton, where he completed both the master's program and doctoral studies in art history, as well as architecture and planning. Schwiebert practiced architecture and planning for many years with a major firm in New York. Twelve years ago, he founded the design and planning group called Ecosystemics, and has provided consulting services to the national park systems of Chile, Argentina, and the United States.

Profiles of his several careers have appeared in *The New York Times, The Washington Post,* and *The Philadelphia Inquirer,* and in *Life, Esquire,* and *Town & Country.* His two-volume *Trout* was recently honored by the White House, when it was chosen as a gift-of-state to the Prime Minister of Australia.

When not fishing or working in some remote corner of the world, Schwiebert lives and works in Princeton, New Jersey.

TROUT

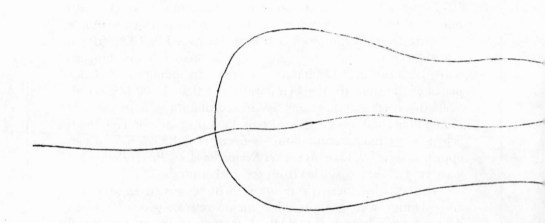

ERNEST SCHWIEBERT

Illustrated by the author

TACKLE
Part One

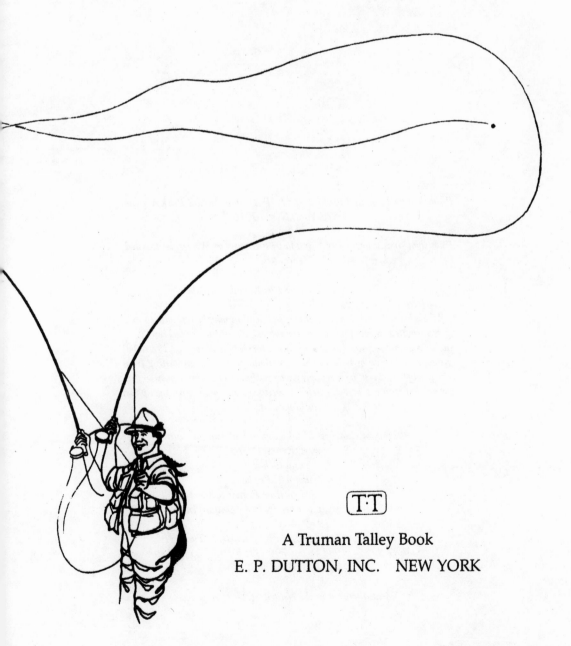

[T·T]

A Truman Talley Book

E. P. DUTTON, INC.   NEW YORK

Published by Truman Talley Books • E. P. Dutton, Inc., 2 Park Avenue,
New York, N.Y. 10016

Published simultaneously in Canada by Fitzhenry & Whiteside, Limited,
Toronto

Library of Congress Cataloging in Publication Data
Schwiebert, Ernest George.
Trout tackle.
"A Truman Talley book."
"Part one . . . is drawn from Ernest Schwiebert's
two-volume Trout, published by E. P. Dutton, Inc., in
1978"—Verso t.p.
1. Trout fishing. 2. Fishing tackle. I. Title.
SH687.S253   1983   799.1'755   83-14190
ISBN: 0-525-48082-X

Manufactured in the United States of America

10 9 8 7 6 5 4 3 2 1

CONTENTS

TROUT
TACKLE
Part One

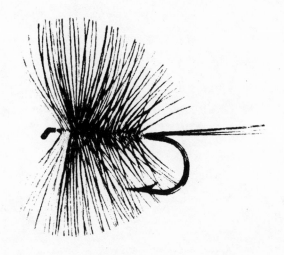

1. The Theory and Practice of Modern Fly Dressing

The flies were exquisitely tied on fine British hooks with gleaming hackles and woodduck wings, and in other drawers there were north-country patterns that glittered with tinsel and junglecock eyes and exotic brightly colored feathers like kingfisher and blue chatterer and macaw. The flies filled their trays by the thousands, and I stood looking at them, pattern by pattern, on that boyhood afternoon, with a sense of awe.

Finely tied flies have always held a fascination for trout fishermen, since their patterns have an elegance and delicate quality and tradition found in no other sport.

The polished mahogany fly chests at Von Lengerke & Antoine in Chicago were a revelation, with drawer after drawer of meticulous dressings smelling faintly of moth crystals. My excitement was so great that my father bought me several dozen patterns, and I examined them for days under my study-table lamp, marvelling at their precision, sense of proportion, and the quality of their materials. It was then that I really determined to learn to tie flies. Fly-tying catalogues began arriving in the mails, and I soon decided to meet some really skilled fly dressers. My first exposure to professional tiers came the following summer, when we travelled north to fish the Michigan rivers.

Our fly-fishing in those early years was often concentrated on the famous trout streams around Baldwin. It was my father who discovered that Harry Duffing tied flies professionally in his barber shop on the dusty main street. Sometimes we stopped to ask him about fly hatches on nearby streams, particularly when the big *Hexagenia* drakes were emerging at twilight in early summer. Sometimes we even went in for unnecessary haircuts to get to know him better—the price was only thirty-five cents in the years after the Depression—and finally Duffing let me see his tying table and equipment and the materials he used in his famous Michigan night-fishing patterns.

There were other famous fly tiers in the years that followed, like Arthur Kade in Sheboygan, where we always stopped on our way north to fish the Brule and Namekagon and Wolf in Wisconsin. Art Winnie tied his caddis patterns and Michigan hoppers at Traverse City, and there were many hours spent with Len Halliday at his cluttered workbench where the spent-wing Adams was born a full fifteen years before I first fished the Boardman. Those were sunlit years in spite of the Great Depression, and few men could smell the growing winds of war.

It was not until after the Second World War that I met William Blades, one of the finest fly dressers who ever lived. It was a complete accident that came about after attending a competition of the North Shore Casting Club in Chicago. There was a young girl casting in the dry-fly accuracy event, and her final score placed second.

That's strange, my father said suddenly. *I believe that girl is in one of my classes at the university!*

Let's try to meet her, I suggested.

The girl caster was the daughter of the famous Frank Steel, the first man ever to make a perfect score in dry-fly accuracy in actual tournament competition. Steel was one of the pioneers who developed our modern arm-casting techniques, not only for distance work but also for working with precision at distances under sixty-five feet. It was a controlled style of casting with a closed wrist. His daughter introduced us to Steel that evening, and when he found we lived in Winnetka, we were invited to the weekly casting sessions held during the winter in the gymnasium at New Trier High School.

It was a distinguished group of casters, with roots dating back to the years when Fred Peet and Call McCarthy dominated the American tournament casting circuit. Fred Peet first became National Casting Champion in 1909, and had won fourteen casting titles before the First World War. Call McCarthy came from Ireland, from a family of Irish river keepers and fly dressers. His titles included three American national championships between 1914 and his tragic death in 1921, not long after he had successfully defended his title. At the time we met him, shortly after the Second World War, Frank Steel was a worthy heir to that tradition of great Chicago tournament casters, and William Blades was the unchallenged court wizard with a fly vise.

Blades did not publish his remarkable *Fishing Flies and Fly Tying* until many years later, but he was already a legend in the trout country of Michigan and Wisconsin. For some reason, he adopted me through two winters while he cajoled and criticized and coaxed me into tying better flies. Blades was a difficult and demanding teacher. His lectures about proportions and tapered fur bodies and the proper winding of hackles were all delivered with bulging eyes and a reedy intensity of voice; the echoes and admonitions still ring naggingly in my mind more than twenty-five years later. Blades accepted nothing short of perfection, and although I never really became such a complete disciple that I tied only his extended-body mayfly dressings and nymphs with moose-mane legs, his uncompromising proportions and standards are still part of my yardstick when I look at flies today.

Fly dressing has a long tradition reaching deep into the history of fishing itself. The hook is certainly among the oldest tools, and probably evolved from the gorge shortly before primitive metallurgy emerged some 7,000 years ago. The gorge was a piece of stone, antler, shell, or bone. It was sharpened at both ends and attached to the line at its middle. The bait was used to hold a gorge parallel to the line, so that a fish might swallow it easily and unsuspectingly. Once the bait had been ingested by the fish, tightening the line turned the gorge crosswise in its gullet. Primitive hooks of fish bone appeared in Neolithic times, probably in the cultures evolving between Egypt and Turkey, just on the threshold of later metalworking civilizations.

Artifacts of stone were still being polished and ground, but some primitive smiths were already working with copper and iron. Archaeology clearly reveals that the first metal fishhooks were made of copper, and more than ten centuries would pass before the combination of copper and tin produced an alloy that proved strong and easy to work. Bronze marked the beginnings of new civilizations, particularly on Crete and throughout the Mediterranean. Bronze hooks with barbed points and needlelike eyes in their flattened shanks are known to have come from Crete more than 5,000 years ago. Fishhooks fashioned of bronze are also known to have appeared in China about a thousand years later, and gold hooks are recorded together with lines of silk and bamboo rods in *The Book of Odes* written about 3,000 years ago. The first artificial flies apparently evolved before the *Chuh Tzu* manuscripts, slightly more than 2,000 years back into the prehistory of China. Such flies were dressed with pheasant and kingfisher feathers on delicate hooks of gold.

Ironworking probably emerged in Egypt about 4,000 years ago, and had already spread into southern Europe centuries before the Christian epoch. The precise origins of steel remain unclear, although such metallurgy already existed from Damascus to Toledo when fly-fishing first developed in Macedonia during the third century.

Modern hooks probably evolved in Europe approximately seven centuries ago, although the industrial production of hooks can be traced to London in the seventeenth century. Its evolution coincides with the rise of needlemaking there, and perhaps the most famous early manufacturer of hooks and needles was the celebrated Charles Kirby. His firm was already well known for its fishhooks when Walton published *The Compleat Angler* in 1653. Kirby greatly improved the tempering and hardening of his steel. His Kirby hook pattern is still copied across the world, and his methods of hookmaking provide the basis for hook manufacturing in our time.

The plague that decimated the population of London was followed by terrible fires in 1666, and the hookmaking industry was scattered across England. Almost a century passed before it had gathered again at Redditch in Worcestershire, where both needles and clothing hooks were made. Another century found all of the world's hookmaking centered in Worcestershire, and the quality of the hooks made by manufacturers like Allcock, Farlow, Bartlett, and Sealey has never been surpassed. Their absolute dominance of the industry would last almost 150 years, although the subsequent growth of Mustad in Oslo, after its founding in 1832, was a prelude to the decline of British dominance in hookmaking. Today Viellard-Migeon also makes a fine line of fly-dressing hooks in France—both wet-fly and dry-fly designs in a full range of sizes.

Fishhooks were not high among the industrial priorities of the British Government during the Second World War, and the Attlee Government placed no importance on reviving the industry. The British hookmakers were ordered to concentrate on needles, and British hooks were no longer available in good numbers. Mustad rapidly filled the vacuum in the postwar fishing world, and now thoroughly dominates the trade, in spite of hook manufacturing in Japan, France, and the United States.

Although fishhooks were made almost entirely by hand until surprisingly recent times, modern hooks are made completely by factory methods. Only the most expensive fly-tying hooks are still partially made with hand methods, particularly in the small trout sizes. Our hooks are formed of eighty to eight-five percent fine carbon steel. It is cut into precise lengths of the proper diameter for each hook size. Both ends are ground to fine points and the wire is cut in the middle, forming two separate hooks in a single operation. Machines taper the wire slightly and shape the eye, and form the point into the proper bend. The barbs are sometimes cut by hand and the points on the best hooks are often hand-sharpened slightly. The eyes are left ringed, and turned up or down according to their type. The hook bends are then forged slightly flat. Although the hook is fully shaped, its wire is still untempered enough for fishing. Heat treatments are applied to harden and temper the unfinished ones. Such heating leaves them covered with a coarse scale that is ultimately removed by tumbling them in abrasives. Scouring is followed with a bronzed finish. Counting, inspection, and packaging complete the typical hookmaking process.

The character and quality of hooks are absolutely critical to making flies that will fish well and imitate natural prototypes. Beautifully tied flies on poor hooks are virtually worthless. Hook character and quality start with wire diameters and sizes, and each hook size requires a different wire. The wire diameter of hooks is designated in terms of its X-rating and the terms Stout or Fine. Hooks that are labelled 1X Fine are formed of wire usually found in hooks a size smaller, and 2X Fine hooks have the wire diameter of hooks two sizes smaller. Hooks are seldom manufactured in wire sizes smaller than 3X Fine, like the Mustad 94833, although Orvis is marketing an excellent 4X Fine hook manufactured in England to its own

Mustad 94840

light-wire specifications. Such fine-wire hooks are intended primarily for fine leaders under three-pound test and dry flies, although emerging nymphs fished in the film also demand light-wire types. Heavy-wire types are labelled in a reverse progression. Hooks marked 1X Stout have been shaped with wire normally used in the next larger size, and a 2X Stout hook is twice as heavy as normal hooks of that size. Wire diameters heavier than 4X Stout are rarely made, and are usually found in salt-water and steelhead hooks.

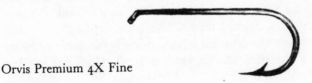

Orvis Premium 4X Fine

Wire temper and hardness are important too. Heavy hooks are strongly made and hook well, but are obviously unsuited for imitations intended to float or fish awash in the film. Light-wire hooks that bend and spring sometimes work themselves free, although their sharpness tends to penetrate the jaw membranes easily and hook well. Some light-wire hooks are too brittle and break with the slightest strain, while others have too soft a temper and spread open when a fish is hooked. It is important to fish a delicate tippet with extremely light-wire hooks. Obviously the perfect hook is not so brittle that it breaks easily, and not so soft that its gap opens under bending strain.

Mustad 3906

Although it is often alleged on trout water, few hooks are actually broken in fish. They are usually broken on the stones or ledges behind a fisherman when his backcast drops too low or when a working cast ticks the fly into the flexing rod. Any fish that subsequently takes is quickly lost, and when inspection reveals a broken hook, the fault probably lies in sloppy casting. If you often find broken hooks, the remedy undoubtedly lies in your backcast and not in the quality of your hooks.

Mustad 94720

Hook shanks are also rated in terms of X-numbers, with the supplemental description of Short or Long. Such coding means a hook labelled 1X Long is made with a shank length normally found in hooks one size larger. Hooks 2X Long and 3X Long have shanks twice and three times as long as standard lengths in their size. Such extra long hooks are seldom found with shank lengths exceeding the Mustad 94720, with its 8X Long specifications. Moderately long hooks are commonly used for nymphs requiring a slender silhouette, and the extra long types are used for streamers. Fly-tying hooks are also manufactured in short-shank designs. Spiders and variants are often dressed on 4X Short hooks like the Mustad 94825 or 5X Short types like the Mustad 95235. Such hooks have reduced shank lengths, four and five sizes shorter than normal. Hook shanks less than 9X Short are seldom made.

Mustad 94825

Hook eyes found in typical trout flies are either turned up or turned down, and are finished in three basic ways. The ball eye is formed without any deviation from the wire diameter of the hook shank. It is usually found in rather inexpensive hooks for nymphs, wet flies, and streamers. The tapered eye is shaped with a gradually reduced wire diameter slightly behind its ring and in the eye itself, and is commonly used for dry flies and the more expensive grades of sunk patterns. Loop-eye hooks are most typically found in salmon flies, for both their strength and the smoothness of their eyes. The loop eye is formed with a finely tapered eye looped back and laid along the shank. It is used extensively in trout fishing for big nymphs and streamers on designs like the Mustad 9575, a superb Limerick style hook with a 6X Long shank.

Mustad 9575

Hook sizes are not measured in terms of their overall configuration, but by the dimension of their gaps. Hook gap is measured from the point to the shank in a vertical line, while the throat of the hook is measured from its point to the inside of its bend. The shank is the relatively straight shaft between the bend and the eye. Hook points are measured from the barb slice to the apex itself.

Hook points in trout fishing are commonly found in four basic styles. Spear points are relatively inexpensive to manufacture, lack the quality of quick penetration, and are not often used for first-grade flies. Needle points are hand polished, have excellent hooking qualities, and are relatively expensive. Most well-tied flies are dressed upon hollow-point-style hooks. Such points are designed for excellent penetration and hooking, and are called hollow because they are sharpened into a convex curve between the tip of the barb and the apex of the point. Barbless hooks are made both without barbs or kinked points which do not tear the jaw membranes when they are worked out, and since the Mustad 94845 has been made in sizes twelve through twenty-two, it has become quite popular. However, hollow points are the most popular.

Mustad 94845

Hook styles are the Bartlett-type sneck bend, the Limerick-type bend, the sproat-style bend, and the round or Model Perfect design. Few flies tied on American waters still employ the sneck-type hooks, although the other three types are relatively common. Sproat- and Limerick-style hooks are used primarily for wet flies, bucktails, and streamers. Most dry flies are tied on round or Model Perfect bends, since they offer optimal strength in the light-wire hooks designed for high-floating performance. Turned-up and turned-down eyes are also a factor in both function and style. It is doubtful that any measurable difference in hooking qualities exists between turned-up and turned-down eyes in normal sizes, but in sizes below eighteen or twenty, the turned-up eyes offer a completely open hook gap that is free of the eye itself. Some flies are more easily constructed on down-eye hooks and are usually dressed on them in spite of their small sizes. Since my boyhood years and the elegant Hardy flies my father sometimes bought, such patterns dressed on turned-up eyes have always been my yardstick for esthetic perfection—particularly in the imitations of mayflies and sedges.

The scale of hook sizes is rather unusual. Trout and salmon flies are tied on the sizes above and below number one at the middle of the scale. The smaller sizes are manufactured in standard numbers from two to twenty-eight, with hook size decreasing as the numerical designation increases. Larger sizes work upward from 1/0 to 9/0 irons, and flies as large as 3/0 are sometimes used on big trout in heavy-water tactics.

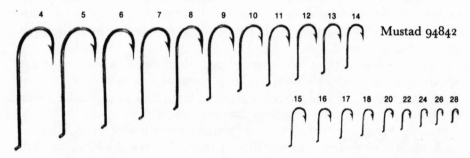

Mustad 94842

Modern flies can be traced back along a conscious line of evolution and lineage since the *Treatyse of Fysshynge wyth an Angle* in the middle of the fifteenth century. The primitive dressings prescribed in Berners included a hackleless version of the British March Brown, and several soft-hackled patterns of partridge and grouse. Simple down-winged wet flies had their literary genesis in the *Treatyse*, although it was Charles Cotton who elevated such dressings to the level of art in *Being Instructions on How to Angle for a Trout or Grayling in a Clear Stream*, which was published as an appendix to the edition of *The Compleat Angler* that appeared in 1676. Superb fly dressers and

Stewart Wet Fly

fishermen like Bowlker and Chetham rallied the faithful during the century that followed, and the modern wet fly was fully evolved a full quarter century before Alfred Ronalds published his *Fly-Fisher's Entomology* in 1836. Stewart revived the soft-hackled border patterns on the Whitadder in Scotland at midcentury, and except for the hairwings that first evolved in Canada and the United States before 1900, the wet-fly method was complete.

Hampshire Wet Fly

However, there were surprising regional variations in style throughout the British Isles. The relatively sparse flies described in the *Treatyse* had dominated English fly dressing for two centuries by the time Charles Cotton mentions the differences in styles found on the streams near London and his own Derbyshire flies. Typical Hampshire wet flies were dressed with slender tails imitative of mayfly spinners, roughly dubbed bodies, rather full hackles, and generous wings of duck quill sections set at about forty-five degrees. The basic wet-fly wing is fashioned with both conventional- and reversed-wing styles, setting the paired wing-quill sections both on top of the hook and at its sides. These variations result in four distinct configurations of wet-fly winging techniques. Such flies still dominate the American wet-fly school.

Cotton fished flies of totally different proportions and style. Their tails were less dramatic in length, suggestive of freshly hatched mayflies. Although their bodies were rather fully dubbed, they were relatively short, and the hackles were quite sparse. Their slender wings were shaped from duck quill sections and set quite high, at an angle of eighty to eighty-five degrees. Such flies would sink readily, breathing with both their hackles and wings when retrieved, offering a completely different silhouette and

Derbyshire Wet Fly

behavior in the water. Wingless flies are still popular fished wet on the rivers of Yorkshire and Devonshire. The Yorkshire style has slender bodies that utilize only sixty percent of the hook, extremely long hackle fibers sparsely dressed, and no tail filaments. Devonshire hackle wets are more fully dressed, with tail fibers, fully dubbed bodies, and heavily tied hackling. Fly dressers on the Teme evolved rather long-tailed patterns with fat bodies, relatively full wings laid back at about thirty degrees, and sparse hackles. Kilbreda dressings from Ireland in the eighteenth century were often tied with a sparse rolled wing, no throat hackles, rather elegantly dubbed bodies mixed with a few guard hairs at the wing, and delicate tails. Such Irish flies had their wings laid back at a thirty-degree angle over their bodies. Similar flies evolved on the Tweed in Scotland, except that their bodies used only half of the shank length, and their wings were virtually upright and divided like the dry-fly wings that evolved in Hampshire before the middle of the nineteenth century. Wet flies dressed on the Usk had slender bodies, divided wings with their concave sides set together and low over the hook, and sparse hen hackles. Usk patterns were tied without tails. Remarkably sparse wet flies also evolved on the Tummel and Clyde, their slender wings set slightly forward of the vertical. Tummel dressings displayed delicate dubbed fur bodies that commonly occupied less than half

Usk Wet Fly

of the hook shank, and hackles proportioned slightly smaller than conventional hook sizes would dictate. Clyde-style patterns had proportionately longer bodies and hackles.

Such variations in style are interesting when they are studied for parallels in stream entomology. These patterns are all dressed with slate-colored wings and dun hackles and bodies dubbed from a hare's mask, except for the Yorkshire and Devonshire types that omit the wings. Each is a regional version of the classic Blue Dun.

However, wet flies in a larger sense are dressed to imitate drowned aquatic insects and terrestrials, as well as some species that emerge or lay their eggs under water. Strictly speaking, the Blue Dun is tied to suggest

Tweed Wet Fly

any number of small mouse-colored mayflies in many sizes from twelve to twenty-eight. Yet these patterns are tied both with and without wings, and several omit the tail fibers. Clearly the winged and tailed flies popular on rivers like the Itchen and the Teme are mayfly imitations, and the exaggerated length of their tails suggests that, when they are dressed on small hooks, they are intended to simulate drowned spinners or *Baetis* flies that lay their eggs under water. The Derbyshire pattern, with its sparse wings and hackles and short tail, is obviously intended as a hatching mayfly dun. So is the heavily hackled Devonshire style, but the Yorkshire hackle

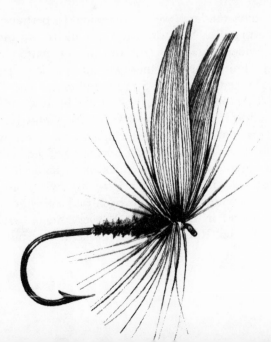

Clyde Wet Fly

Tummel Wet Fly

version is tied without wings or tails, and is perhaps better suited to imitating a hatching caddis pupa. The down-wing patterns typical on the Usk water are also dressed without tails, and from their proportions are superb imitations of either a drowned sedge or caddis that goes beneath the surface to lay its eggs. Although they are also dressed without tails, the upright wings on the wet flies of the Tweed, Clyde, and Tummel suggest that they are intended as mayfly patterns. Perhaps they were dressed to imitate a hatching dun, its wings working free of the epicuticle, while its legs and tail are still tangled in the membrane, its silhouette lost in the splitting nymphal skin.

However, the standard wet-fly dressing is perhaps too much an imitation of the mayflies, both drowned specimens and those genera that lay their eggs under water. Several rolled-wing patterns with tails are excellent stonefly imitations, and there are many sedge-type flies that have been fished wet for centuries. Paul Stroud used to monitor fly production at Von Lengerke & Antoine in my early years in Chicago, and he insisted that wet flies were caddis imitations. For that reason, his fly drawers were filled with wet patterns that were not just conventional down-wing styles, but literally placed the wing sections along both sides of the body, like an adult sedge. Modern vinyl-type feather lacquers have made it feasible to dress really durable stonefly imitations in a flat-wing style. Some version of the palmer-tied wet fly without wings has been tied since the time of Berners' *Treatyse*, and is found in the fly lists of every major writer of the four centuries that followed. Ronalds included several caterpillar imitations in

Idaho Hairwing

his *Fly-Fisher's Entomology*, and palmer-tied wets that imitate beetle larvae are popular on many waters. Hair-wing wet flies evolved almost a century ago on the Henry's Fork of the Snake in Idaho, and are found tied in both down-wing and flat-wing styles. Typical flat-wing wet flies tied with hair are the several big stonefly imitations popular on many western rivers, and there are also a number of down-wing caddis-style flies that have evolved in recent years on the Pacific Coast. Hair-hackle wet flies also evolved in the fly vises of western anglers, particularly Franz Potts and the incredibly creative George Grant in Montana.

There are a number of wet-fly dressings designed to imitate terrestrials, dating back to the fifteenth century patterns, in both the *Treatyse* and the fly lists of Charles Cotton. Patterns like the Cowdung, Sawfly, Hawthorn fly, Marchfly, Oak fly, Soldier fly, Bottle fly, and Marlow Buzz were common in 1800. There are even wet-fly imitations of leafhoppers in the Ronalds *Entomology*, and patterns tied to suggest wasps, bees, beetles, and ants are centuries old. The modern lacquer-body ants, both with and without wings,

McCafferty Ant

undoubtedly evolved in the fly vises of many anglers—although history credits the late Bob McCafferty with their invention on the famous limestone streams of Pennsylvania more than a half century ago.

Wet flies reigned alone through the first two millenniums of fly-fishing history, although a number of angling writers discussed dapping and fishing their wet flies in the surface film. The precise origins of the dry-fly style are unknown, except that its genesis clearly lies on the smooth, fly-rich currents of the Wiltshire and Hampshire chalkstreams. It is logical that the beginnings were found on such waters. Wet flies would float on relatively windless days, and the rich palette of fly hatches on these rivers led naturally to large numbers of surface-feeding trout.

History tells us that legendary fly dressers like James Ogden of Cheltenham were making dry flies as early as 1840, about the time that George Pulman published his first edition of *The Vade Mecum of Fly-Fishing for Trout*, the book that introduced the dry-fly method in print. Such flies

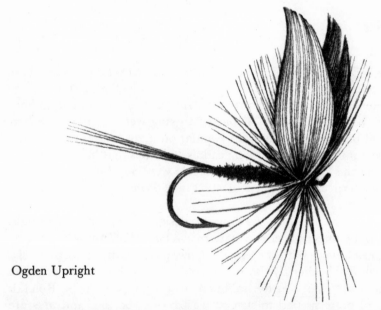

Ogden Upright

were already well known in England at midcentury to have Wilfred Foster of Ashbourne supplying upright-wing dry flies for the trade as early as 1854, which proves that the theory and technique had reached the Dove, Derwent, and Manifold in Derbyshire. Stoddart also describes using the dry fly on Scottish rivers as early as 1853, in his second edition of *The Angler's Companion*, unquestionably demonstrating that dry-fly theory had journeyed completely northward throughout Britain.

History also demonstrates that the divided-wing upright and fan-wing styles of dressing evolved quite early. James Ogden credits himself with both types in his book titled *On Fly Tying*, which was published in 1879. No evidence to discredit his claims is found anywhere in the literature of angling. His elegant divided-wing uprights were tied with double thicknesses of duck-wing-quill sections laid back-to-back, imitating the upright wings of a floating mayfly dun. Their two hackles were wound on both sides of these gracefully cocked wings, holding them securely in their upright position. Slender bodies and tails completed the mayfly imagery. Palmer-tied uprights also evolved before 1850, and although many patterns were dressed with tails, such flies are most effective as imitations of fluttering sedges. The sheen and density of their hackles, the dark silhouette of their duck-quill wings, and their performance during Trichoptera hatches and egg-laying swarms all point to their role as caddisfly patterns. Local styles involving reverse-wing and forward-wing dressings also evolved on many rivers, for both mayfly and sedge imitations.

Ogden also developed the fan-wing dressing to imitate the large *Ephemera* drakes that hatch on the lakes and slow-flowing rivers of the British Isles in early summer. His elegant patterns can still be studied if you have access to a copy of Aldam's *Quaint Treatyse on Flees and Artificial Flee*

Ogden Fanwing

Making, which includes both the actual fan-wing drakes tied by Ogden and their materials. Fan wings are designed to suggest the large, delicately mottled wings of big mayfly duns and spinners, and their lineage is more than a century old since their genesis on the Derbyshire Wye.

Sedge-type dry-fly dressings with their down-wings also evolved in the eighteenth century. Such flies have their roots in palmer-tied down-wing wet flies, like those painted in the several books on fly hatches and their imitations that were published shortly after 1800. Ronalds included such caddis patterns as the Sand fly, Grannom, Cinnamon Sedge, and Red

Cinnamon Sedge

Sedge in his *Fly-Fisher's Entomology*, and the transition to similar palmer-tied flies dressed with dry-fly quality hackles is logical. Before the close of the century similar down-wing caddis imitations like the Giant Red Sedge, Cinnamon Sedge, Black Silverhorns, Caperer, and Welshman's Button all evolved on British trout streams.

Extended- or detached-body imitations of large mayflies were also common before 1900, and Frederic Halford included such flies in his fly lists. These early detached bodies were tied on stiff cores of silkworm gut, and the late William Blades, who was a primary American advocate of such fly patterns, regularly used foundations of hard nylon. Detached bodies of cork and buoyant hair are also found on some rivers, and extended bodies of hair are popular in the West for imitating larger mayflies. Soft adhesive rubber was briefly popular for translucent mayfly-type bodies, but it was a short-lived material that soon became tacky and discolored, and is seldom used today. I first learned the nylon-core extension system from Blades himself, not long after the Second World War, and later stumbled on a surprisingly easy method of tying detached bodies in 1956.

It was during the years when I was part of the government agency established to design and build the United States Air Force Academy. One morning when I stopped to visit a contractor on the Cadet Quarters Complex, I found a spool of delicate .008 stainless music wire on his desk and asked him about it. Stainless music wire is available in a number of finer sizes down to .0025, and I was immediately intrigued with its potential as the core for detached fly bodies. My first experiments worked in the standard Blades method, tying the wire to the hook shank with heavily waxed silk, cutting it to proper length, fastening in the tail fibers, and constructing the body conventionally. Such flies were the best detached-body flies I had ever seen, but they were still extremely difficult to tie. It was easier when I began leaving the wire foundation long enough to hold it

Schwiebert Drake

taut with my left hand, and not trimming it off at the base of the tails until the fly was completed.

One afternoon in the winter months I happened to glance at two fly vises lying on my work table, and suddenly thought about a surprisingly simple method of making a detached-type body on a delicate wire core. Quickly I mounted both vises on the table, jaws facing each other, and stretched six inches of wire between them. The wire was quickly wound with working thread at the proper length, the tails were tied in, and a dubbed body was wrapped over the waxed base. Both body and tails were prefabricated on the tautly stretched wire, and suddenly I realized that there was room to tie three or four more sets of bodies and tails on the same core. The wire was released from the vise and the prefabricated fly bodies lay in a circular coil. It was easy to cut them free from the coil, trimming the wire precisely at the tails and leaving some seating length at the opposite end. The seating length was then wrapped firmly to the hook shank, its free end projecting beyond the hook eye, and then bent back and tightly wrapped with working silk. The wire remains flexible and springy underneath the fully dressed body, and such music wire cores are a superb method for making a detached body. The wings and hackles are then dressed conventionally, concealing the hook perfectly.

In recent years I have been experimenting with a remarkable British hook that has just appeared on the American market, and it achieves the same balance and silhouette as the mayfly imitations I developed with music wire cores almost twenty-odd years ago. The new Yorkshire

Fly-body Hook

extended-body hooks are much easier to use in dressing such flies; they can be seated with the extended shank projecting out for the bodies and tails and reversed with the hook eye projecting in the conventional manner to complete the pattern. The hooks are like all creative ideas—deceptively simple once someone conceives them—and consist of a single wire forming both the body core and a short shank hook which lies in the finished hackles. The structure and silhouette of these new flies is remarkably lifelike, and I have found them singularly effective on difficult and selective fish throughout the United States.

During the heavy *Ephemerella* hatches on the Au Sable in Michigan this past spring, we were dressing flies long after midnight at the Averill place on the Whippoorwill water downstream from Stephan's Bridge. The fish are picky there, having been caught and released regularly during the first week of the season, and we turned to the Yorkshire-style hooks in desperation. Walter Averill was also dressing flies, while Don Phillips and Arthur Neumann offered a stream of criticism and sardonic advice. The Yorkshire-style hooks were unknown to them, and they were greeted with excitement.

They're really something! Walter Averill marvelled. *Now why didn't we think of them first?*

We dressed our imitations with full hackles in the thorax style and parachute style for the swifter currents below Black Bend and the Recreation Club water, and there were also a few no-hackle versions tied for the Whippoorwill Stretch. The flies were a remarkable success, particularly on fish that refused conventionally tied imitations.

Fly-body Drake

In *Modern Dry-Fly Code* Vincent Marinaro describes another type of detached-body mayfly imitation using natural and dyed porcupine quills to suggest the almost translucent bodies of spent Ephemeroptera once their eggs are laid. Marinaro dresses his porcupine-quill imitations without wings, simply trimming their hackles out above and below the hook to create the illusion of spent wings, in a structure suggested earlier in the

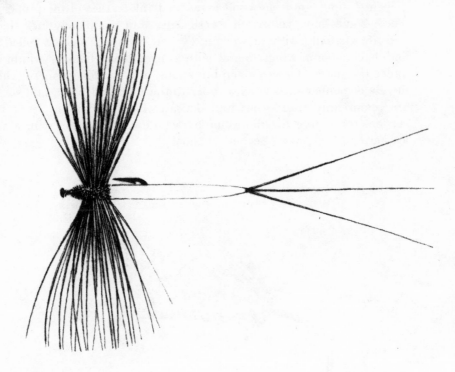

Marinaro Porcupine Spinner

works of British thinkers like Mottram, Dunne, and Colonel Harding. Such Marinaro spinners are elegant and original patterns.

Another interesting method of imitating the translucent bodies of mayflies is the Darbee extended-feather technique, which was developed by Catskill tier Harry Darbee and has grown popular with a number of fine American fly dressers. It is used widely on the difficult western spring creeks, with considerable success on their selective rainbows and browns. The feather-body dressings are the essence of simplicity itself, shaping the

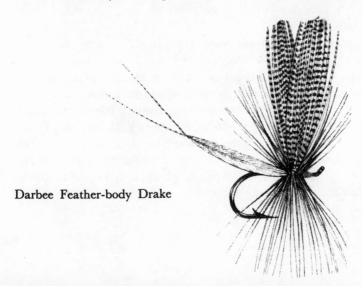

Darbee Feather-body Drake

detached silhouette from a soft breast or flank feather of the proper color. These bodies have color and translucency, but completely lack thickness and are virtually without weight. Typical dressings include rolled wings and hackle-point wings, along with conventional hackles trimmed out under the thorax for subimago imitations, and flat for spinners. Tails are merely cemented with vinyl lacquer to the extended body, and such flies are remarkably translucent and delicate. Poul Jorgenson ties a hybrid version, combining the thorax or parachute configuration with a shaped feather body extending beyond the hook.

Holberton Reverse-style Wet Fly

Wakeman Holberton was granted a patent for a reverse-tie wet fly in 1886, in the normal down-wing style. It was believed that such a dressing would cast with less atmospheric friction and that its wings and hackles would flutter when retrieved. Reverse-tied floating flies are also found on some American streams, with the theory that full dry-fly hackling conceals the hook. Such dry flies are currently popular on the Nantahala in the mountains of North Carolina.

Spent-wing spinner imitations evolved on British rivers late in the nineteenth century, possibly in the talented hands of innovators like William Lunn, the famous riverkeeper of the Houghton Club on the Test. Lunn worked out a number of excellent spent-wing imitations, particularly the Sherry Spinner, Houghton Ruby, and the Lunn's Particular. Large spinner patterns, like the spent stages of big *Ephemera* drakes on the British chalkstreams and Irish limestone lakes, are often imitated with four hackle points tied spent to suggest their large wings. Perhaps the most popular American spent-wing pattern is the Adams, which is typically successful during caddis hatches and mating swarms in spite of its tails. Its hackle

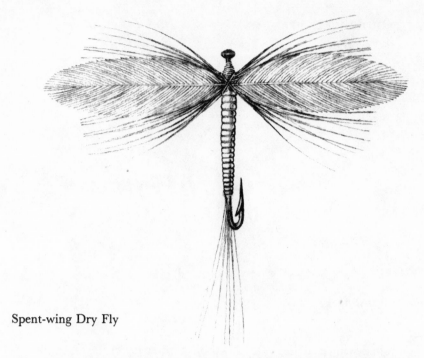

Spent-wing Dry Fly

color-mix and silhouette suggest a fluttering sedge. Several regional patterns like the Woodruff and Whitcraft are similar American spent-wing flies, but most spent dressings are intended to imitate mayflies.

Split-wing flies tied with hackle points tied flat and trailing at thirty to forty-five degrees were developed to suggest such insects as flying ants, saw-flies, midges, soldier flies, oak flies, gnats, marchflies, and several kinds of winged beetles. Some fly tiers have also tied small stonefly imitations with split-wing dressings to imitate the fluttering split-winged Plecoptera of early spring. Sail-wing dressings are not common in modern trout flies, although sail-wing flies were typical in the early history of fly-fishing. The locally famous Madsen pattern is a palmer-tied sail-wing popular on the Au Sable in Michigan, and was first tied by the late Earl Madsen, who guided fishermen below Grayling.

Sail-wing Dry Fly

Gordon Rolled-wing Dry Fly

The rolled-wing dry flies achieved their popularity in the Catskills late in the nineteenth century, and the technique perhaps originated with Theodore Gordon on the Neversink. Gordon dressed several early Catskill patterns with single rolled-wings of woodduck, tied upright in a single bunch like the wings of a mayfly held closely together. Both the yellow-bodied Gordon and the classic Gordon Quill had such wide influence that Gordon himself became the lone wellspring of the Catskill school. It subsequently included such famous tiers as Roy Steenrod, Herman Christian, Reuben Cross, and William Chandler in the generation that followed Gordon, and their skilled fingers were responsible for rolled-wing patterns like the Hendrickson and Light Cahill. Living members of the Catskill school include Walter Dette and Harry Darbee, who live along the Willowemoc above its junction with the Beaverkill, and Art Flick on the Schoharie. Preston Jennings and John Atherton are both dead now but their works, *A Book of Trout Flies* and *The Fly and the Fish*, are still with us, helping to codify the theory and practice of the Catskill school. Fly patterns like the March Brown and Gray Fox are original with Jennings, and the Red Quill was developed by his protégé Art Flick. Both the Light and Dark Cahills, as well as the Light and Dark Hendricksons, are typical Catskill dressings too.

Such rolled-wing flies of woodduck and mallard flank have evolved into divided-wing dressings since Gordon and Steenrod, who was Gordon's principal disciple. Bergman described such a divided rolled-wing dressing in *Trout*, with a series of step-by-step photographs in the making of a Cahill pattern. Rolled spent-wings of woodduck and mallard are also found on some watersheds. Such divided-wing flies are typical of the modern Catskill school, and are a significant American contribution to the history of fly dressing.

Cross Rolled-wing Dry Fly

Variant-type flies originated on the rivers of Yorkshire in 1875, where sparse wet flies had always been tied, and it is logical that dry flies with exaggeratedly long hackle fibers should evolve there. Doctor William Baigent originated the variant-style dry fly, and evolved a series of twelve patterns that became known commercially as Refracta flies. Baigent believed that the shiny fibers of his long gamecock hackles created the illusion of fluttering life, as well as floating his flies easily on relatively swift currents. The Refracta series mixed hackle colors, or used badger and furnace hackles. The dark colors were intended to suggest the legs, and the longer fibers created both the illusion of fluttering and a distorted refraction in the surface film that could deceive a selective fish. Baigent's flies included four spinner imitations and eight variants of different subimago patterns. His flies included the basic insect colors found on British rivers, and I can remember the baskets of heavy trout we took in my Colorado boyhood summers after the Second World War, using exquisite Baigent Red Variants that arrived in elegant little Hardy boxes.

Baigent variants were conventional flies with upright divided wings, bodies, tails, and hackles of exaggerated-length fibers. Bergman advocated multicolor variants, long-hackled patterns dressed of radically different hackle colors that originated with Albert Barrell on the Housatonic at Pittsfield. Bergman defined the variant-type fly as having long hackle fibers, tails, foreshortened bodies, and slightly undersized wings. His definition has not survived past midcentury, however, since Flick patterns like the Gray Fox and Dun Variants completely omit wings, and famous western dressings like the Donnelly Dark and Donnelly Light Variants have rather long hackle-point wings. These western flies are the work of Roy Donnelly, who lives on the Pacific Coast and developed his Variants in the Jackson Hole country of Wyoming. The late Bob Carmichael, who

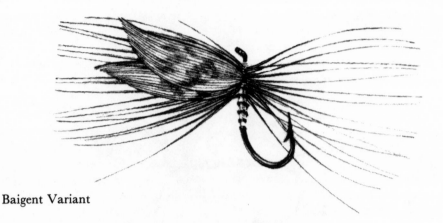

Baigent Variant

operated a famous tackle shop at Moose Crossing in the halcyon Wyoming days after the Second World War, used to rate the two Donnelly Variants essential flies for any western dry-fly man.

Donnelly developed his Variants in Jackson Hole fishing with us, Carmichael explained the summer before his death. *But the credit for them is entirely his—they're a little like the Dark and Light Cahills for you boys back east.*

They're that good? I asked.

Bet your sweet ass! Carmichael grumbled happily. *Wouldn't step into the Snake or Gros Ventre without them!*

Carmichael was right about his Donnelly variants.

Such flies have superb floating qualities for their hook sizes, and it is understandable that they would prove popular on strong swift-flowing rivers. They are most effective during hatches of big fluttering insects, and are often deadly on meadow streams having good numbers of clumsy, long-legged craneflies. The success of the Flick patterns on large eastern

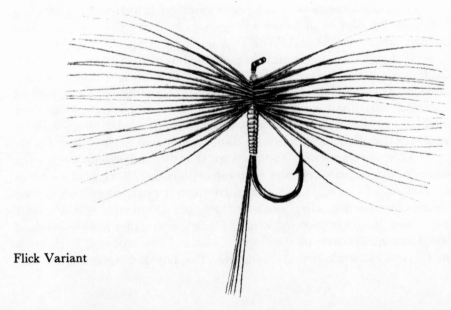

Flick Variant

waters like the Upper Connecticut, Esopus, Delaware, West Canada, Neversink, Lower Beaverkill, and the West Branch of the Ausable are ample proof of the theory. The Donnelly variants are equally popular on heavy western rivers like the Yellowstone, Big Hole, Madison, Snake, Beaverhead, Gros Ventre, and Salmon, and such long-hackled flies are superb big-water patterns.

Bivisible flies were developed to provide optimal floating qualities as well as dressings visible to both fishermen and fish alike. Bivisibles were invented by the incomparable Edward Ringwood Hewitt, who tells us in *A Trout and Salmon Fisherman for Seventy-five Years* that he was experimenting with them well before 1900. Bergman recommends them highly in both *Just Fishing* and *Trout*, particularly the brown, black, and grizzly patterns developed by Hewitt, and the badger-hackle pattern first tied by Charles Merrill of Detroit. Bivisibles are also favorites of Charles Ritz on European streams. The flies consist of hackle-fiber tails, primary hackle colors tied in tip-first and tightly palmered the length of the shank, and finally several turns of white hackle at the head. The palmer-style dressing floats high and its white face hackling is readily visible in marginal light.

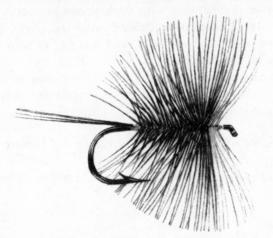

Bivisible

Many fishermen who dislike the theory of matching the hatch point happily to the bivisible, believing its success is a complete rebuttal to concepts of fly imitation. However, over the years I have attempted to correlate success with bivisibles to fly hatches coming off the water. Their floating qualities alone ensure a consistent level of success in swift-flowing pocket water, but their success on selective fish in flat water was puzzling until I discovered a curious parallel between sedge hatches and bivisibles. Many times a soggy bivisible fished awash in the film was deadly when caddisflies were hatching clumsily, drifting along tangled in their pupal skins. Other times a high-floating bivisible worked well during mating swarms of Trichoptera and hatching sedges, although a bivisible does not seem to resemble such flies. It was a puzzle that worried me for several months, until I sat studying a box of bivisibles one morning.

That's it! I thought suddenly. *Maybe bivisibles are just caddis imitations tied in reverse—sedges tied backwards!*

It was a simple explanation.

The problem had been my inability to reconcile the tails on the bivisible, since sedges and caddisflies lack tails completely. The naturals also have dark forewings and pale rear wings, while the relationship of dark and light hackles are exactly the opposite on a bivisible. But I had been fallaciously comparing bivisibles and caddisflies, assuming the hook eye of the artificial equalled the head of the naturals.

The reverse is true, but you must ignore the position of the hook to see the parallels between sedges and bivisibles. The antennae of a caddisfly can suggest the tails of a bivisible. Its dark palmer-tied hackles imitate the dark forewings, while its pale face hackles suggest the milky or hyaline rear wings of the naturals. Such juxtaposition of color and silhouette and form seem to explain the marked success of bivisibles during sedge flights.

Edward Ringwood Hewitt also developed spiders and skaters on his famous Neversink pools and flats. These long-hackled flies are much simpler than the variants that originated in Yorkshire, and it is believed that Hewitt began experimenting with such dressings shortly before the First World War. His spiders were dressed with tail fibers, stiff hackles palmered tightly on a short-shank hook, and a facing of white gamecock. Bergman was a strong advocate of such Hewitt spiders, and both *Just Fishing* and *Trout* are filled with anecdotes about using them from the Owens in California to the Ausable in the Adirondacks, where Bergman often fished from the late Byron Blanchard's famous little country hotel at Upper Jay.

Neversink skaters were a refinement of the earlier Hewitt spiders and were dressed completely without tails or white facing hackles. Hewitt tied his skaters to dance and hopscotch across the current, using only two

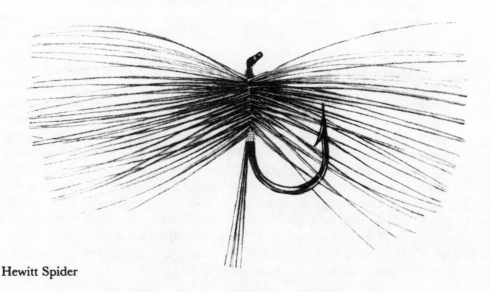

Hewitt Spider

hackles of a single color. Honey, badger, furnace, brown, ginger, black, and natural dun are all popular skater colors. Structurally, the skater was not possible until the development of nylon shortly before the Second World War. Nylon working thread left slippery and unwaxed is the secret. The unwaxed nylon is used to form a smooth thread foundation, and the rear hackle is wound tightly and tied off, with its shiny face toward the bend of the hook. Then it is pinched between the forefingers and thumbnails of both hands, and compressed as tightly as possible. The second hackle follows, its shiny face toward the hook eye, and is pinched tightly against the initially tied hackle. Once the entire fly is hackled, it is compressed together as much as possible at mid-shank, until the tips of both hackles come together at the perimeter. The slippery elasticity of the nylon made this possible, and the stiff rim of hackle fibers form a springy circle that will hop, skip, and jump on cue from the rod tip. Such skaters were designed to fish dead drift and cocked high, or skittered across the film like a fluttering cranefly, and Hewitt often fished a combination of both techniques on a single cast.

Hewitt is also credited by some angling historians with development of flat-winged dry flies designed to imitate the Plecoptera, particularly the small stoneflies that emerge in April on the Catskill streams. His little patterns used a pair of duck-quill sections laid with their convex surfaces together, stroked as straight as possible, and set in clear feather lacquer. Such wings imitated the wings of a stonefly folded absolutely flat over its dorsal abdomen. Since these early Hewitt flat-wings, many other fly dressers have tied stonefly imitations in this style. Most are using flat-wings of hair to suggest the big Plecoptera that hatch on our western rivers in early summer, but some use a wing layered of three or four hackles tied flat over the body, and Dan Bailey has long dressed a stonefly imitation with a body of woven nylon under a wing of veined synthetic material.

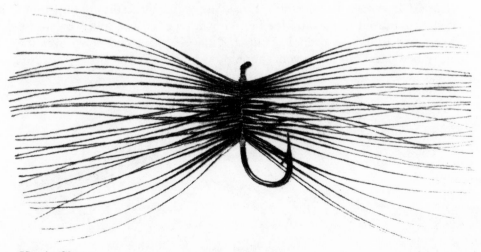

Hewitt Skater

Bumblepuppy

Bucktails have their roots in the Bumblepuppy patterns that Theodore Gordon developed on the Neversink in 1880, and William Scripture was dressing hair baitfish imitations before the close of the century. Herbert Welch constructed feather-winged imitations of smelt on his Maine lakes and rivers as early as 1902, and the true feather-winged streamer is probably the work of Alonzo Stickney Bacon.

Baitfish imitations fall generally into three basic categories: bucktails with wings made entirely of hair, streamers with wings fashioned completely of feathers, and patterns which mix their wings in combinations of both feathers and hair, like the famous Muddler Minnow.

Hair-wing minnow imitations are dressed in several styles. The old Scripture-type bucktails have a down-wing laid tight along the hook, and the Reuben Cross method tied in dark bucktail above the shank, with light-colored hair underneath the hook. Paul Young tied a type of split-winged bucktail on the Michigan rivers as early as 1925, with hair slightly flared on either side of its body. Salt-water bucktails are sometimes used on big trout water, and the best-known type has two hair wings—the first is tied in like an oversized tail, and the second is laid down over the entire body and tail like a conventional bucktail.

Scripture Bucktail

New England Streamer

Feather-wing streamers incorporate wings of both hackles, and softer fibers like ostrich and marabou. Streamers dressed with wings of neck and saddle hackles have their origins in New England, along with dressings that mixed such feathers with sparsely tied hair. Alonzo Stickney Bacon, Carrie Stevens, Herbert Welch, and Herbert Sanborn are responsible for several of the better known patterns. The original marabous were dressed by the late A. M. Ballou of Dighton, Massachusetts. Mylar is a shiny, reflective plastic originally developed for inflated communications satellites, and it has found its way into a number of fine baitfish imitations. Adhesive sheet-mylar is used extensively as shiny overwings along the flanks of marabou streamers. Fine tinsel mylar is sometimes mixed into the marabou like glittering synthetic hair, and it is also woven into mylar tubing, which is slipped over

Ballou Marabou

a body foundation of tapered white curon. Western fly tiers also favor bodies wound from Christmas rope-tinsel and trimmed to a pencillike diameter under both saddle hackle and mixed marabou wings. Such rope-tinsel and mylar flies move through the water with an enticing flash-and-glitter, catching the light like a crippled shiner tumbling weakly in the sunlight. Their light-catching qualities often cause them to dramatically outfish conventionally tied bucktails and streamers.

Muddler minnows were born in 1948, when a Cree Indian was guiding Don Gapen on the famous Nipigon in Ontario. The guide caught a sculpin among the bottom stones, telling Gapen it was the principal diet form of the large brook trout in the river. It was the late Joe Brooks who probably carried the Muddler west to Montana, where its success led Dan Bailey to dress it commercially in vast numbers. Muddlers were tied and fished from big sizes like 1/0 to small hooks like size twelve. Its big sizes were probably taken for sculpins, while the middle sizes are taken both for baitfish and big nymphs. Some fishermen report that small Muddlers are effective during hatches of big *Hexagenia* and *Ephemera* flies, and I have taken fish on a Muddler fished slow and deep when they were feeding on big dragonfly nymphs. Others have caught fish when they were taking big grasshoppers and stoneflies. It was the remarkable Dan Bailey who first combined marabou with the Muddler concept, adding a body of Christmas rope-tinsel. Bailey tied several patterns, using thick marabou wings of white, brown, yellow, gray, and black fibers. Gordon Dean, who once operated the fishing department at Abercrombie & Fitch in New York, developed the yellow-winged variation of the standard pattern. His Yellow Muddler was based on the conventional turkey wing mixed with hair and the clipped deerhair collar and head. The Spuddler is another variation on the sculpin-type fly which uses wings mixed of hair and darkly mottled saddle hackles. It is also a pattern developed by Dan Bailey on the Yellowstone in Montana. Perhaps the best Muddlers yet tied are the multicolored dressings developed by Dave Whitlock, using flattened heads and bodies of woven mylar tubing. However, these Whitlock patterns are imitations of silvery baitfish rather than the sculpins that were prototypes for the original.

Hair-wing flies had their beginnings on the Henry's Fork of the Snake before the First World War, when Benjamin Winchell and Carter Harrison first concocted them in honor of Alfred Trude, their host at a large ranch in Idaho. The first hair wings subsequently travelled with one of the party, Colonel Lewis Thompson, to the salmon rivers of the Maritime Provinces. These primitive flies were dressed down-wing over the body, and it was not until shortly before the Depression years that hair-wing dry flies evolved. Ralph Corey lived on the Muskegon in Lower Michigan, and his Corey Calftails were down-wing dries that became widely popular after the First World War. Wings tied upright and divided of hair appeared almost simultaneously on the Beaverkill and the Ausable of New York in about 1929.

Corey Calftail

The hair-wing Royal Coachman dry fly was the creation of L. Q. Quackenbush, one of the early stalwarts of the Beaverkill Trout Club a few miles above Lew Beach. Quackenbush liked the fan-wing Royal Coachman, except that it was fragile and floated badly, and in 1929 he suggested to Reuben Cross that white hair wings might work better. Cross tied some using upright wings of calftail and tail fibers of natural brown bucktail. It worked perfectly, and Catskill fishermen soon labelled it the Quack Coachman in honor of its peripatetic inventor.

Lee Wulff also worked out his famous Gray Wulff and White Wulff patterns in the Adirondacks in 1929, in a successful effort to find imitations of the big *Isonychia* duns and *Ephemera* spinners that would float well on the tumbling Ausable at Wilmington. These Wulffs have proven themselves superb flies, from Maine to California and British Columbia, and have spawned a large family of patterns using different bodies and hackles.

Wulff Dry Fly

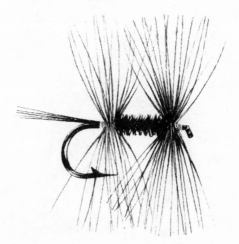

Fore-and-Aft Fly

Wulffs have so completely dominated the upright hair wings that L. Q. Quackenbush and his hair-wing Coachman are almost forgotten, and his innovation is now commonly called the Royal Wulff.

The heavy early-summer hatches of large *Pteronarcys* on our western rivers have led to a number of dry-fly patterns intended to imitate these big stoneflies. Don Harger developed an early hair-wing salmon fly with a raffia body over a kapok core. Bird's stonefly and the sofa pillow pattern soon followed, and a number of other imitations with hair wings have evolved in the fly vises of professionals like Granny Granstrom, André Puyans, Polly Rosborough, Bob Jacklin, and Phil Wright. Similar down-wing caddis patterns are found on many western rivers, and hair wings are a staple on heavy currents.

Fore-and-aft flies are not terribly new, and Ray Bergman was tying commercial fore-and-aft grasshoppers about the time that *Trout* was published some forty years ago. Such winged flies with hackles at both the head and the tail were popular on the limestone streams of Pennsylvania for many years, and Charles Fox was still using these Bergman grasshoppers on the Letort as late as 1956. Fore-and-aft dry flies have become quite popular on western rivers since the Second World War, and the Renegade is probably the best known of these patterns. Harry Darbee ties a pale little fore-and-aft pattern to imitate the delicate yellow and honey-colored Plecoptera that hatch on Catskill streams, and I have long believed that the hackle silhouette of the wingless fore-and-aft dressing is a workable imitation of a fluttering stonefly or sedge.

Parachute dressings had their beginnings in the inventive mind of William Brush, the distinguished automotive engineer from Detroit who once fished from the Pere Marquette Rod and Gun Club. Brush developed

Brush Patent Hook

a special loop-eye hook for tying parachute dry flies, about the same time that Quackenbush and Wulff were experimenting with hair-wing patterns, and he applied for a patent in 1931, which was granted three years later. Parachute flies are tied in the normal manner, except for the hackles, which are wrapped horizontally around the hackling spindle on the Brush-patent hook. Such hackling provides an aerodynamic effect which settles the fly softly and hook-down on the surface. It also provides a unique light pattern of hackle fibers—flush and full in the surface film—not found in a conventional hackle structure. Since they were developed there originally, parachute flies were around during my Michigan boyhood years, but I had never used them until an afternoon on the Little South Pere Marquette, fishing with the late Gerry Queen of Detroit.

It was a warm afternoon, with sunlight bright on the pale bottom gravel and casting deep shadows under the trees. The morning had been productive. Small sedges with mottled wings had hatched sporadically, and we had taken fish steadily with a conventional spent-wing Adams. We stopped for lunch on a cedar deadfall, shared our sandwiches and two chocolate bars, and drank gratefully from the river itself.

Two fish started rising along a brush pile upstream where the willows shaded the current. Their rise forms did not come often, but they were showy and made strong dimples that travelled downstream and disturbed the quiet currents. The rises concealed a brace of fine trout.

You try them, Gerry Queen suggested.

The earlier success of the small Adams made it a logical choice, and I waded carefully into position. The second fish was lying in the eddying currents below a willow stick that hung throbbing in the flow. It came up several times before I was sure of its position, and when I had marked it down, I finally made the cast. The little Adams settled perfectly, flirted briefly with the willow stick, and floated over the fish without drag. It was refused without inspection.

He doesn't want the Adams, I said.

Three or four good floats confirmed that diagnosis, and I waded back toward Queen. *Try one of these*, he said.

It was a parachute-tied Adams.

But they've already rejected an Adams, I frowned. *What makes you think a parachute will work?*

Try it! Queen smiled.

It was a conventional Adams with mottled spent wings, except that its brown and grizzly hackles were wound flat in the plane of the surface film. It settled like a pancake in the meniscus, riding so low that it was difficult to see on the water. It reached the fish and disappeared in a quiet rise.

He took your parachute! I yelled happily.

It was a fat thirteen-inch brown, it surrendered after a brief struggle, and I carefully dried the bedraggled parachute fly. The first fish looked a little bigger and it was still working. The parachute Adams worked out and dropped softly, and it was also taken without hesitation.

They both took it! I said with satisfaction. *I've got to check their stomachs and find out why.*

The gullets of both fish were crammed with caddisflies, except for about two dozen *Asilus* flies, their mottled wings and slender bodies in a tangled mass.

What were they taking? Queen asked.

Robber flies, I replied.

It was a striking case of selectivity to light pattern in the film. Color, size, and silhouette were virtually identical, and only the indentations of the parachute hackles in the surface film were different. It was simply a problem of giving the fish the spraddle-legged light pattern they were looking for that warm afternoon in early summer.

Clipped-hair bodies were added to upright and divided wings of hair when fly makers like Harry Darbee in New York and Joseph Messinger in West Virginia developed flies with bodies shaped of deer and elk hair. Such flies became popular on eastern streams shortly before the Second World War. History tells us that Darbee experimented with them first, although Messinger was highly skilled in dressing clipped-hair bass bugs and frogs, and boasts a number of partisans who argue that his Irresistible was the first trout pattern with a clipped deer-hair body. It had deer-hair wings and tails, and with its dark bronze-blue hackles, the Messinger Irresistible closely resembled the earlier Gray Wulff. It floated like a cork and is quite popular on rivers that are notorious for their angry currents.

Percy Jennings exploited the early clipped-hair experiments of Harry Darbee with a Catskill pattern his family named the Rat-faced McDougal. It is tied both with upright wings of natural hair, and with spent wings of grizzly hackle points. Since those beginnings a whole family of clipped-hair patterns has evolved for big water fishing, and other hair-body dressings like the Humpy and the Goofus Bug have been developed on our western rivers. The original hair-body flies had imitated big mayflies, but these patterns were juicy-bodied patterns suggestive of beetles and other terrestrials. There are also several clipped-body grasshoppers and stoneflies, like the salmon fly imitation developed by Philip Wright on the Big Hole in Montana.

Since midcentury several other remarkably creative fly dressers have been experimenting with basic fly-tying theory and practice. Dry-fly theory began with imitations of the Ephemeroptera, and although these recent studies include mayfly patterns, other common aquatic insects have also been studied. Such American flies owe some debt to the theories of Skues, Mottram, Harding, and Dunne. Their books were interested in the relationships between fly configuration, light, translucence, refraction factors in both atmosphere and water, surface-film effects, silhouette, and the visual perceptions of the fish. Their speculations have caused a profound impact on fly tying in the past twenty-five years, and that impact has triggered some remarkable echoes in the United States.

Perhaps the best known of these men is Vincent Marinaro, whose

Modern Dry-Fly Code was published in 1950, and quickly became the focus of an underground cult. It was not fully recognized as a book of major stature and its original sales were disappointing. Its reputation grew steadily over the years, until it commanded prices on the collector's market that rivalled and surpassed the books of Halford and Skues. It was singled out as the most literate fishing book published in America since George La Branche's *Dry Fly and Fast Water* made its debut in 1914, and that critical judgement came from Professor James Babb, Curator of the Wagstaff Collection of Angling Literature at Yale. Its lyric style and technical originality richly deserve such praise.

Marinaro and his studies with the equally famous Charles Fox are the subject of an entire chapter in my book *Remembrances of Rivers Past*, which describes both these men and their fishing on Letort Spring Run in Pennsylvania. It points out that difficult fish have been the principal catalyst for most innovations in fly-fishing theory and practice. Anglers are always shaped by the character of their rivers, and the shy fish of the Itchen and Test that originally produced British dry-fly theory have equally shy counterparts in the work of Fox and Marinaro.

The brown trout of the Letort are fished only with flies and are seldom killed. Their wariness and selectivity are honed to a fine edge, and each successive capture and release makes them even more shy and skittish. Certain fish become old friends and worthy adversaries, and their holding and feeding lies are well known to the Letort regulars.

Marinaro was a Halford disciple in the beginning, completely committed to the dry-fly code worked out on the British chalkstreams a century ago. *It was the fish that spoiled my religion,* Marinaro admits unhappily. *Our limestone trout simply rejected imitations based on the Halford formulas!*

It was a nagging revelation for a disciple.

Halford argued for exact imitation in terms of size, color, and silhouette, yet his flies often fell short of those criteria. The bodies were opaque and their wings were almost totally obscured by the color of their hackles. J. W. Dunne also recounts his difficulties using the Halford patterns in his book *Sunshine and the Dry Fly*, when the selective browns on the Longparish beats of the Test began refusing them. The naturals on the Longparish water were ethereal insects, with hyaline wings and pale bodies the color of fresh honey and amber and wine in a crystal goblet. Some duns had wings the color of woodsmoke, and others had dark slate gray wings or wings of a remarkable purplish dun. The first Blue-winged Olives that Dunne collected were such a revelation that he believed the hatches at Longparish were a different species. Their richly olive bodies had no echoes in the dark thinly dressed bodies of the Halford imitations, and the Halford patterns performed miserably on difficult fish.

Dunne tells us that he composed imaginary letters to angling periodicals, pointing out that his collections indicated a whole spectrum of natural flies apparently not included in the Halford series of imitations. The truth was painful when he finally realized that the naturals he was collecting were the living prototypes of the dour Halford dressings. Marinaro experienced a similar pattern of self-education on Letort Spring Run when he found its selective brown trout less than enthusiastic about imitations of its hatches that were based on the Halford formulas.

The conventional dry fly largely evolved from the work of thinkers like Ogden, Marryat, and Halford in England. It was carried to fruition during the last half of the nineteenth century, and was modified slightly with the rolled woodduck wings of Theodore Gordon and the Catskill school.

Such dry flies have both wings and hackles just behind the hook eye, body materials occupying most of the hook shank, and tails that were rather exaggerated in length. Wings were upright and divided, shaped of fragile wing-quill sections or duck breast feathers. The stiff gamecock hackles and tail fibers were designed to support and float the imitation on the surface film. Stiff hackles and tails were combined to float the flies as high as possible, and a whole liturgy of high-floating flies evolved. It was argued that the physical presence of the hook made exact imitation virtually impossible, and that fine hackles and long tails could obscure the hook by holding it above the surface meniscus. Ray Bergman echoes these theories in *Trout*, complete with diagrams showing the floating characteristics of Cahills tied on light- and standard-weight hooks, and adds the following observations:

> To begin with I doubt that close imitations are essential for success. As a matter of fact I believe that it is impossible to create an artificial duplicate of a natural insect. No matter how cleverly we tie our flies we can never attain that ethereal lightness, delicacy and definite lusciousness which is so apparent in the real thing.

Few modern fly dressers who fish our really difficult waters, like the western spring creeks or the limestone streams of the Appalachians, or any river within two hours of a major city, would agree that imitation is unimportant to their success. The regulars on Letort Spring Run have mercifully refused to collect innumerable wagers from strangers who insist that their favorite patterns will work anywhere. Letort trout are simply not interested in conventional Cahills and Hendricksons and Royal Wulffs, unlike their cousins in less demanding freestone streams.

However, the most creative tiers will agree that an exact duplicate of the naturals is impossible. Their elegance, ephemeral coloring, and hyaline character are beyond our reach in absolute terms. We are after an effective duplicate that creates the illusion of a natural insect and deludes a selective fish. Such difficult trout are the final yardstick of our skills.

Bergman was clearly unconvinced by the whole history of imitation, reaching from the *Treatyse of Fysshynge wyth an Angle* through Cotton and Ronalds to Halford and his *Dry-Fly Entomology*. Fishing was easier in the Bergman years, even on the Catskill streams and the rivers of northern New Jersey that he fished regularly and wrote about, and it is easy to understand that fly patterns seemed less important forty years ago. Fishing writers are a little bewildered by the recent changes in our sport, but demographers understand what has happened. There are now more people living within five hours of the Catskills than the total population of the entire United States when Theodore Gordon began to fish their storied rivers.

Bergman knew that the hook was obviously essential to fishing and believed that its necessity formed an insurmountable handicap to exact imitation. It is unquestionably true that no natural possesses a hooklike appendage hanging from its body. However, Bergman also believed that a dry fly floating high on its hackles and tail fibers concealed the hook and cancelled out its existence:

> There are some qualities which tend to make our manufactured flies more lifelike and so more productive. One is the lightness of wire of which the hook is made. There isn't any doubt that a fly tied on a light wire hook is more advantageous to the angler than one tied on a heavy wire hook. For one thing, the light wire hook enables the flytier to use less hackle and yet have a fly which will float. Besides, if on a light wire hook you use the amount of hackle needed to properly float a heavier hook, you would have a fly that would float higher and so prevent the hook from penetrating as far under the surface, surely an advantage; that is working along the idea that we should imitate a natural as nearly as possible. After all the hook is the one thing we can't do without and also it is the most glaring discrepancy between an artificial and a natural. Therefore, if it can be kept above the surface of the water, that part of the artificial fly which touches the water should appear more like a natural than it would if the entire hook could be seen under the surface.

Light-wire hooks are undoubtedly important in floating a dry fly with the least dubbing and hackle necessary to float it properly on a given piece of water. No modern fly tier would challenge that premise, but the rest of the argument is no longer valid, although an entire generation came to manhood religiously accepting such orthodoxy.

It is still possible to overhear similar dogma on the porches of venerable fishing camps on rivers across the United States. Halford informed the world that mayflies rode the water on their toes, and surprisingly few men challenged him despite the obvious evidence of their own eyes. Mayflies do not ride the current on their toes, despite the drawings in Halford's *Dry-Fly Entomology* or the mayflies depicted in Jennings' *Book of Trout Flies* half a century later. Mayflies ride the current dumpily, their thoracic segments and belly sternites riding flush in the surface film, and their legs straddled clumsily at the sides. Sometimes they ride the current well, wings together and balanced like Halford's perfectly cocked dry flies, but sometimes their float is less than perfect. Their wings flutter and ride asymmetrically, sometimes getting trapped in the surface film, and a hatching dun is often skated and blown off balance until one wing is awash and the other rides upright. Sometimes the entire body and its tails are pinioned in the surface too, and *none* of these conditions, including the normal belly-flat posture of both body and thorax, is imitated by a dry fly floating high on its hackles and tail fibers—with both hook and body held above the surface film.

There is a whole generation of innovative fly dressers who discovered these fallacies for themselves. J. W. Dunne went so far in *Sunshine and the Dry Fly* as to argue that body color and translucency were the principal factors in selectivity, and Colonel E. W. Harding guardedly supports that theory in *The Fly-Fisher and the Trout's Point of View*. The first American fishing writer to challenge orthodox dry-fly philosophy was Vincent Marinaro. In his *Modern Dry-Fly Code* Marinaro not only rejected the Halford formulas but also proposed a wholly new theory of dry-fly structure.

Halford chose his palette of materials for dry flies in the following system: hackles were correlated to leg color; wings imitated the wing color and configuration of the naturals; bodies were interpreted in terms of the sternite or belly-segment colors; and the caudal filaments were imitated by the color of the delicate tail fibers.

Marinaro tied his early imitations of the Pennsylvania fly hatches using the Halford formulas faithfully. His prototypes worked reasonably well, but the hyperselective fish of Letort Spring Run rejected them consistently. Something else was obviously needed. His Letort experience convinced Marinaro that two conceptual errors flawed the Halford theory of fly dressing. Choosing leg color for the hackles obscured the more important color and silhouette of the wings, distorting the principal color mix of his flies. Halford also failed in his interpretation of wing position as well as thorax and body length. Mayflies typically ride the current with slightly upturned bodies, foreshortening body length in both the surface film and the vision of the fish. Halford interpreted body length literally in his imitations, and ignored thorax length entirely. Wing mass in the naturals slants backward toward the center of thorax and body length. The most cursory observation of mayfly anatomy will prove that a sizeable percentage of overall body length lies in the head, plus those thoracic segments lying ahead of the wings. That percentage of total body silhouette is completely ignored in conventional dry-fly theory, and hackle color based on leg color is unworkable when its fibers completely obscure both wing color and silhouette.

Experiments along the Letort confirmed the Marinaro theory that hackles should ignore leg color on most dry flies and should be chosen to reinforce wing color. His wings were designed to suggest wing color and silhouette, and should be seated farther back along the hook, both to echo their real position in fly silhouette and to make room for the thorax. Doctor Edgar Burke anticipated these thorax-style dry flies in his writings, but his dressings merely omitted the thorax and constructed the wings and hackles with a bare shank well behind the hook eye.

The Marinaro fly structure is revolutionary. It places trimmed hackle-point wings toward the center of the hook shank, working the hackles around them at exaggerated crossing angles. The trimmed wings were worked out by William Bennett, who collaborated with Marinaro in much of his work.

Similar cut-wing theories are advocated by J. W. Dunne in his *Sunshine and the Dry Fly.* The Marinaro body material is tapered in a slender cigar shape, both behind the hackles in a conventional body and ahead of the hackles to imitate the thorax. Body length behind the hackles is shortened proportionally, since the curving, upward posture of a mayfly body tends to foreshorten its apparent length when viewed from below. Marinaro

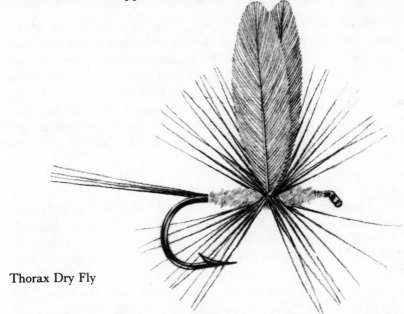

Thorax Dry Fly

sometimes trimmed out his hackles under the thorax, in the style of J. W. Dunne, and sometimes cross-wound them to expose the thorax. Such flies were designed to float the fly solely on the hackle and body structure, ignoring the presence of the hook, and laying a light pattern of thorax, body, and hackles in the surface film. Its imagery echoes the thoracic structure, sternites, and legs lying in the meniscus. Marinaro cocked his tails high, just as mayflies hold their setae high and free of the water in many cases, although this subtlety is probably unnecessary. The thorax style of dressing has since proven itself thoroughly on the selective fish of Letort Spring Run, and my own slight modifications of the concept have regularly proven themselves in my daily fishing.

Marinaro did not stop with his thorax-fly theories.

His work also focused on the unique problems found in imitating terrestrial insects like ants, beetles, and leafhoppers. Other fishermen had developed ant imitations for subsurface fishing, and flying-ant patterns already existed in the seventeenth century, but it was Marinaro who first worked out minute ants designed to float in the surface film. His patterns included seal-fur dressings with delicate little hackles between their thorax and gaster segments, and the intriguing horsehair ants were tied without working silk. The hair both formed bodies and secured their hackles.

But there had been ants before, even if they were not tiny imitations dressed to float awash in the film, and perhaps the most remarkable Marinaro contribution lies in imitating the leafhoppers. Although Ronalds surprisingly mentions these tiny terrestrials in his nineteenth-century *Fly-Fisher's Entomology*, his imitations are ineffective as leafhopper patterns. It was Marinaro who discovered both the contemporary importance of these insects and an approach to fly dressing that could imitate them with precision.

The ultimate day of discovery is eloquently recorded in his *Modern Dry-Fly Code*, which describes fishing the Letort with Charles Fox near their little fishing hut. No insects were visible on the water, but the fish were working busily in its glassy channels. Conventional flies had failed consistently in the past and proved no better that frustrating afternoon. The rise forms were the familiar bulge rings so familiar on Letort Spring Run. Fox and Marinaro tried fish after fish in the meadows, resting first one and then another, and exchanged helpless gestures as they moved along the stream.

Marinaro writes that his increasing frustration finally proved too much for him, and he stopped fishing to study the current. Lying prone in the warm grass, Marinaro watched the silken current slide hypnotically past. Considerable time elapsed in pleasant daydreaming before he suddenly became aware of almost-invisible insects on the water. Marinaro rubbed his eyes in disbelief, but there they were: tiny mayflies struggling in their diaphanous nymphal skins, beetles so small they looked like bubbles in the meniscus, minute ants awash in the surface film, and countless other minutae pinioned helplessly in the tension of the smooth current.

His mind stirred with excitement.

Marinaro hurried to the fishing hut and fashioned a fine-mesh seine with sticks and mosquito netting. Its meshes quickly collected a delicate residue of insects at its water line. There were tiny mayflies with wings less than one-eighth of an inch in length, beetles less than three-thirty-seconds of an inch in diameter, tiny black and rusty pink ants, and minute leafhoppers in astonishing numbers.

It was the moment Marinaro discovered the jassid.

Modified conventional patterns consistently failed to take fish feeding on leafhoppers in the days that followed. New fly-dressing theories were clearly needed. The basic concepts of the jassid-style tie were painfully slow in coming, and early attempts were less than fruitful.

It was not a problem of really imitating a jassid, Charles Fox explained thoughtfully at his bench on the stream one evening. *It was more a problem of suggesting silhouette and light pattern in the film.*

The actual shape and thickness of the leafhoppers was ultimately forgotten, and a silhouette theory of terrestrial imitation evolved. Since many of the tiny *Cicadellidae* or leafhoppers have banded multicolored wings, Marinaro chose a down-wing dressing with a similarly colored junglecock feather. The first patterns were tied with conventional hackling, and although they caught some fish, the jassid imitations were not really effective until Marinaro trimmed the hackle fibers to lie flat in the surface film. Their success was striking, and it was clearly the result of his fresh theory: that fish cannot really sense the thickness of small insects drifting over them, and that opacity and silhouette and light-pattern distortion in the film are the secret of the jassid-type fly and its success.

Since the prototypes were dressed with junglecock feathers, many anglers assume that such leafhopper imitations are impossible without wings that use these rare little eyed feathers. Nothing could be farther from the truth, since leafhoppers come in virtually the entire range of colors, from milky white and pale green to richly mottled purples and dark blackish browns.

Jassid

Leafhoppers can be imitated with any number of small feather types set in clear vinyl lacquer, in various colors and hackle combinations, depending on the naturals you observe in the grass. The jassid-type imitation did not die out when the Asian junglecock was declared rare and endangered, and the importation of their capes was forbidden.

Marinaro also developed a silhouette-style imitation of the Japanese beetle in those years. The selective trout of the limestone streams were quick to discover that these destructive little Coleoptera from the Orient were both abundant and food-rich. Some fish clearly disliked them, and we laughed at the occasional trout that shook its head disdainfully after taking a beetle, disturbed at the wriggling and crawling in its gullet. Others took them readily, and a dedicated beetle-feeder was often so stuffed with them that they literally crunched and rattled when we handled it in the net. It was a totally new problem in imitation.

Beetle imitations soon proved surprisingly difficult. Small coffee beans were first tried; and they were filed and mounted on the hook with cement in the manner of tiny bass bugs. These imitations floated too low and landed too hard, and the fish apparently wanted none of them. Cork and balsa wood beetles were not much better. Clipped and folded deer-hair patterns worked, but they also absorbed too much water and were not ovoid enough to simulate the Japanese species. Black sponge rubber was tried; although it worked surprisingly well, it tended to twist on the hook, making it difficult to hook a rising fish. All of these flies took fish on most limestone streams, but the wary Letort trout remained skeptical.

Like the jassid-style dressings, the full configuration and thickness of the beetles were ultimately forgotten, and the Marinaro principles of opacity and silhouette were applied. Marinaro used large junglecock eyes in his first patterns. Their opacity was quite good, and they took fish rather well, although such flat-tied wings tended to be fragile. The silhouettes were too linear for the oval-shaped beetles, and the tendency of the feathers to split led me to abandon them quickly. Obviously, other fly-dressing options were needed, although Marinaro had already worked out the basic structural principles involved.

Ross Trimmer and I were cooling out in the Turnaround Meadow on the Letort one afternoon late in August. I was lazily dressing flies and accidentally noticed several pheasant-skin pieces in a hackle canister. One fragment had a few dark little throat feathers from a ringneck cock-bird.

Look, I said, *they're the exact color of the beetles!*

You're right, Trimmer agreed.

It was not long before I had palmered three black gamecock hackles on a sixteen hook and trimmed them flat along the top of the shank. Two ringneck feathers were laid with their concave sides together and saturated with vinyl lacquer. Once fully dried, these feathers were trimmed into an oval beetlelike shape, pressed flat over the hook, and tied into cement. Finally, a single untreated neck feather with a greenish bronze sheen was laid over the underwing and trimmed to shape. When the hackling under the hook was trimmed out, the little feather-wing beetle would ride flat and opaque in the surface film.

Looks pretty good, Trimmer said eagerly.

What should we call it? I said.

Well, Trimmer cut himself some fresh chewing tobacco, *what about the Schwiebert beetle?*

I've never liked naming flies that way. I shook my head.

Letort beetle? he suggested.

Better, I said.

Our success with the new beetle was instantaneous. We tried them over the beetle-feeding trout in the Barnyard and Otto's Meadow. The first fish was working under the big willow in the Barnyard, and it took without hesitation. We worked upstream slowly, stopping well above the trestle, and took twenty-one fish between us. Such a score on the difficult beetle-feeders was unbelievable.

Letort Beetle

The small Marinaro ants also proved themselves in my first few seasons on the Letort, and I soon began experimenting with ant imitations dressed with dubbing. Crewel wool picked apart and spun on the tying silk made excellent wet flies, using the dubbing to shape the configuration of head, thorax, and gaster that suggests the silhouette of an ant. Soft webby hackling completed the sunk patterns. Various types of natural fur and synthetic dubbing was tried on my ants dressed to float awash in the surface film. Seal's fur and dyed kapok proved themselves, and now we have nylon wools and the more exotic polypropylene fibers to pick apart and dub on the tying thread. Their specific gravity is so much lighter than water that their floating properties are good, they shape into elegant little ants, and a few turns of stiff gamecock hackle completes the pattern. However, Gary Borger has developed a series of parachute-hackle ants on the limestone streams of southern Wisconsin. These ant patterns lie superbly in the surface film, providing a better light pattern than my conventional dressings, and I have started using these tiny ants extensively.

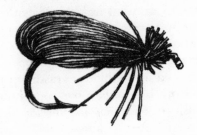

Crowe Beetle

Grasshoppers are another staple in the midsummer trout diet, particularly on meadow streams like Letort Spring Run. Marinaro and his collaborator, William Bennett, developed a so-called pontoon hopper made of feather quills. Such patterns are difficult to tie and they cast rather clumsily. I have not used them much, although they have produced some Olympian fish for Marinaro and his friends.

Art Winnie was an old-time tier in the Boardman country of Lower Michigan, and once reigned as King of the Kalkaska Trout Festival. Many traditional Michigan patterns originated in his prolific fly vise, including his Michigan Caddis and Michigan Mosquito dressings. Perhaps his best-known pattern is the Michigan Hopper, which has fathered a number of offspring like the widely sold Joe's Hopper, the elegant Kade dressings in Wisconsin, and the modern variations born in the skilled fingers of Dave Whitlock in Oklahoma

The conventional grasshopper pattern is found in the color plates of Bergman's *Trout*, and Bergman himself tied a fore-and-aft variation of these typical turkey-wing dressings. Such flies were found in the fly boxes of most fishermen on the Pennsylvania limestone country, but the selective Letort browns seem more difficult every year, and they started refusing these old-time imitations with an irritating frequency.

New patterns seemed necessary. Like the neck-feather beetle imitations, our first attempts were tied in the Turnaround Meadow on Letort Spring Run. My western experiments with hair wings and clipped-hair bodies had worked well on big cutthroats in the Jackson Hole country, on the picky rainbows of Silver Creek in Idaho, and the fat brown trout lying under the grassy banks of the Madison in Yellowstone Park.

Many good fishermen were reporting success with a Muddler Minnow soaked in silicone paste during late summer orgies of grasshopper feeding. *It worked beautifully on Flat Creek,* the late Wayne Buszek once explained. *It floated like a cork, and when we plopped them down hard—those big cutthroats came after them like crocodiles!*

His experience provided our catalyst.

It was still early summer, and the grasshoppers in the Letort meadows were relatively small. Size sixteen hooks seemed about right, and my first attempts were relatively simple flies. The bodies were nylon wool picked apart and dubbed; the nylon wool was chosen both for its ability to hold color when wet and for its specific gravity. Since the naturals were small, we tried a wingless imitation consisting only of a three-quarter collar of deer body hair. Its strands trailed back in a tight hopperlike silhouette, and its flaring butts were trimmed into a blocky grasshopper-shaped head. These prototypes seemed to work better than our conventional patterns, but not many early summer fish were actively looking for them that week.

The grasshoppers in the meadows grew larger as the summer progressed. Subsequent refusals and successes finally caused us to restore the familiar turkey-section wings and alter the deer-hair dressing slightly. The silhouette of the wings folded over trailing underwings of deer hair, with a

Letort Hopper

trimmed collar and trailing outer layer of hair, proved itself on the stream. The absence of conventional hackling permitted the full bulk of the fly and its yellow-dubbed body to float flush in the surface film. We floated it over a small mirror in a shallow pan with a live grasshopper, and its light pattern looked hopperlike and promising.

Looks pretty good, Ross Trimmer observed. *Maybe we'll name it the Letort Hopper.* Trimmer cut some chewing tobacco.

It's christened, I agreed.

The selective fish liked it fine. We devised additional refinements as the summer reached the end of the season, modifying body color and exaggerating the trimmed hair into grasshopper-shaped heads. Sometimes we added trailing legs of knotted condor quill, dying their tips to suggest the red-legged hoppers that were everywhere along the stream. It was important to remember that the flaring deer hair had to be carefully trimmed out underneath to insure that the dubbed body laid flat on the surface. Our modern polypropylene dubbings have a lighter specific gravity than nylon, and provide several hopperlike body colors with exceptional floating properties.

It was not long before Edward Shenk and his collaborator Edward Koch developed their Letort Cricket. It was an entirely black pattern using the same principles of silhouette, floating properties, and light pattern as our Letort Hopper. The grasshopper took several three- and four-pound fish in its first few seasons, and I had an even larger brown break off in the moss on a slough near the Beaverhead.

But the cricket imitation had a more impressive launching ceremony when Ed Koch took a nine-pounder with it from Otto's Meadow on the Upper Letort. It was taken early in the morning, well into the 1962 season, and it has been verified as the largest dry-fly trout ever caught in Pennsylvania.

Succeeding summers found our tree-sheltered mountain rivers infested with pale green inchworms. These larvae vary from three-eighths of an inch in length when the fish begin taking them, to slightly more than an inch when they are fully grown and about to build their cocoons. Such larvae have no leg structure, so no hackles can be used to float an imitation, and only the body material itself serves this function. It was the late Paul Young who tied the first green inchworms that I ever used, and these were fashioned of apple-green deer hair tightly bound along the hook shank with strong nylon working thread. The flaring tips and butts were trimmed off close. Some versions were tied with extended bodies and others are dressed on long-shank hooks. It was a deadly pattern in inchworm season, and it took some muscular deep-bellied browns on the foliage-dark rivers of my Michigan summers—particularly the South Branch of the Au Sable.

Edward Ringwood Hewitt also tied some primitive inchworm imitations that had apple-green bodies dubbed on slender hooks with a sparse collar of olive hackles. His pattern was sold by William Mills & Son in New York as late as a dozen years ago. Ray Bergman also recommends this pattern in his first book *Just Fishing*, and similar patterns are still fished both wet and dry on many eastern streams.

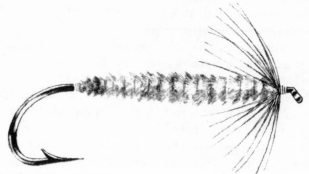

Hewitt Inchworm

Such flies work well enough on broken water, but the fish on our glassy Brodheads flats were another matter, and we clearly needed better dressings. The behavior of the inchworm larvae was the secret. The delicate green worms performed their midday acrobatics up and down their silken cords over the current, and they often worked so far from the foliage that they actually trailed in the water. It was usually their almost imperceptible wakes that attracted attention and started the fish working on them, and a delicately dragging fly was needed.

The solution had to float with nothing more than its dubbing materials, and that meant a relatively delicate hook. Structurally the imitation should also skim like an aquaplane in the current, and its color should have the intense green chroma of the live inchworms. Wet imitations sometimes worked, tied with pale greenish synthetic yarn on long-shank hooks with a fine wire ribbing, but such patterns refused to float except on relatively still currents. It was a stubborn problem until I thought of tying dubbed bodies on cores of fine stainless wire.

The stainless core material was stretched taut between two fly vises, and a bright green synthetic wool was picked apart and dubbed on waxed silk. Five or six bodies were quickly prefabricated on the .005 wire, and I sealed their ends with vinyl lacquer. When the wire-core bodies were snipped from the wire, they were virtually weightless, and I selected tiny little lightweight hooks to secure under them. The hooks were wrapped with waxed pale green working nylon and then lashed at either end of the shank, with their eyes about a quarter of the body length back from the head. Soaked with silicone paste, these flies proved reasonably buoyant, and the position of the hook eye caused them to skim perfectly on a light nylon tippet.

The principle of buoyant synthetic dubbing, shaped in a linear silhouette without other distortions of the light pattern, proved itself again with the gypsy moth larvae. These insects are sombre slate-colored worms before they become fully grown caterpillars. Wet-fly imitations were tied of black wool dubbing and palmered with a grayish saddle hackle, its fibers trimmed to about one-sixteenth of an inch in length.

Black polypropylene or seal's fur dubbing on a fine stainless core also worked well, before the gypsy moth larvae were an inch long, and they regularly took selective fish. These imitations were also fitted with tiny hooks hanging underneath their bodies, and sometimes they hang suspended on their silken cords, trailing in the current like inchworms. Gypsy moths have not been important for many seasons on our eastern streams, but the eager response of our trout this past summer to imitations of proper color and silhouette and size indicates that this tree-killing pest is an important new trout food.

It's like the Japanese beetles all over again, Alvin Grove observed recently on the Battenkill. *Mixed blessings.*

Many innovative fly tiers are still working with experimental patterns and fly structure, and knowledgeable anglers are aware that we are

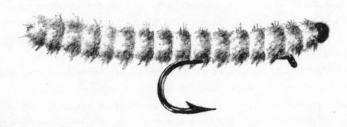

Wire-body Inchworm

experiencing a period of considerable creativity and innovation. Most dry-fly types are focused on the Ephemeroptera, but there are also some remarkably creative imitations of stoneflies, caddis, and damselflies on widespread waters.

Perhaps the first fly dresser to experiment with structural hybrids, combining extended bodies with parachute-style hackles and both fan wings and rolled wings, was the late John Gaylord Case. His elegant little upright-wing drakes were dressed with woodduck tails and extended bodies spun from natural and dyed kapok. His wings were either slender fan wings or conventional rolled wings of mallard, woodduck, and teal, depending on the wing color of the hatches. Although he was an eastern fly-fisherman from New York—and my first editor on *Matching the Hatch*—Case did a lot of fishing on our Rocky Mountain spring creeks. His experimental patterns reflected a knowledge of the mottled-wing naturals on many American rivers—particularly the *Stenonema* flies on our eastern waters, and the several *Callibaetis* speckle-wing hatches found in profusion on slow-flowing western streams.

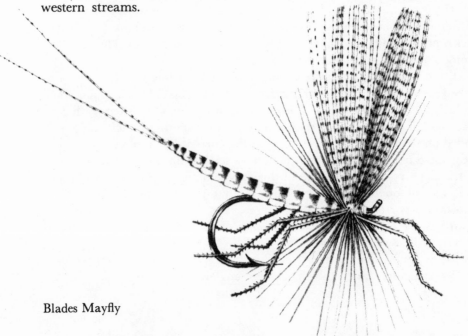

Blades Mayfly

The wing image and extended-body silhouette of these dressings is superb. The parachute hackling at the root of the wings creates a light-image illusion of spreading legs, and floats the body and thorax right in the film. Case achieved a synthesis of several centuries of fly dressing theory with his mayfly work, although he never wrote a book about his studies. His fragile imitations were superbly conceived for eastern fishing and the western spring creeks he loved over many summers, and it was not long before other tiers were working with the same structural theories and more buoyant synthetic materials.

Paradun

In *Selective Trout* Douglas Swisher and Carl Richards describe extensive experiments with parachute-style imitations using various types of rolled wings and fan-wing type dressings. These so-called paradun dressings are quite effective, and a number of hair-wing parachute ties have evolved in recent seasons using both calftail and elk in rolled upright sail-wings. Swisher and Richards also detail the techniques of making an elk-wing mayfly imitation with a detached body of deer hair. Such adaptations of the detached-body parachute dressings provide rough-water floating qualities that the delicate Case-type imitations lacked. Perhaps the best of this elk-wing school are tied by Andre Puyans of San Francisco, and I have several samples of his *Ephemerella grandis* drakes on my table as I write. They are dressed for the heavy early-summer hatches of big Lead-winged Olives on the Henry's Fork of the Snake, perhaps the best trout stream in America.

Swisher and Richards are certainly better known for their no-hackle dun and spinner imitations. It is these patterns that have made *Selective Trout* extremely successful since its publication in 1971—although it is perhaps more important for its original studies in entomology and previously unknown fly hatches, its work on fly and nymph behavior, and its emphasis on hatching nymphs. Most fishermen are fascinated with the no-hackle and parachute dry flies, believing them a totally new contribution to fly dressing. Such opinions could come only from fishermen who do not tie themselves, or from fly tiers who are not knowledgeable students of the history of their art.

No-hackle flies have unquestionably been fished in the film since Cotton and Bowlker and Pritt, and the original dozen patterns described in the *Treatyse of Fysshynge wyth an Angle* were similar no-hackle dressings from

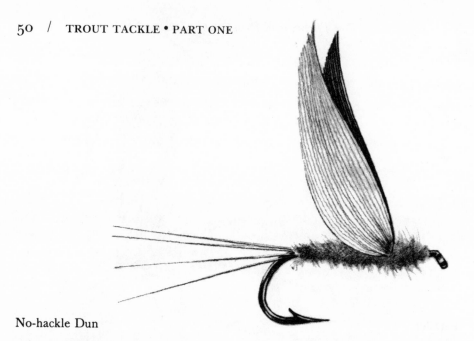

No-hackle Dun

the fifteenth century. Skues mentions the remarkable performance of the Hare's Ear on the heavy *Baetis* hatches that literally cover the Itchen late in April. It is a relatively ancient pattern with roots several centuries deep in the history of fly-fishing. It has no-hackle dressing, like many of the north-country patterns of Yorkshire and Roxburgheshire. It also has a roughly dubbed body of hare's mask ribbed with fine gold tinsel, completely unlike the olive green sternites of the hatching Medium Olives. Skues devotes a brief chapter of *The Way of a Trout with a Fly* to the puzzle of matching these Olives, wondering both about its lack of conventional hackling and its coloring. His observations clearly indicate that the Itchen trout do not take the Hare's Ear as a lure, but take it when specific insects are hatching. Skues' experience with this no-hackle pattern more than a half century ago is intriguing, both because it is clearly a problem of imitating a hatching dun only half-free of its nymphal skin and because it underlines an almost continuous history of no-hackle dressings in the United Kingdom.

Selective Trout is unique not so much in its discussion of the structure of the no-hackle pattern as in its authors' recognition that a no-hackle dressing offers some unique elements of light pattern and silhouette, particularly in the smaller sizes. Detached bodies, parachute-style hackling, and spent parachute-hackle spinners have also been tied and fished for many years in both Europe and the United States.

Such criticism is not aimed at the remarkably original content of *Selective Trout*, but for those who believed these theories were completely new, and without antecedents in the history of fly-dressing. Their contribution can be traced directly from the fifteenth-century flies listed in Berners to the contemporary observations of Skues, Mottram, Harding, and

Marinaro. The no-hackle duns and hen-wing spinners are also a result of modern synthetic dubbings like polypropylene, as well as the structural proportions and refinements worked out by Swisher and Richards. Such original concepts would justify *Selective Trout* in themselves, but the book offers many other fresh theories in its cornucopia of ideas.

These past two weeks I have been fishing with Carl Richards and Doug Swisher on the Au Sable, in Michigan. The difficult trout on the fly-water of the North Branch, and the river itself between Stephan's and the Wakeley Bridge, were the critics that helped shape their no-hackle theories. Heavy fly hatches and smooth currents characterize both stretches. Most of the fish can be taken on conventional flies during a good hatch, but there were a number of selective browns that made a believer of me—when they inspected and refused conventional flies before accepting a carefully dressed no-hackle imitation.

Other innovators are working in these years too, and their fly vises have produced several unusual imitative mayfly patterns. Some use completely new synthetic materials, and others employ old fly-tying materials in fresh ways. It was Chauncey Lively of Pittsburgh who originally developed the intriguing wonder-wing style of tying, using small body feathers tied in by their tips, drawn upward into their final slender configuration, and trimmed off. His flies can be tied in surprisingly small sizes, and their wings are both lifelike and durable. Another strikingly original use of conventional materials is the work of André Puyans of San Francisco. His little loop-wing duns and spinners are tied in both upright and spent-wing versions, using goose quill and other feather fibers to suggest only the outlines of the wings. It is a remarkably simple method of suggesting the crystalline wings of mayfly spinners, and Puyans even mottles the leading edge of some loop-wing patterns with lacquer to

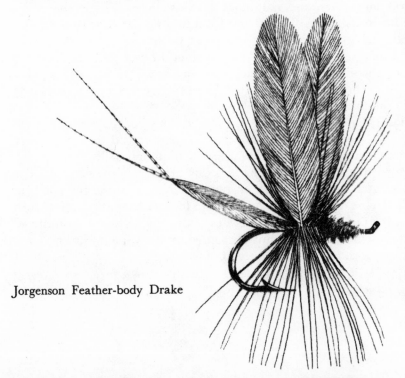

Jorgenson Feather-body Drake

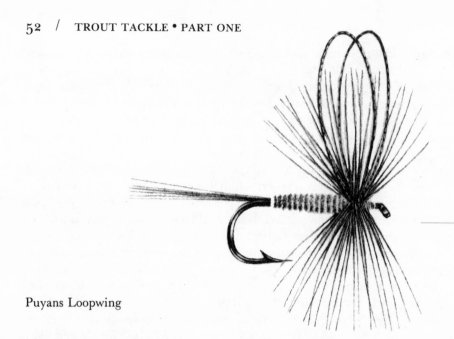

Puyans Loopwing

simulate such speckle-wing mayflies as *Callibaetis nigritus.* It is also possible to dress these Puyans loop-wings with thin nylon monofilament, and their performance during a fine spinner fall of *Callibaetis* on Silver Creek proved their worth—its selective Idaho rainbows are the acid test of any imitation, and we took fish after fish on a windless evening.

Mayflies are not the only fly hatches on our trout streams, and on many American rivers their importance is waning. Pollution, warming rivers, and water drawn off in reservoirs and irrigation networks have decimated the Ephemeroptera and made other insects more important. During recent years, experimental flies dressed to imitate stoneflies, marchflies, damselflies, and caddisflies have displayed considerable originality. Edward Ringwood Hewitt also liked to dress flat-wing stoneflies for his Neversink hatches. During recent years we have experienced serious flooding from rains triggered by late-summer hurricanes. The scouring damage of these floods both decimated and eradicated many aquatic species; until the stoneflies and the sedges have become increasingly important on our eastern streams.

Almost twenty years ago, we experienced some heavy hatches of small brown-mottled caddisflies, and once our fish had gorged themselves they became extremely selective. The usual dry-fly imitations failed consistently, and one afternoon I stopped fishing and caught a few of the naturals. The fly vise was attached to the table in my corner room above the porch at Henryville House, and I was rooting around in my material canisters when I knocked the little box of live caddisflies to the floor. The insects fluttered around the room, and several quickly settled on the window screen. Their dark silhouettes suddenly caught my attention.

They're like a big jassid, I thought excitedly, *except for the notch-shaped silhouette of the wings!*

It proved a workable solution. Brown partridge hackles were saturated with vinyl lacquer, and stroked into a thin caddislike shape before they dried. Once they were fully dried, I trimmed them with the V-shaped notches to suggest the silhouettes of caddisflies with their wings folded. Brown and grizzly hackles were palmered the length of a sixteen hook, and trimmed out along the belly and the back, so the imitation would lie flat in the film. The notched partridge hackle was laid jassid-style in two drops of cement, and pressed flat along the shank of the hook. It was both simple and effective.

It was so successful with the selective fish on our Brodheads flats that I tried it with small Plecoptera imitations the following spring. These fluttering little stoneflies were taken more readily by the trout that season than usual, perhaps because our mayfly hatches had not yet recovered from the flood damage in 1955. Since stoneflies often lie awash in the current with their wings folded flat along the body, imitations in the jassid-style seemed promising. Pale rusty pink and black and dark brown bodies were dubbed along the entire hook, with short tail fibers and a single dun hackle delicately palmered behind the hook eye. The hackles were trimmed out along both the back and bottom of the shank, and either gray or dun-colored hen hackles shaped like stoneflies and set in vinyl lacquer were tied flat over the dubbed bodies. The patterns worked extremely well.

The following season we experienced unusually heavy hatches of dark little *Bibio* flies, and the fish in our eastern streams fed on them eagerly. It was the same pattern of feeding behavior that had occurred with the caddis two years earlier. The trout took so many marchflies that they became stuffed and stopped taking them, but in the succeeding days there were sporadic hatches that the fish took well. These *Bibio* hatches came in the middle hours of the day, and the fish became typically selective in their feeding. These red-legged marchflies were not easily imitated, and we tried several patterns before finding a workable dressing. The naturals are rather

Flat-wing Sedge

antlike, with their black bodies and reddish-tinged legs, except that their pale grayish wings are folded flat over their bodies. The basic jassid-type theories of silhouette, light pattern, and color worked again. We dressed a body and thorax of black seal's fur with a dark reddish furnace hackle tied parachute between the segments. Pale grayish hen hackles were shaped and set in vinyl lacquer and laid flat across the back once the upper fibers were trimmed flat. The dressing took many selective fish during the times the *Bibio* flies were hatching in good numbers.

Our western spring creeks exhibit the unusual characteristic of sporadic and predictable feeding on adult damselflies. The large numbers of these slender-bodied Zygoptera on such streams clearly demonstrate the fact that their weedy alkalinity provides an optimal habitat for damselflies. Particularly on famous Silver Creek in Idaho, the local fishermen have begun tying extended-body damselflies with flat monofilament dyed bright blue, bright green, and several shades of brown. Both conventional hackling and parachute ties are seen. Such flies are surprisingly deadly in late summer when the damselflies are mating.

Several tiers have been experimenting with other caddisfly imitations on widespread waters in recent years since sedge hatches have become more important on streams depleted of their mayfly populations. Hair-wing patterns like the Woodchuck were sedge imitations in wide use on my Michigan boyhood streams, and their simplicity was striking. Woodchuck dressings were tied without bodies, simply using down wings of mottled body hair and a conventional hackling of mixed brown and grizzly. Although the Michigan Mosquito has slender pheasant-fiber tails, it also has duck-quill sections tied down over its quill body. The pheasant tails were fragile and broke off quickly, leaving an effective sedge imitation.

Damselfly Nymph

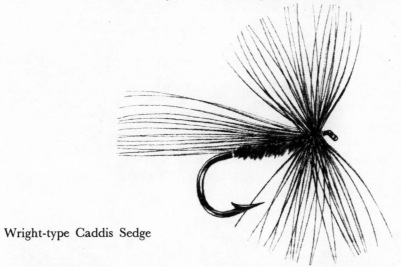

Wright-type Caddis Sedge

Similar dressings are found in *Fishing the Dry Fly as a Living Insect,* a recent book by Leonard Wright, in which both the sedges and their fluttering behavior receive attention. Larry Solomon is a first-rate tier from New York who is tying a flat-wing sedge using two flaring hackle points over the body. Such dressings are not totally new, since they have a prelude in the work of chalkstream thinkers like Skues and Lunn, but the revival of the Trichoptera found in the work of both Solomon and Wright is long overdue on our waters.

Perhaps the most unusual caddis imitation in recent years is the work of two British anglers. John Goddard is the author of *Trout-Fly Recognition,* which has been called the definitive book on fly hatches in the United Kingdom. Clifford Henry is a remarkably innovative fly dresser who illustrated Goddard's book with sketches and diagrams, and their collaboration has produced a strikingly original clipped-hair caddisfly. Goddard has two small photographs of their clipped-hair sedge in his recent book, and its ingenious character is not fully apparent.

Like many innovative solutions, the concept is both simple and obvious. It consists of a heavy strand of darning cotton that matches the body color of the natural being imitated tied in under the hook, trailing off toward the rear. Two antenna fibers are tied in lying forward from the eye. The beginning is not unusual, but the next step is remarkable: the entire hook shank is filled with bunched body hair of deer, caribou, elk, or antelope, depending on the wing color of the hatch. The hair is densely flared along the hook like a bass bug, and then trimmed into the tent-shaped bulk of a sedge. The fly body is formed simply by dubbing fur or polypropylene on the darning cotton rather roughly, and stretching this cotton core taut along the underside of the shank. The fly is conventionally hackled, and the upper fibers are clipped off at the thorax. The concept has been widely adopted on the white-water rivers of our Pacific Coast, and André Puyans dresses large versions of these clipped-wing sedges for the

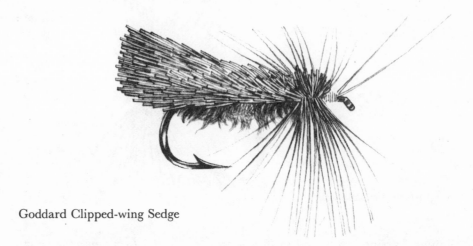

Goddard Clipped-wing Sedge

rivers north of San Francisco. His variation also razor-trims a tapering notch at the center of the flaring wing mass to simulate the V-shaped space between the wings. These clipped-wing sedges are a remarkable mixture of sophisticated British silhouette theory and the floatability of clipped deer hair, which developed on the rough-and-tumble American rivers.

Except for hatching imitations like the Hare's Ear, and the soft-hackled border patterns that suggest emerging sedge pupae, our imitations of aquatic nymphs, larvae and pupal forms are largely a product of this century. Skues is the father of both the mayfly nymph imitation and its chalkstream fishing techniques. His nymphs were already fully developed when *The Way of a Trout with a Fly* was published in 1921, and the exquisite watercolors of Captain Sainte Barbe Goldsmith illustrate the Skues-style nymph in a pair of color plates. Skues tied his nymphs with short soft-fiber legs and tails, bodies roughly and delicately dubbed on colored silk, and a thickly dubbed thorax. This slightly exaggerated thorax was covered with a

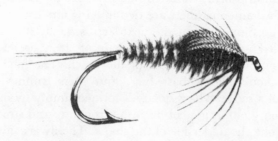

Skues Nymph

wing case formed of pheasant-tail fibers. The proportions of these flies are elegant and studied, and the remarkable Skues-style nymph is still the principal influence in our thinking today.

Both Mottram and Harding dressed similar nymphs, and our own Preston Jennings advocated conventional wet flies with their wings clipped or tied short in his *Book of Trout Flies*, which created a silhouette in the Skues tradition. Edward Hewitt tied flat-bodied nymphs of similar proportions, but his hard lacquer bodies were only lifeless echoes of the elegant Skues prototypes.

Both James Leisenring and Art Flick tied patterns closely matched to American nymphal forms, but their proportions and style are not unlike their English antecedents. It was Charles Wetzel who started a nymph-tying school of precise imitation, complete with individual wing pads and legs of knotted moosemane. However, Wetzel was not a highly skilled tier in the sense that his patterns were beautifully wrought works of art, and it was William Blades who developed the tying of precise nymphal patterns to the point of excellence. Blades was my fly-dressing mentor for several years, and although his exacting patterns have a strange, lifeless quality to them, no one has excelled their craftsmanship. Blades was an artisan of exceptional talents, and disciples like Poul Jorgenson and Ted Niemeyer are superb fly dressers in the Blades tradition.

Edward Sens is another American nymph fisherman, and although he never wrote about his entomological studies, his fly patterns were outlined by Ray Ovington in his *How to Take Trout on Wet Flies and Nymphs*. The Sens dressings were also keyed to familiar dry-fly hatches, with wing cases of cut feathers rather than the Skues-type feather sections tied down over the thorax. The basic proportions of the Sens nymphs are still obvious echoes of the Skues prototypes, but his little caddis pupae are completely original. These imitations of hatching sedges consisted of little more than rough dubbing along the body, two half-developed wings along the sides, and a thorax of darker dubbing mixed with rough guard-hairs. These emerging caddis were the prelude to a whole philosophy of hatching nymphs and pupae found in the work of writers like Hidy, Swisher, Richards, Rogowski,

Sens Pupa

Rosborough, and in my own book *Matching the Hatch*. Such a philosophy is a modern American innovation of considerable importance.

Frank Sawyer wrote his book *Nymphs and the Trout* in 1958, and his two favorite patterns for the Avon above Salisbury are unquestionably derivative of the half-century Skues tradition. His small Pheasant Tail, Grey Goose, Pale Watery Nymph, Spur-wing Nymph, and tiny pinkish cream shrimps are pure simplicity. The three mayfly patterns are very much in the Skues style, except that they dispense entirely with leg fibers. The late Major Oliver Kite was a dedicated Sawyer disciple, and Kite also fished the chalkstreams near the cathedral town of Salisbury. Kite was so convinced that the Sawyer pheasant-tail dressing was sufficient for his home waters that his *Nymph Fishing in Practice* recommends carrying only that pattern in a number of hook sizes.

Ted Rogowski is an eastern fly-fisherman transplanted to Seattle to work as a federal attorney for the Environmental Protection Agency. During his years in Manhattan with a distinguished Wall Street law office, he was an active member of the Anglers' Club of New York and one of the founding officers of the Theodore Gordon Flyfishers. Rogowski is a tier of nymphs that are consciously descended from Skues, but his dressings are

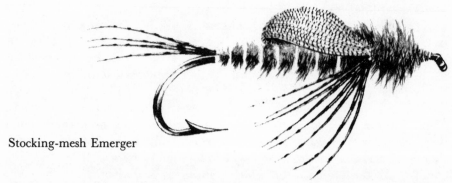

Stocking-mesh Emerger

also thorax-style configurations adapted from the dry-fly theories of Marinaro. His work is described in *American Fly-Fishing* in a long, discursive chapter dealing with experimental fly dressing; about fifteen years ago his studies included emerging wings shaped from sections of women's nylon stockings. The air held in the stocking meshes tends to buoy these fur-bodied nymphs, holding them just within the meniscus like a hatching fly. Such emerging patterns are a major step after the beginnings found in the work of Sens.

George Grant is a skilled fly dresser from Butte, with a lifetime of fishing on Montana rivers like the Ruby and Beaverhead and Big Hole. His work is described in a paperbound folio entitled *The Art of Weaving Hair Hackles for Trout Flies*. His woven-body nymphs with hair and plastic hackle fibers are his most famous innovations, but it is the hybrid nymphs that are perhaps his most important work. These patterns combine both traditional

Swisher-Richards Emerger

soft hackles like grouse, ringneck pheasant, and woodcock and bodies of flat nylon monofilament wound smoothly over cores of synthetic wool and floss. These underbodies are mottled, edged with indelible felt pens, and marked to suggest the body coloring of the naturals. Flat nylon monofilament is an unusually effective material for simulating naturals that have bodies glowing with inner chroma, like the bright greens muted inside the loosening pupal skin of a hatching sedge.

Polly Rosborough is a professional tier from Chiloquin in the mountains of Oregon, and his fur-bodied nymphs are widely known on American rivers. His roughly tied patterns are practical, easily tied, and effective on difficult fish. Some are frankly impressionistic in concept, capable of suggesting a number of subaquatic diet forms. Others are clearly imitative nymphs focused on a particular hatch. Rosborough has assembled his fly patterns and philosophy of nymph technique into a slim book titled *Tying and Fishing the Fuzzy Nymphs*, and its tying concepts are an intriguing synthesis. His exaggerated heads are painted dark on their dorsal surfaces, obviously intended to suggest the thoracic structure of the naturals. Some smaller mayfly and stonefly forms are dressed without leg fibers, while his larger nymphs have sparsely tied legs. Rosborough ties his wing cases with various fibers like mallard, lemon woodduck, and marabou, sometimes leaving a few sparse fibers trailing to suggest emerging wings. Other Rosborough dressings clearly suggest hatching nymphs with soft, feather-wing cases reaching back more than half the body length. The full series of patterns includes several important western mayflies and stonefly species, along with caddis larvae and the pupal imitations of hatching sedges. Midge pupae and freshwater shrimps are also found in the Rosborough fly books, and his patterns are an important facet of American nymph tactics.

Dave Whitlock and Ron Kusse are two nymph experts whose patterns are not focused on specific hatches. They tie general imitations that suggest groups of major species. Both men like soft body-hackle fibers in their nymphs. Their skilled use of fur dubbing for imitating the abdomen and thoracic structure of their nymphs, and the delicate light-catching qualities of tinsel ribbing to suggest both body segments and a loosening nymphal skin, is clearly in the Skues tradition. Their feather wing cases of peacock and dark quill sections of turkey are tied in the same manner found in the watercolors of *The Way of a Trout with a Fly*, and their tying style is quite similar to my own. Whitlock also experiments with new materials, and his vinyl-backed freshwater shrimps are typical of his inventive mind. His shrimp imitations also work with bent hook shanks to suggest the body posture and swimming motions of the naturals. Ron Kusse also works with distorted hook shanks, particularly in his slender imitations of big Ephemeroptera and damselflies, because he believes that a living nymph does not hold its abdomen ramrod straight in life—and that slender nymphs tied on long-shank hooks look lifeless unless they are kinked to suggest restlessness and movement.

Steenrod Rolled-wing Dry Fly

Although their no-hackle dry flies have perhaps attracted the most attention, Douglas Swisher and Carl Richards have included a number of important observations on nymphs, larvae, and pupal forms in their book *Selective Trout*, as well as their emphasis on emerging subaquatic insects. Their work in these areas closely parallels my own, although our basic studies are concentrated in different geographic regions.

Swisher and Richards have explored the all-fur nymphal imitations first worked out by W. H. Lawrie in his *All-Fur Flies and How to Dress Them*, which covered conditions in the United Kingdom, and other patterns in *Selective Trout* were entirely constructed of fur dubbing except for their throat hackles and tails. Some patterns are dressed in precisely the Skues style, while others have wing cases of bunched peacock and ostrich herl. Although the first detached-body nymphs were described in my writings over fifteen years ago, *Selective Trout* has expanded on my work, which was devoted only to damselfly nymphs. Swisher and Richards have worked out delicate detached-body mayflies, using both feather section and breast feathers set in vinyl lacquer. Their hatching mayfly nymphs have been dressed with wings of hackle points, hen hackles, and rolled wings of soft hackles and duck flank feathers. Similar tying methods are used in their emerging sedge pupae, with soft, roughly tied materials that trap tiny air bubbles and glisten with moisture, working almost imperceptibly in the current. My recent book *Nymphs* catalogues most of the important American subaquatic species and their imitations, using all of these fly-dressing techniques.

Although Charles Wetzel outlined the first midge pupal imitations in his *Practical Fly-Fishing* more than thirty years ago, and my own *Matching the Hatch* included both larval and pupal imitations of these tiny insects, many young tiers are adding to our knowledge of selective patterns for these minutae. Some of the most knowledgeable midge-fishing experts are tiers like Edward Koch and Sidney Neff in Pennsylvania, Eric Peper and Robert Linsenman in the Catskills, John Alevras and Len Codella in northern New Jersey, and Swisher and Richards in Michigan.

But perhaps the most unusual innovation in *Selective Trout* is the concept of a nymph tied with an articulated body, designed to wriggle and flutter in the water. These so-called wriggling nymphs are a remarkable concept for imitating the many swimming species as well as those ecotypes which struggle clumsily in hatching. Frank Sawyer discusses his inability to imitate the Blue-winged Olive nymphs in his *Nymphs and the Trout*, and his British experience has parallels for the many related fly hatches found on our own rivers. Such nymphal forms are poor swimmers. These nymphs are clambering types that crawl awkwardly along the bottom, and the fish often take them most readily when they are struggling clumsily just under the surface to hatch.

The Blue-winged Olive nymph is a wriggler, Sawyer writes to explain his lack of success, *and it is necessary to imitate the wriggle as well as the nymph.*

Wiggle Nymph

Sawyer is absolutely correct. Our rivers support many species closely related to the Blue-winged Olives of the United Kingdom, and our fish relish them as much as their chalkstream cousins. Their hatching behavior is a series of erratic, undulating motions as they struggle toward the surface. The trout take them with showy rise forms, obviously excited by their writhing bodies and half-emerging wings and working legs. Such helpless movements invariably attract the fish into seizing its prey. The wriggle nymphs are the kind of creative fly dressing that continues to evolve in these latter years of our century, and the healthy ferment that has produced such innovations is nothing less than a fly-fishing renaissance.

2. Some Notes on the Modern Fly Line

It was a birthday gift of fly tackle that firmly launched me on the odyssey that has carried me throughout the trout-fishing world. The fly line was a braided level type with a hard enamel finish and it lay coiled and stiff in its box. Stretched and finally broken in along the river, it would work and shoot as well as my boyhood skills could fish it. However, when its brittle finish began to crack and wear, my enamel line refused to float and cut ragged grooves in the guides.

Line like that's impossible, one old-timer on the Pere Marquette observed. *Cut the guides right off the rod!*

It was a bright morning in early summer on the willow-lined Baldwin when another fisherman watched me fishing and gave me my first silk line. The trout were working eagerly to the hatching *Ephemerella* flies, and I had already taken several when a friendly voice startled me.

You're fishing beautifully. The strange fisherman stepped into the stream. *How old are you?*

Ten, I replied shyly.

The man nodded and smiled. *May I see your equipment?* he asked. *It's fishing well for you already.*

He took the rod gently, flexing out a series of elegant false casts, and dropped my fly along a deadfall. *It's well balanced,* he smiled, *but this linoleum line you've got is too stiff and clumsy for real dry-fly work.*

Linoleum line? I echoed.

We call them linoleum lines, the man laughed, *but they're not really made of linoleum—they're not so bad!*

What should I have? I asked.

British silk, he replied. *British double tapers woven of silk are the best fly lines in the world.*

What does one cost?

They're pretty expensive, he smiled, *but you walk up to my car and I'll show you.* We waded across the current, and his trunk was a cornucopia of beautiful split-cane rods and reels and mahogany tackle boxes filled with flies and assorted fishing gear.

The man rummaged down in a leather duffel and came up with a half dozen Hardy leaders of exquisite silkworm gut, tapered down to .007 at the tippet. The leaders were shiny and hard, and their delicate calibrations were a revelation, with a breaking strain of a pound listed on the elegant rice-paper envelopes.

They're beautiful! I exclaimed.

Yes, the man agreed, *but an English silk line is even more beautiful, and together with a fine silkworm-gut leader, it can be nothing less than poetry!*

The man searched deeper into his gear and held out an elegant Halford fly line, its darkly gleaming coils lying in its rice-paper wrappers. It was in my hands now and it was supple and smooth, its solid woven core flexing easily in my fingers, and its oil finish felt rich to the touch. Its oily, faintly waxen odor is unforgettable almost thirty-five years later.

It's yours, the fisherman said in a voice that would take no back talk, *along with the silkworm-gut leaders.*

You're serious? It was incredibly generous.

Yes. We shook hands.

The silk fly line and the half-dozen leaders were worth thirty-odd dollars during the Depression years, but it was some time before I fully understood his generosity. The man waded off downstream while I was still soaking a coiled leader in the shallows, and I never thought to ask his name. The synergy between my new silk line and its matching gut leaders was poetic, and although our modern polyvinyl fly lines and nylon leader materials are a technical revolution in trout fishing, the superb handling qualities of silk have never been equalled.

The evolution of the fly line has occupied the span of many centuries, with the first recorded use of a braided silk line dating to the Chou Dynasty, and Chinese fishermen on the Chi River in Hunan Province. Unlike the fishing reel, the braided silk line apparently did not migrate to Europe with the trading caravans, since Claudius Aelianus described a horsehair line in use by the ancient fly-fishermen of Macedonia almost five centuries later. Dame Juliana Berners still recommended a horsehair line in *Treatyse of Fysshynge wyth an Angle,* and even described preparing lines of different colors for different seasons and types of water. It was Charles Cotton, in his *Being Instructions How to Angle for a Trout or Grayling in a Clear Stream,* who first described a finely tapered line in 1676:

> Now to have your whole line as it ought to be, two of the first lengths nearest the hook should be of two hairs apiece; the next three lengths above them of three; the next three above them of four; and so of five, and six, and seven, to the very top; by which

means your rod and tackle will, in a manner, be tapered from your very hand to your hook; your line will fall much better and straighter, and cast your fly to any certain place, to which the hand and eye shall direct it, with less weight and violence than would otherwise circle the water, and fright away the fish.

Such lines were common on the trout streams of Europe and North America until the close of the nineteenth century, and some tradition-minded anglers were still using braided horsehair forty years later. Cotton-braided lines enjoyed a brief vogue on British waters in the latter half of the nineteenth century, and enamel-finished lines were first developed shortly after 1860.

Compound braided lines of horsehair and silk preceded the pure silk lines that emerged in these same years. Level lines of oiled and raw braided silk were available in the United States from Dame, Stoddard & Kendall of Boston as early as 1875. These primitive oil-finished lines were apparently an American development, although the first tapered fly lines woven of silk and cotton clearly originated in England. The Manchester Cotton Twine Spinning Company and Eaton & Deller of London were simultaneously responsible for perfecting these tapered designs. The Manchester product was fashioned of both cotton and silk, and was twisted rather than actually woven, while Eaton & Deller developed the first truly woven fly line tapered in silk and oil-dressed. These technical innovations were perfected about 1880, and the Eaton & Deller lines were clearly the prologue to our modern tackle.

Orvis still advertised silk-tapered fly lines with enamel finishes in 1884, when Frederic Halford was already working with a surgical instrument manufacturer to develop a solid woven-silk line with a fast-taper construction. Other makers experimented with hollow fly lines because of their obvious floating potential, but hollow lines proved extremely fragile. Walter Durfee Coggeshall, who was a good fishing friend of Skues on the Itchen, carried Halford's research even further with his excellent tapered silk lines. Coggeshall finished his delicate lines with several thin coats of linseed oil and varnish, each coat being allowed to dry thoroughly and hand-rubbed before the next coat was applied. When the silk braid was completely covered and sealed under these oil-finish layers, the entire line was hand-polished to a hard gloss. Some companies introduced an evaporating agent to their finish formulas, to accelerate the critical drying process. American tackle companies were quick to copy these innovations, but they were slow to catch on with our fishermen. Abercrombie & Fitch, the famous sporting goods store in New York, apparently did not carry them in stock until after 1910.

Silk fly lines tapered to the Halford calibrations and finished according to the final Halford patents were the bench mark of quality for the first fifty years of this century. Their character and workmanship were superb. The soft oil finish was a revelation to generations of Americans accustomed to the brittle enamel-finished lines that often chipped and cracked and coiled tightly on the reel, and the new lines seemed to sweeten and become more supple with time. Tackle catalogues early in this century described a so-called secret process in the manufacture of these lines, but this was a fabrication. The lines were braided solidly of silk and immersed in a pressure tank containing a mixture of refined linseed oil and Kauri-gum varnish. Atmospheric pressure in the finishing tank was then sharply reduced, drawing the air entrained in the braiding from the line and permitting a controlled quantity of the oil-finish formula to saturate the silk. The foundation created in the pressure tank formed the base for a series of oil-and-varnish coats, each carefully rubbed down with rottenstone and pumice before the next layer was applied. Talcum powder was finally used to polish the finished product.

Silk lines had a lithe and supple poetry about them, partially because of their inherent properties, and partially because they are heavier than nylon lines of the same diameter. This means a four-weight silk line is thinner than a four-weight nylon taper, and its reduced wind resistance played a considerable role in its casting qualities.

However, these beautiful lines of oil-finished silk had problems as well. The finishes were relatively soft and wore away quickly, and the lines readily absorbed water when fishing. It was necessary to dress them daily to repel the water and keep the lines floating, and it was wise to strip them from your reel each night onto the skeleton frame of a line drier. Many anglers bought two lines, which enabled them to fish one and dry the other simultaneously. Oil finishes also oxidized and became quite tacky. Although immersion in a highly alkaline solution neutralized their tackiness, it also removed much of the finish, and it was necessary to refinish the braided core with successive coats of linseed oil and varnish. The silk was also highly susceptible to fungus and rot. Such problems were easily avoided by purchasing a new line, although it was painful to discard an expensive Halford fly line in any condition.

These double-taper lines were the peak of fly-fishing theory and practice until midcentury, although weight-forward line theories had been advanced for salmon fishing in Ireland as early as 1885. Hardy Brothers had developed primitive forward tapers for trout in concert with Philip Trench of Dublin twenty-five years later, although another quarter century would pass before the superb distance casters of our western American steelhead rivers would adapt and refine weight-forward tapers and shooting-head designs into our modern tools for long-range work. Such line theories evolved to perfection on our Pacific rivers and tournament-casting platforms, along with the double-haul technique capable of exploiting their distance qualities, particularly in the hands of pioneers like Dick Miller, Marvin Hedge, and Peter Schwab.

Nylon fly lines were first developed during the Depression years, but were not available in commercial quantities until after the Second World War. The potential of nylon was obvious, since it was stronger than silk and did not rot with protracted exposure to fishing. It was also considerably more elastic than silk. The traditional oil finishes simply could not cope with this exaggerated elasticity; and finding a synthetic finish with a compatible modulus of elasticity proved difficult. The elasticity of the nylon core literally stretched and shattered its outer finish, and the line was quickly ruined. All fishermen remember how short-lived these early nylon lines were, and what damage their cracked finishes did to rod guides. Nylon fly lines were held in low esteem in those years, and their longevity was the butt of many streamside jokes.

The first true sinking lines had been manufactured and sold just before the end of the nineteenth century by Foster Brothers, whose shop is still near the British Dove in Ashburton. It was a silk line braided over a brass core, and similar lead-core lines are currently popular on our Pacific coastal rivers for deep-water tactics.

However, laboratory technicians were busily working to solve the problem of a synthetic finish with an elasticity equal to the braided nylon cores. The solution finally came in 1949, when practical methods of using polyvinyl chloride in fly-line finishes were perfected. It was first used with a hollow-woven line of nylon, but such lines had the same defects as earlier hollow lines of silk and cotton and other fibers. Such lines were much too fragile, their hollow cores eventually shipped water and sank the lines, and their tapers were achieved by varying the thread counts at various points in the line. Such hollow cores were difficult to fabricate and control with precision, and they were expensive.

Three years later, another milestone was reached in the development of the modern fly line. It became possible to control the design taper in the polyvinyl chloride finish rather than taper the woven core itself.

It was a remarkable technical breakthrough, and it had an immediate impact on the cost of manufacturing tapered fly lines, placing them within the economic reach of the average fisherman. It also permitted linemakers to produce tapers with unbelievable precision, virtually identical in their finish calibrations and with tolerances of less than .001 inch. Manufacturers suddenly found themselves capable of producing lines of uniformly consistent density and weight.

The first polyvinyl chloride finishes were conceived with minuscule bubbles and low specific gravity, and were designed to float faultlessly. Chemists soon perfected synthetic finishes capable of producing compound sinking-tip lines, as well as sinking lines of varied specific gravity and sinking ability. The short-lived sinking lines braided entirely of dacron were soon rendered obsolete. The sinking polyvinyl lines offered anglers a whole new spectrum in their sport, permitting them to fish nymphs and wet flies and streamers with more precise control of depth than had ever been possible in the past.

The series of remarkable technical developments since midcentury had a revolutionary impact on fly-line construction and manufacture. Our lines differ considerably from the wonderfully sophisticated innovations of

Halford and Coggeshall and Marryat in the nineteenth century. Polyvinyl chlorides make it possible to braid a level core of simple construction with a precisely tapered coating, instead of the intricately woven solid or hollow tapers of the past. The synthetic vinyl finishes are heat-cured and can be applied to control density and, through their specific gravity, the sinking and floating qualities of the lines themselves.

Such heat-cured plastic finishes made mass production of fly lines possible for the first time in history. Manufacturers can fabricate them continuously in long skeins, duplicating a controlling taper formula in virtually exact copies. Diameters are controlled within .001 of an inch and total line weight is monitored to within 1/500 of an ounce. Such precision is achieved through variable dies having a controlled orifice that can modify both line diameter and weight at any point along the core.

Production becomes relatively simple. It begins with a core of braided nylon, fiberglass or monofilament in the floating lines. Dacron is usually used in the sinking tapers because of its high specific gravity. The core is treated with bonding agents to implement adhesion of the polyvinyl finishes. The treated core is then passed through its first plastic bath and is forced through the operable die system. Its controllable aperture shapes the polyvinyl chloride into its final calibrations and tapers. Heat curing hardens the plastic and fuses it to the core material. The ends of each double- or forward-taper line are marked when its die sequence is complete, and a run of several lines is wound on a storage reel. The completed fly lines are finally cut apart for coiling and inspection, and are ultimately wrapped and packaged for shipment.

Precise control of diameter and the wide variation of weight within a single diameter soon made a new designation system necessary for our modern fly lines. It has been a century since the manufacturers evolved a scale of measurements based upon line calibrations, and a system of designated letter equivalents. The American and European calibrations in the old system are as follows, with the metric measurements in rounded figures:

EUROPEAN AND AMERICAN LINE CALIBRATIONS

SIZE	1/10 MM	1/100 MM	1/1000 INCH
A	15.0	150	.060
B	14.0	140	.055
C	13.0	130	.050
D	11.5	115	.045
E	10.0	100	.040
F	9.0	90	.035
G	8.0	80	.030
H	7.5	75	.025
I	6.0	60	.022

Obviously, the earlier nomenclature for fly lines based solely on diameter became unworkable with the perfection of polyvinyl chloride finishes, since two lines of identical diameter and taper systems could vary radically in weight. Most knowledgeable trout fishermen in my boyhood years were using rods that called for HDH and HCH double-tapered lines. Some big-water anglers in our western mountains could even be found wielding GBG tapers on heavy currents, and there were already skilled light-tackle men fishing rods with calibrations delicate enough to balance elegantly with an HEH line in oil-finished English silk. Some variation in the specific gravity and weight of these lines was possible too, because of weaving technology and the specifications for the oil finishes, and HDH lines from one manufacturer were not always identical to HDH tapers from another maker in terms of casting with a specific rod. Balancing rods and lines was a difficult kind of alchemy.

Originally, silk fly lines were designed in three basic types. The level line had a constant diameter over its entire length and was relatively easy to manufacture. It was inexpensive, and therefore the type purchased first by many beginners, but in the larger diameters, it delivered the leader clumsily on the water under difficult conditions and has largely disappeared from the market. Single-taper silk lines were also popular because of their lower price, and consisted of a relatively fine level head of about three feet, ten to twelve feet of front taper, and the remainder of their ninety feet in the heavier belly diameter. Since few anglers could cast more than fifty to sixty feet, and fewer still ever experienced actual fishing problems that required such casting, fishermen soon discovered that when a single-taper line was worn out, almost half of its level belly remained brand new and gleamingly intact in the inner windings of the reel. The silk double-taper design was therefore conceived in terms of its long-range economy, even though it was more expensive to make. It was literally two single-taper designs joined back-to-back in a single line. Double-taper specifications resulted in a perfectly symmetrical design that could be reversed when one end was worn out, doubling the fishing life of the average silk line.

Multiple tapers remained in their infancy in the years before the Second World War, and the knowledgeable men who really knew something about their theory and design were a relatively small group of tournament casters and steelhead fishermen who were as closed-mouthed about their secrets as a medieval guild.

These men spliced varying lengths of level fly line together in hundreds of experimental homemade tapers for distance casting. Tackle cranks like Dick Miller, Peter Schwab, and Marvin Hedge badgered Pacific Coast rodmakers and line manufacturers into producing precisely what they needed, even though many of their more radical concepts were unworkable for less skilled casters and were virtually unmarketable. Peter Schwab had a favorite weight-forward design that consisted of a five-foot steep taper from .025 to .045 with no level head, ten feet of level .045 working into ten more feet of .050, followed by ten feet of homemade back taper between .045 and

.037. The shooting line consisted of fifty-five feet of .037 lovingly polished with graphite, and with the entire multiple head weighing only 140 grains, a fisherman skilled with a fine eight-and-a-half-foot rod could deliver the whole fly line while waist-deep in a heavy steelhead riffle.

The empirical work taking place on our Pacific Coast exploded into the world of international tournament casting in 1938, when Marvin Hedge demonstrated the double-haul techniques he had worked out to exploit these new multiple tapers to their full distance potential. It was a method conceived to instantly exaggerate line velocity, a velocity perfectly matched to shooting long lengths of the level running line behind the weight-forward head. Tournament distances in the trout-fly class quickly cartwheeled beyond 150 feet, and when Dick Miller reached 179 feet in registered competition, the weight-forward line and the double haul utterly ruled the world of distance fly casting.

Early weight-forward theory was so esoteric that tackle men like Marvin Hedge actually made and sold compound Hedge tapers designed for specific distances. Hedge had specifications for casts of 75, 100, and 150 feet. The tournament casters and steelhead crowd all wanted the extreme distance model, but few had the tackle, physical strength, and timing to lift it cleanly from the water.

Our modern weight-forward lines evolved rapidly from these hand-made prototypes. Typical early specifications for factory-produced lines offered approximately two to three feet of level head, nine to ten feet of relatively steep taper, twenty-odd feet of weight-forward belly, two to three feet of exaggerated back taper, and the remaining lengths a fine running or shooting line of constant diameter. Such lines radically lengthened the casting distances of most fishermen, even before they fully mastered the double-haul methods that could take them beyond seventy-five or eighty feet.

However, mere distance without delicacy is limited to broken water and big rivers, since the velocity of a double-haul tends to drop the weight-forward belly rather harshly on the surface. Fishermen quickly discovered that it was difficult to straighten an uncoiling front taper without gently snubbing its shoot late in the cast, and that even this refinement dropped their terminal tackle too crudely for a selective fish in relatively smooth currents. Obviously, future developments were needed to wed the distance capabilities of the new multiple tapers with the reasonable subtlety of a double-taper fly presentation. Such hybrids are never fully successful, but the modified long-belly designs that have evolved in the past five years are certainly a step in that direction. Their specifications call for lengthening the belly of the weight-forward head from twenty to twenty-five and thirty feet, which helps dampen the clumsy velocity of the longer shots and turns the line over smoothly with a properly timed checking of the shoot. It is doubtful whether a hybrid taper capable of both fishing fine and fishing at distances that Charles Cotton never dreamed possible is fully workable.

These early fly-line concepts all involved floating lines, and their tapers were described in terms of the letter designations familiar to almost all fly-fishermen. Level lines were labelled with a single letter equivalent to their constant diameters. Most fishermen on trout water worked with level lines from E to B designation or calibrated between .040 and .055 inches. Single-taper lines were typically HE lines for fishing fine, HD and HC tapers for all-around work, and an occasional GB design was seen on big water. These designations translated into a taper from .025 to .040 on difficult fish, lines that ran from .025 to either .045 or .050 to balance the average trout rod, and big-water lines that varied from .030 to .055. Double-taper lines are still the most popular, and under the old system of sizing them, their trout-fishing types commonly ranged from HEH to a relatively muscular GBG. The HEH specified a taper that progressed from .025 through .040 and back to .025 in a perfectly symmetrical design. HDH and HCH lines were perhaps the most popular models in America at midcentury. Their tapers were also symmetrical, running from .025 through bellies of .045 and .050 back to .025 at the opposite head. Few anglers wanted to work hard enough to muscle a GBG double taper all day, with its taper of .030 to .055 and back to .030, but a surprising number were sold and used on western rivers.

Multiple-taper distance lines were also described with the letter nomenclature when they were first developed. Big-water and bassbug tapers were the most common early designs, and the HCF, GBF, and GAF weight-forward lines were popular from the beginning. These were the so-called three-diameter types. The HCF had a compound taper ranging from .025 to its belly of .050, and its running line measured .035. The popular GBF size ran from its head of .030 to a shooting belly of .055 and tapering back to its .035 running diameter. Fishing a rod that could handle a GAF silk forward taper in split cane was not easy, and hauling a line that varied from .030 to .060 in its belly and head, dropping back to a shooting diameter of .035 produced some Herculean fatigue.

The perspective of time indicates that both the double-taper and weight-forward lines were manufactured with level heads that were much too long until recent years. Level heads of six to ten feet were common and typically failed to deliver a complete cast and turn over the leader under fishing conditions. It was often necessary to cut back a series of trial-and-error lengths from these level heads to find the proper behavior with a specific rod. It was a little like shortening the legs of a table, cutting and cutting until the sorry moment when you realize that you have sawed off too much and the table is ruined. Thousands of fly lines were damaged just like that, snipping and trimming the level heads to balance a particular rod. Our lack of knowledge was certainly a factor, but erratic standards of manufacturing and consistent diameter-to-weight ratios were perhaps the worst problem in balancing lines, leaders, and fly rods.

The basic tapers were all woven of silk and finished in linseed oil and Kauri-gum varnish, made by different manufacturers, and varied somewhat in weight-per-foot. Nylon core lines were somewhat lighter when fabricated in the same tapers and diameters. The nominal length of casting line worked in the air without double-hauling was a maximum of forty to fifty feet in the double tapers, and about fifty to sixty feet in the forward-taper designs. Behind that nominal casting length lies a so-called holding length of level running line that is constantly chafed back and forth while casting.

The length of line which defines the maximum loading weight that a fly rod can accommodate before it is overstressed is its lift capacity. It is the maximum free length of line that can be held in motion during false casting, using only a single left-hand casting haul. The maximum free-line loading with double tapers consists of the forward taper plus about sixty percent of the belly, depending on casting skills and rod action. Maximum loading with weight-forward type lines equals the level head, forward taper and belly and back taper, the holding line, and as much as the caster can handle of the shooting length to about seventy-five feet.

Basic comparative considerations between double-taper and weight-forward lines in actual fishing have not changed since the development of our modern polyvinyl chloride finishes, except that sinking lines are thinner than floating lines of equal weight, and will work better in both the atmosphere and a wind because of less wind resistance.

Double-tapered lines are superb fishing tools at ranges of fifteen to seventy-five feet, delivering and turning over smoothly without frightening a hard-fished trout. Since their belly length is heavier, casting rhythms are relatively slow, and line velocity on delivery is quickly dampened by the inertia of the level belly diameters. Long casts are slowly developed by false casting to build line velocity, while velocity is quickly achieved with a weight-forward taper. Such forward-taper lines are demonstrably more effective in a wind, regardless of their specific gravity. Since windy weather invariably riffles a smooth current holding selective fish, a weight-forward line is sometimes a good choice on a stream where it would normally be too clumsy when sufficient wind is present to mute mistakes. Casting rhythms and line velocity are relatively fast with a forward taper, which means presentation to a cruising fish is quicker. Speed of presentation is important under some conditions, and the most important quality of the weight-forward line is unquestionably its distance capability.

It is interesting to compare typical weight-forward specifications for lines having .050 belly diameters from several major manufacturers when *Matching the Hatch* was published twenty-odd years ago. Some makers varied their three-diameter designs radically, even changing belly length as much as eight to ten feet in their own lines with diameters from .050 to .060. The short level heads, short front tapers, and relatively constant belly lengths were already standard among the Pacific Coast linemakers even then, and the influence of thinkers like Schwab and Hedge is obvious. It is also apparent from these specifications that some eastern manufacturers were already aware of the optimal criteria for a weight-forward design.

Both manufacturers and fishermen soon became aware that the new polyvinyl chloride finishes, with their nylon and dacron cores under plastic tapers of widely varying specific gravity, were rapidly making the old letter designations obsolete. Lines could no longer be compared in terms of diameter alone, and the traditional HDH and GBF labels were utterly unworkable. Weight became the basic criterion in sizing lines, yet radical variations in weight were possible in the same diameter with finishes of air-impregnated plastic or high-density polyvinyl. The traditional alphabetical designations were now meaningless, yet no standard system of classification had emerged to replace them.

New standards were finally worked out by the fishing-tackle industry in concert with casting clubs in both Europe and America, and these standards were based primarily on weight. Since thirty feet was a reasonable average of maximum line loading before line velocity was built with the double haul, it was adopted as the bench mark by which weight could be measured and compared. The weight of the front thirty feet, regardless of taper specifications, was determined in grains. The unit of measure is derived from the average weight of wheat, with approximately 7,000 grains per pound. It was a complicated system of comparative measurement, but it translates into a simple formula for the modern angler. The system was defined in a code based on weight in grains for the terminal thirty feet of any taper, and the maximum allowable variation in that weight ranged from six to twelve grains. The standard code was resolved in the following terms:

STANDARD MANUFACTURING LINE-WEIGHT CODE

LINE CODE	WEIGHT IN GRAINS	MINIMUM TOLERANCES	MAXIMUM TOLERANCES
1	60	54	66
2	80	74	86
3	100	94	106
4	120	114	126
5	140	134	146
6	160	152	168
7	185	177	193
8	210	202	218
9	240	230	280
10	280	270	290
11	330	318	342
12	380	368	392

These new designations based upon line weight for the first thirty feet in grains correspond approximately to several of the past alphabetical designations familiar to most fly-fishermen. It might prove helpful in this period of transition from the old system to the new code to study the following table:

COMPARATIVE TABLE OF FLY-LINE SIZES

CODE	WEIGHT IN GRAINS	DOUBLE-TAPER	FORWARD-TAPER
3	100	IFI	IFG
4	120	HFH	HFG
5	140	HEH	HEG
6	160	HDH	HDG
7	185	HCH	HCF
8	210	GBG	GBF
9	240	GAG	GAF
10	280	G2AG	G2AF
11	330	G3AG	G3AF
12	380	G4AG	G4AF

The tackle industry also outlined an alphabetical code to identify taper specifications and relative specific gravity in each line, since a cornucopia of performance specifications had quickly evolved after the introduction of synthetic cores and polyvinyl chloride finishes in fly lines. Level lines were identified with an L-designation, and ST-type lines indicated a single-taper design. Double tapers were coded with the letters DT, an obvious choice, and WF was the code selected for weight-forward lines. Specific gravity finishes designed to sink were identified with an S-coding, and air-impregnated plastic coating designed to float was given an F-designation. Sinking-tip lines received a coding FS to note their hybrid floating and sinking capability, in which the initial ten feet of their tapers sink readily, and the remaining line is designed to float. Such lines permit a skilled fisherman to fish with precision at intermediate depths, and a running line that floats will pick up from the water and shoot readily. The new alphabetical code, with its identification of taper specifications and floating or sinking qualities, was combined with the numerical weight code. The combination defines a modern fly line with a precise and workable standard description.

It is a relatively simple system. The designation L6F means a level fly line weighing 160 grains in its first thirty feet and having an air-impregnated finish that floats. Lines labelled ST5S are single tapers weighing 140 grains in the terminal thirty feet and finished with a high-density plastic that sinks. The package marked DT5F contains a familiar double-taper line that weighs 140 grains and floats like a bobber, and a WF8S label identifies a weight-forward taper weighing 210 grains that sinks like an anchor. The relatively new sinking-tip lines are usually forward tapers, and a WF7FS designation points to a line weighing 185 grains that is built to sink its forward taper, with its remaining eighty feet designed to float. The new line code is simple, concise, and defines the full specifications and character of a modern fly line.

The design tapers of the contemporary Aircel floating and Wetcel sinking lines contain much valuable data, and are produced by the firm that pioneered the polyvinyl chloride lines. The Aircel lines in both double-taper and weight-forward specifications clearly demonstrate the comparisons between the new coding method and the past alphabetical system. The Aircel weight-forward models found in the chart on pages 76–77 provide an interesting comparison with the earlier tapers described in this chapter, the pioneer forward-taper lines produced by several manufacturers twenty-odd years ago.

Sinking lines have a higher density than plastic floating lines of equal weight, and therefore have a much smaller diameter. Both their specific gravity and their reduced atmospheric friction make a polyvinyl sinking line seem much heavier than its actual weight in casting. Such sinking-line effects are well known to manufacturers and anglers alike, and linemakers have compensated by actually reducing the weight of their sinking lines within the same line-weight coding. For example, rods matched perfectly with a DT6F floating double taper are handling a line that weighs approximately 165 grains in its first thirty feet. Those same fly rods cannot handle a high-density sinking line of 165 grains, and to avoid overstressing its line capacity a comparable DT6S line should be reduced to only 155 grains. Such reductions are obvious in the diagrams on pages 78–79 of the Wetcel double tapers and weight-forward lines.

These modern fly lines with their synthetic cores of nylon and dacron are remarkable technical innovations, and they offer our generation a rich spectrum of fishing methods never available before. Our fathers fought constantly to keep their double-taper lines dressed and floating, and tournament-distance casts of seventy-five to eighty-five feet were exceptional. The distances on modern competition platforms are easily twice that, and we owe them both to better technique and our sophisticated weight-forward lines.

High-density lines were totally unknown thirty years ago, and the modern angler is fishing his flies at depths unthinkable in the past. These innovations are perhaps only a prelude, since manufacturers are now experimenting with plastic finishes on fiberglass cores and clear polyvinyl chloride tapers formed over a translucent monofilament core. Cortland has just perfected a line finish of a synthetic foamlike material, and its microscopic air chambers are formed over a delicate dacron core. Pacific Coast fishermen have been experimenting widely in recent years with shooting heads of lead-core trolling lines spliced to special running lines or monofilament. Such rigs can reach distances of 150 feet under actual fishing conditions, and can fish a big nymph or bucktail right on the bottom in the heaviest currents. Technical breakthroughs in line construction are evolv-

Double-taper Floating Lines

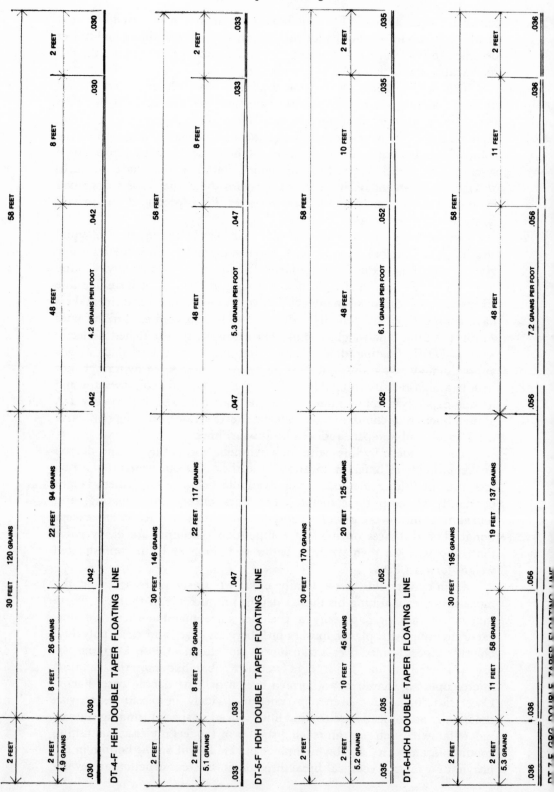

DT-4-F HEH DOUBLE TAPER FLOATING LINE

2 FEET | .030 | 8 FEET 26 GRAINS | 4.9 GRAINS | .030 | 30 FEET 120 GRAINS | .042 | 58 FEET | 4.2 GRAINS PER FOOT | .042 | 22 FEET 94 GRAINS | 8 FEET | .030 | 2 FEET | .030

DT-5-F HDH DOUBLE TAPER FLOATING LINE

2 FEET | .033 | 8 FEET 29 GRAINS | 5.1 GRAINS | .033 | 30 FEET 146 GRAINS | .047 | 58 FEET | 5.3 GRAINS PER FOOT | .047 | 22 FEET 117 GRAINS | 8 FEET | .033 | 2 FEET | .033

DT-6-HCH DOUBLE TAPER FLOATING LINE

2 FEET | .035 | 10 FEET 45 GRAINS | 5.2 GRAINS | .035 | 30 FEET 170 GRAINS | .052 | 58 FEET | 6.1 GRAINS PER FOOT | .052 | 20 FEET 125 GRAINS | 10 FEET | .035 | 2 FEET | .035

DT-7-F GBG DOUBLE TAPER FLOATING LINE

2 FEET | .036 | 11 FEET 58 GRAINS | 5.3 GRAINS | .036 | 30 FEET 195 GRAINS | .056 | 58 FEET | 7.2 GRAINS PER FOOT | .056 | 19 FEET 137 GRAINS | 11 FEET | .036 | 2 FEET | .036

Weight-forward Floating Lines

WF-5-F HDG WEIGHT FORWARD FLOATING LINE

2 FEET   30 FEET   139 GRAINS   58 FEET   41 FEET

2 FEET   8 FEET   30 GRAINS   19 FEET   100 GRAINS   3 FEET   9 GRAINS   17 FEET   58 FEET   41 FEET

5 GRAINS

.033   .033   .047   .047   .036   .036   .033   .033

WF-6-F HCF WEIGHT FORWARD FLOATING LINE

30 FEET   163 GRAINS   58 FEET   41 FEET

2 FEET   9 FEET   37 GRAINS   19 FEET   116 GRAINS   2 FEET   10 GRAINS   17 FEET   58 FEET   41 FEET

5.5 GRAINS

.035   .035   .052   .052   .037   .037   .035   .035

WF-7-F GBF WEIGHT FORWARD FLOATING LINE

30 FEET   197 GRAINS   58 FEET   41 FEET

2 FEET   9 FEET   46 GRAINS   18.5 FEET   133 GRAINS   2.5 FEET   18 GRAINS   17 FEET   58 FEET   41 FEET

6.5 GRAINS

.037   .056   .056   .041   .041   .035   .035

WF-8-F GAF WEIGHT FORWARD FLOATING LINE

30 FEET   220 GRAINS   58 FEET   40 FEET

2 FEET   10 FEET   55 GRAINS   18.5 FEET   155 GRAINS   1.5 FEET   10 GRAINS   18 FEET   58 FEET   40 FEET

7.2 GRAINS

.037   .037   .061   .061   .041   .041   .037   .037

Double-taper Sinking Lines

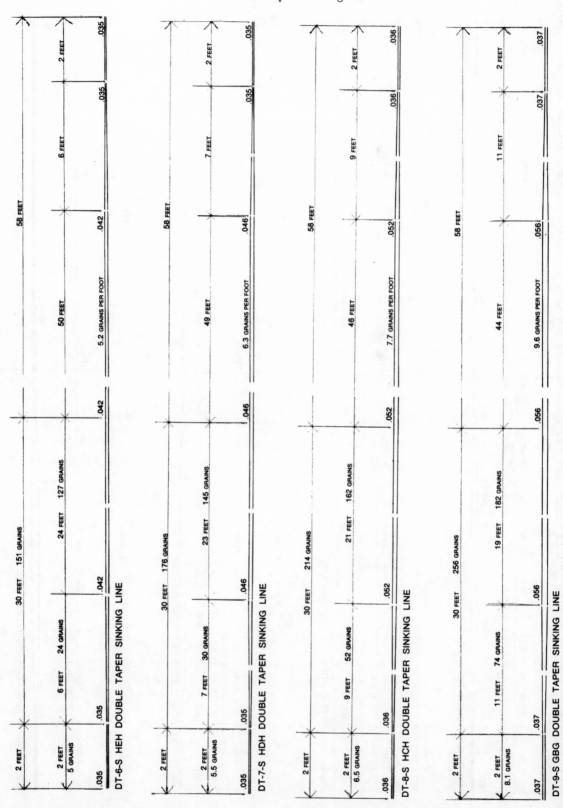

DT-6-S HEH DOUBLE TAPER SINKING LINE

DT-7-S HDH DOUBLE TAPER SINKING LINE

DT-8-S HCH DOUBLE TAPER SINKING LINE

DT-9-S GBG DOUBLE TAPER SINKING LINE

Weight-forward Sinking Lines

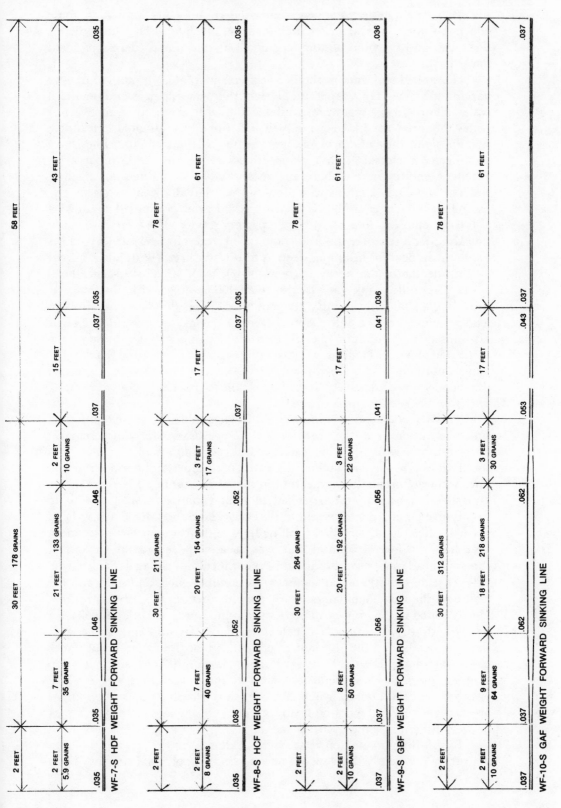

ing at a remarkable pace, and our modern lines are providing more effective fishing time with less maintenance, reaching fish at unthinkable distances, and catching bottom-feeding trout that our predecessors could never have taken.

Controlled sink rate is another refinement created to provide lines of varying specific gravity, taper, and weight that will fish at several depths of water. Slow-sinking types are available that fish about three to five feet below the surface of a lake or reservoir, and are perfectly suited to fishing a nymph along the bottom of smaller streams. Medium-sinking lines have also been developed to fish at intermediate depths; they provide an excellent choice for a fisherman whose budget is limited to a single sinking-type line. High-density lines were originally conceived for fly-fishing in salt water, since its buoyancy and tidal currents demanded a polyvinyl chloride line of extreme specific gravity. However, fishermen quickly discovered that the exaggerated sink rate of these salt-water lines made them ideal for fishing as deep as fifteen to thirty feet in lakes, and at feeding depths in the heavy currents of big trout streams and steelhead rivers. Controlled sink rate is also available in lines with sinking tips, providing a floating line with a ten-foot head designed to drown a stubborn leader quickly, and a full shooting-head that sinks quickly ahead of its air-impregnated running line. The latter design will offer most of the tactical advantages found in a fast-sinking taper, yet its floating back taper and shooting line can be readily mended to get the current-swing deep and dampen fly speed effectively. It is also possible to shoot the buoyant running line from the surface more easily.

Thirty-foot shooting tapers are also available in these controlled sink-rate finishes, and they provide an average fisherman with a remarkable distance tool. Shooting heads consist of thirty-foot sections from standard weight-forward tapers, minus the back taper and normal running line, and were originally worked out in steelhead country. The front tapers and shooting bellies were attached to light running lines of twenty to twenty-five pound monofilament in the early years, and later shooting-head experts spliced light polyvinyl running lines to their weight-forward tapers. One hundred feet of running line was usually spliced to the thirty-foot shooting head, and regular dacron backing filled out the reel. Such tackle will generate remarkably long casts with minimal effort and skill, and the new oval-shaped monofilaments are proving themselves as running lines ideally suited to shooting-head tactics. Shooting heads will seldom deliver a fly with dry-fly accuracy. Delicate presentation is also impossible with shooting heads, and they are not recommended for fishing shy trout under most conditions, since the forward tapers land too hard and the limp running line makes it difficult to control fly speed with precision. Yet lake or big-water conditions in which distance outweighs all other considerations are so perfect for the shooting-head technique that it should become a part of every fisherman's repertoire of tactics.

British line manufacturers Philip Tallants and Terrence Collingbourne have recently developed a new concept in polyvinyl designs. Their

Masterline series employs new plastics technology, making their finishes vulnerable to other line cleaners, and a fresh concept in shaping both tapers and finishes. Taper specifications vary with changing line weights, and the tips are designed to float just under the film, casting a smaller shadow. The weight-forward tapers utilize a series of long-belly designs to improve their fishing qualities, but the finish of the Masterline is perhaps its most surprising feature. The finish is made intentionally irregular, rather than die-smooth like the other plastic lines. Contrary to popular mythology, which holds that the smoothest lines cast more effortlessly, these irregular finishes hopscotch through the guides with considerably less casting friction. Masterlines come in the relatively expensive Chancellor grade, the medium-priced Oxbridge series, and the moderately priced Graduate grade. Although the design concepts in these lines are quite new, their exceptional performance has led several American manufacturers to experiment with similar line specifications.

Most modern fly lines are packaged on vinyl spools designed to help in transferring them to the reel, once an adequate length of twenty- to thirty-pound dacron backing is in place and spliced to the running-line tip. The backing provides a filler that occupies enough space on the reel spool that the line itself is stored in the largest possible coils. It also enables a fisherman to play a fish with more efficiency, since a single turn of the reel recovers more line when the spool is nearly filled than when it is empty and nearing the spindle. Backing is also insurance against the strong fish that strips the entire fly line from the reel in a ratchet-screaming run, for without its extra one hundred to two hundred yards behind the line, such trophy fish might easily be lost. Many anglers use nylon braided line or cheap monofilament as backing, but the elasticity of such materials is dangerous. It can stretch so much under the strain of a really big fish that it can warp or damage a fine-alloy reel during the fight, and salt-water fishermen have had reels literally self-destruct under the elastic stress of a backing line stretched by a big tarpon. The backing line should be twenty- to thirty-pound test, not because its full breaking strain is needed, but because its diameter is thick enough to prevent a big fish from wedging it deeply into the remaining coils, when a strong run is suddenly triggered.

You seldom need backing, is a common observation heard on big-trout rivers from Tierra del Fuego to the Valley of Ten Thousand Smokes. *But when you need backing—you really need it!*

Transferring a new line to the reel begins with turning its packaging spool upside down, twisting it apart, and removing the coil wrappings without disturbing the line itself on its plastic arbor. Unwind about twenty inches of the running tip that is attached to the backing and close the shipping spool, taking care not to pinch the new line. The reassembled plastic spool is then centered on a pencil or small wooden dowel, and with the line under tension from your fingers, wind it clockwise on the reel. Lines are usually supplied with small, pressure-sensitive markers provided to adhere to the reel and identify the line stored on its spool. These markers should not be fastened to the reel spool or frame, but should be trimmed and placed inside the reel-seat foot, making them invisible when the reel itself is mounted on its matching rod.

Maintenance of these modern polyvinyl fly lines is infinitely simpler than taking care of the oil-finished silks of the past. The new lines are a remarkable equilibrium between durability and soft, supple handling. The plastics are unusually capable of withstanding abrasion and water chemistry and wear that would have shredded the finish of a traditional British oil-finished silk in the past.

However, these modern lines are not indestructible. Avoid wedging your line under stones, and when they become fouled there, exercise the patience to free them properly. Pinching a line between the reel spool and flange can bruise its finish, and you should obviously avoid stepping on your line, particularly on ledges and stones, and with hobnailed boots or wading chains. Poor backcast timing can crack-the-whip, developing forces in the terminal length of the line that no material or bonding process can withstand, and it is a common cause of line damage in fishing.

Like a fresh nylon leader, your line should be stretched slightly to eliminate any twisting or coiling when it is new or has been stored on the reel. Anglers who grew up with the fussy intricacies of pampering silk fly lines and their interminable cycles of cleaning and daily dressing and drying are invariably baffled with a line that can simply be left on the reel. It not only can be left there overnight and between fishing trips, but it can also be stored there over the winter. Storage coils that develop on a reel will straighten quickly with a simple stretching. There are fishermen who derive much pleasure from coddling and fussing over their equipment, and who actually enjoyed the daily rituals of cleaning their silk lines, lovingly dressing them with British mucilin—in spite of the containers that could seldom be opened—and stripping the line each night for drying on a wooden frame. The younger members of the angling fraternity will never miss this daily ritual and will welcome the trouble-free character of the polyvinyl chloride lines.

However, there are some problems with vinyl finishes. Solvents found in many suntan creams and lotions, line dressings, dry-fly ointments, fuels, lacquer thinners, and insect repellents are chemically incompatible with their plastic finishes. Modern fly lines should never be stored in hot places or subjected to prolonged exposure to sunlight, particularly inside a locked automobile. Solar radiation is damaging to many synthetic materials and bonding agents after long periods of exposure, which results in a surprising molecular denigration. Ordinary fishing time is no problem in this regard, since solar atrophy of your line will have less demonstrable effect on its lifespan than the abrasion of normal usage and wear.

Polyvinyl lines should be cleaned when they float poorly or begin to shoot grudgingly on long casts. Fishing waters swarm with microscopic organisms that collect on the line and dry after a few days of fishing, accumulating in sufficient numbers to affect its floating and casting qualities. Both these tiny organisms and the residues they attract to the finish absorb minuscule amounts of water than can sink a floating line or make it ride too low in the surface film for an easy line-lift on pickup. Cleaning and polishing these lines will quickly restore their unique qualities. Weekly attention is probably enough, except in exceptionally alkaline waters with their atypically rich concentrations of microorganisms. The line manufacturers all provide excellent fly-line cleaning compounds for their particular products.

Minor repairs on these lines are possible when their synthetic finishes do crack or fray slightly. The best method is to keep a small bottle of fresh synthetic-base varnish in your gear. It should be heated in a saucepan of moderately hot water to thin its viscosity and applied with the index finger in extremely thin coats. Forty-eight hours drying time is about right, and the varnish should finally be polished smooth with talcum powder and a fine wool cloth. Varnish can be applied with a needle to repair a small hinge or chipped place in the line. Fraying and wear typically appear in the few inches of line that ride back and forth in the tip guide during the normal range of casting. The length of this casting wear will vary with individual casting habits and the average length of casts on a particular stream, and such line wear is understandably exaggerated by habitual double hauling.

Line color is perhaps the single failure of the modern polyvinyl chloride fly line. My reservations about the palette of colors now available undoubtedly come from the sensory impressions of boyhood, and my first exposure to the rich, waxy odors of the Halford and King Eider silks, with their gleaming mahogany and pale amber coils wrapped in rice paper. Sensory impressions and esthetics play a surprising role in fly tackle, although many anglers are unwilling to admit it. Given a choice between the olive and richly glistening brown or pale amber fly lines, and the garish pinks and sickly pale greens and blues displayed on our modern tackle counters, my preferences are obvious. Multicolored camouflage finishes and two-color lines are also bothersome, and a simple color spot or indentation in the finish would be enough to tell the eye or fingers where a compound line changes from sinking to floating. The white lines becoming so popular were originally developed for photographic purposes, and I first used them in making a salmon film in the Labrador. The hot orange line had similar origins, since its chroma is remarkably visible in poor levels of light.

These past few seasons, experience on widespread streams would indicate that in floating lines used for dry-fly tactics and nymph fishing just under the surface the white and hot orange photographic lines do not frighten the fish. Berkeley recently introduced a series of beautiful straw-colored floating lines that remind me of the silk lines of my boyhood years, and they performed beautifully in a week of field testing with Doug Swisher on the Au Sable in Michigan. The visibility of these pale lines to the fisherman is useful too, particularly in following a dry-fly float or wet-fly swing at long distances in poor light.

Yet I still use a dark mahogany-colored line for the difficult, hyperselective fish on my home waters in our eastern mountains, and I feel it has been more effective on the shy fish of our famous western spring creeks. Fishing deep I prefer darker colors, like the rich greens of the Wetcel lines or the medium brown finish on the Cortland sinking line over pale sand and gravel bottoms. Pale colors are unwise in a sinking line that works deep among the fish, and is viewed laterally against the adjacent colors of the bottom. It can also be argued that a wooded stream poses identical problems in a floating line, and although a pale line is not readily visible against the sky, it is shockingly visible against a leafy canopy of trees and sheltering alders. Perhaps the line manufacturers should produce sinking lines that echo typical streambed environments, like the deep greens of a big river flowing over a bottom encrusted with fountain moss and algae, the pewter-colored boulders of a western sagebrush stream, and the rust-colored ledges of a foothill river like the Frying Pan in Colorado. Dame Juliana Berners prophetically wrote about keying line-color to stream bottom more than five centuries ago in her *Treatyse of Fysshynge wyth an Angle*, and perhaps it is not too late to listen to her wisdom.

Past books on fly-fishing often provided tables matching fly rods of typical lengths and weights to recommended line weights and tapers. Such tables always seemed a doubtful help, since they said little about the calibrations in two rods of otherwise equal length and weight. Wall thickness in the split bamboo also produced radical differences in the tip speed and power of superficially similar rods and demanded a heavier fly line. Polyvinyl chloride finishes and synthetic cores scrambled these equations even more, and the introduction of modern fiberglass rods produced chaos in past recommendations concerning balanced rod-to-line ratios. Graphite and boron fly rods promise to cause even more confusion in matching lines to rod lengths and weights. These technical changes have largely been introduced since midcentury, and did not intrude upon the relatively simple discussions on matching rods and fly lines in the earlier writings of men like Hewitt and Bergman and Knight.

However, such tables recommending basic rod specifications to fly-line weights are perhaps useful to novice fishermen, provided their assumptions and data are updated to include the world of synthetic rods and lines. Most manufacturers still recommend lines for their production rods, although this traditional convenience is proving difficult in the experimental carbon graphite and boron rods undergoing field research. Carbon graphite has an amazing capability of molding its stress behavior to line weight and loading, and a good caster has virtually no timing adjustments to compensate for using lines from four-weight through eight-weight on the same graphite rod. The perfection of these sophisticated synthetics in rod manufacture will further complicate our theories of tackle balancing. Although I am fully aware of its obvious pitfalls, the following table catalogues the work of several manufacturers who produce first-rate rods in fiberglass, and it may provide some useful comparative data:

FIBERGLASS FLY RODS AND LINE WEIGHTS

LENGTH	WEIGHT	FLOATING	SINKING	OLD CODE
6	$1\frac{1}{4}$	DT4F	DT4S	HEH
$6\frac{1}{2}$	$1\frac{3}{4}$	DT4F	DT4S	HEH
$6\frac{1}{2}$	$2\frac{1}{2}$	DT5F	DT5S	HDH
7	3	DT5F	DT5S	HDH
$7\frac{1}{2}$	$3\frac{1}{4}$	WF5F	WF5S	HDG
$7\frac{1}{2}$	$3\frac{3}{4}$	WF6F	WF6S	HCF
8	$3\frac{1}{2}$	WF6F	WF6S	HCF
8	$3\frac{3}{4}$	WF7F	WF7S	GBF
$8\frac{1}{2}$	$3\frac{3}{4}$	WF7F	WF7S	GBF
$8\frac{1}{2}$	4	WF7F	WF7S	GBF
9	$4\frac{1}{2}$	WF8F	WF8S	GAF
9	5	WF9F	WF9S	G2AF
9	$5\frac{1}{4}$	WF10F	WF10S	G3AF
$9\frac{1}{2}$	$5\frac{1}{2}$	WF10F	WF10S	G3AF
$9\frac{1}{2}$	$5\frac{7}{8}$	WF11F	WF11S	G4AF

Perhaps the most obvious surprise in this table, particularly for fishermen who are more familiar with split-cane construction, lies in the relatively light rod weight and heavy line-weight capacity of these fiberglass rods for their length. These qualities are most striking in the big-water rods, where the distance capability with a relatively heavy line on fly rods as light as three-and-a-half to five-and-a-half ounces can mean a big difference in fatigue at the day's end. Building a bamboo rod capable of double hauling a forward taper WF10S with only nine feet and less than five ounces of cane is clearly impossible.

The carbon graphite and boron rods that I have seen and fished are most unusual, and they include prototypes from Berkeley and Orvis and Fenwick, as well as privately built boron fiber designs. Their performance makes conventional wisdom about rods and matching fly-line tapers a shambles. The rods are light for their lengths and line weights, but even a two- or three-ounce graphite rod cannot be considered delicate. The most delicate synthetic I have fished was a solid wire-core boron prototype that weighed slightly more than a half ounce, and took a four-weight line, like a three-ounce split bamboo. The following table lists several boron and carbon graphite rods with their recommended lines:

BORON AND CARBON GRAPHITE ROD AND LINE RECOMMENDATIONS

TYPE	LENGTH	WEIGHT	FLOATING	SINKING
Boron	6	$\frac{1}{2}$	DT3F	DT3S
Boron	$6\frac{1}{2}$	$\frac{5}{8}$	DT4F	DT4S
Graphite*	$6\frac{1}{2}$	$\frac{3}{4}$	DT5F	DT5S

BORON AND CARBON GRAPHITE ROD AND LINE
RECOMMENDATIONS (continued)

TYPE	LENGTH	WEIGHT	FLOATING	SINKING
Boron	7	I	DT6F	DT6S
Graphite*	7	I	DT6F	DT6S
Graphite	7	$1\frac{1}{2}$	DT6F	WF6S
Boron	$7\frac{1}{2}$	$1\frac{3}{4}$	DT6F	WF6S
Graphite*	$7\frac{1}{2}$	$1\frac{7}{8}$	DT6F	WF6S
Graphite	$7\frac{1}{2}$	2	DT7F	WF7S
Graphite	8	$1\frac{7}{8}$	DT6F	WF6S
Boron	8	$2\frac{1}{4}$	DT4F	WF4S
Graphite	8	$2\frac{3}{8}$	DT7F	WF7S
Graphite	$8\frac{1}{2}$	$2\frac{7}{8}$	DT7F	WF7S
Graphite	$8\frac{1}{2}$	$3\frac{1}{4}$	WF8F	WF8S
Graphite	9	$3\frac{3}{4}$	WF9F	WF9S
Graphite	9	4	WF10F	WF10S

* Solid graphite rods on a wire core

Experienced trout fishermen will recognize the improbability of a three-ounce rod taking an eight-weight line, or double hauling a hundred feet of nine-weight taper on a rod weighing less than four ounces. Boron and graphite will undoubtedly work a revolution in our thinking about balanced rods and fly lines.

The following table of modern split-bamboo rods offers an interesting comparison between fiberglass and the other synthetics and cane, at least in their power-to-weight ratio, and relative casting power. It should be understood that in delicate work with tiny flies, split bamboo still has a clear superiority in skilled hands, and the ultra-light line tapers used with the small cane rods have no workable counterparts in glass construction. Many manufacturers are included in this chart:

SPLIT-BAMBOO RODS AND LINE SPECIFICATIONS

LENGTH	WEIGHT	FLOATING	SINKING	OLD CODE
6	I	DT3F	DT3S	IFI
6	$1\frac{1}{2}$	DT3F	DT3S	IFI
6	2	DT4F	DT4S	HEH
6	$2\frac{1}{2}$	DT4F	DT4S	HEH
$6\frac{1}{2}$	$1\frac{3}{4}$	DT4F	DT4S	HEH
$6\frac{1}{2}$	$2\frac{1}{8}$	DT4F	DT4S	HEH
$6\frac{1}{2}$	$2\frac{5}{8}$	DT4F	DT4S	HEH
7	$2\frac{3}{8}$	DT3F	DT3S	IFI
7	$2\frac{1}{2}$	DT4F	DT4S	HEH

SPLIT-BAMBOO RODS AND LINE
SPECIFICATIONS (continued)

LENGTH	WEIGHT	FLOATING	SINKING	OLD CODE
7	$2\frac{3}{4}$	DT4F	DT4S	HEH
7	$2\frac{7}{8}$	DT4F	DT4S	HEH
7	3	DT5F	DT4S	HEH
7	$3\frac{1}{4}$	DT5F	DT5S	HDH
7	$3\frac{3}{4}$	DT5F	DT5S	HDH
$7\frac{1}{2}$	$2\frac{1}{2}$	DT4F	DT4S	HEH
$7\frac{1}{2}$	$2\frac{3}{4}$	DT4F	DT4S	HEH
$7\frac{1}{2}$	3	DT4F	DT4S	HEH
$7\frac{1}{2}$	$3\frac{1}{8}$	DT4F	DT4S	HEH
$7\frac{1}{2}$	$3\frac{3}{8}$	DT5F	DT5S	HDH
$7\frac{1}{2}$	$3\frac{1}{2}$	DT5F	DT5S	HDH
$7\frac{1}{2}$	$3\frac{5}{8}$	DT5F	DT5S	HDH
$7\frac{1}{2}$	$3\frac{7}{8}$	DT6F	DT6S	HCH
$7\frac{1}{2}$	4	DT6F	DT6S	HCH
$7\frac{1}{2}$	$4\frac{1}{4}$	DT6F	DT6S	HCH
8	$3\frac{3}{4}$	DT6F	DT6S	HCH
8	4	DT6F	DT6S	HCH
8	$4\frac{1}{8}$	DT6F	DT6S	HCH
8	$4\frac{1}{2}$	DT6F	DT6S	HCH
8	$4\frac{1}{2}$	WF7F	WF7S	GBF
8	$4\frac{3}{4}$	WF7F	WF7S	GBF
8	5	WF7F	WF7S	GBF
$8\frac{1}{2}$	$4\frac{1}{4}$	DT5F	DT5S	HDH
$8\frac{1}{2}$	$4\frac{1}{2}$	DT6F	DT6S	HCH
$8\frac{1}{2}$	$4\frac{3}{4}$	WF7F	WF7F	GBF
$8\frac{1}{2}$	$4\frac{7}{8}$	WF8F	WF8S	GAF
$8\frac{1}{2}$	5	WF8F	WF8S	GAF
$8\frac{1}{2}$	$5\frac{1}{8}$	WF8F	WF8S	GAF
$8\frac{1}{2}$	$5\frac{1}{2}$	WF8F	WF8S	GAF
$8\frac{1}{2}$	$5\frac{7}{8}$	WF9F	WF9S	62AF
$8\frac{1}{2}$	6	WF9F	WF9S	G2AF
9	$4\frac{3}{4}$	WF7F	WF7S	GBF
9	5	WF7F	WF7S	GBF
9	$5\frac{1}{8}$	WF8F	WF8S	GAF
9	$5\frac{1}{4}$	WF8F	WF8S	GAF
9	$5\frac{1}{2}$	WF8F	WF8S	GAF
9	$5\frac{3}{4}$	WF8F	WF8F	GAF
9	6	WF8F	WF8S	GAF
9	$6\frac{1}{8}$	WF9F	WF9S	G2AF
9	$6\frac{1}{2}$	WF9F	WF9S	G2AF
$9\frac{1}{2}$	$5\frac{1}{2}$	WF8F	WF8S	GAF

SPLIT-BAMBOO RODS AND LINE
SPECIFICATIONS (continued)

LENGTH	WEIGHT	FLOATING	SINKING	OLD CODE
9½	5¾	WF8F	WF8S	GAF
9½	6	WF8F	WF8S	GAF
9½	6¼	WF9F	WF9S	G2AF
9½	6½	WF10F	WF10S	63AF
9½	6¾	WF10F	WF10S	63AF
9½	6⅞	WF10F	WF10S	G3AF

The obvious comparison between typical nine-foot glass rods taking a nine-weight G2AF line with a total weight of slightly more than five ounces and nine-foot bamboo rods that must be fifteen to twenty percent heavier to throw the same line is remarkable. The nine-foot graphite rod weighing three and three-quarter ounces and taking the same 250-grain taper is even more remarkable. The variables in cane density and design calibrations that affect the performance of bamboo fly rods are evident in these comparative tables, along with the weight differences of their reel seats. Glass and graphite are obviously excellent materials for average fishing and distance problems, while bamboo is still the optimal solution to problems of delicacy and precision.

However, our discussions of fly-line development and the technical revolution in lines that has taken place since midcentury are only partially helpful in matching lines to specific rods and fishing conditions. There are such variables in rod performance that only empirical casting can really balance a fly rod and its matching line, and such casting is the only viable test, because there are also critical variables in casting style.

Rod length and weight are an important clue to line weight, but they give us only a general impression of actual rod dynamics under the stress of casting. Rod taper can produce soft tip action with a stiff butt, relatively stiff action that carries from the tip guide well into the butt section, and the progressive taper which flexes with a slow, smooth power into the grip itself. Each action is possible within surprisingly similar rod length and weight, and each will take lines of different specifications.

It is important in line selection to remember the basic physics of rod-and-line dynamics. It is the weight of the fly line that is cast, not the fly we are presenting to the fish. It is the weight of the line working beyond the rod tip that causes it to flex and cast. Short-range tactics with a typical double taper find too little line extended, so false casts are often used to build enough line velocity to compensate, working them in a rapid flick-flick rhythm.

Such false casting often lacks sufficient line weight to stress the rod properly, and the line travels in an exaggeratedly narrow loop. It often fails to unroll properly, taking the leader with it, and the fly often catches the leader or the line. Average casting ranges provide enough line weight to accommodate the character of the rod, the casting rhythms slow as line is lengthened, and the fly works out in a graceful loop that unrolls and turns over cleanly. However, the double-taper line quickly reaches its performance ceiling, since a distance cast soon dies when the velocity of its shoot is equalled and dampened by the belly weight it is pulling behind.

Each fly rod has a definite ceiling on the length of line it can strip cleanly from the water, and another limit to the line weight and length it can load and carry in the air when false casting. Such limits are quickly reached with double-taper lines. Weight-forward lines are designed to exploit and overcome these limiting factors, placing most of their weight beyond the tip guide where it is instantly available for the left-hand shoot. Its thin shooting line lies immediately behind, and its weight imposes infinitely less drag on the velocity of the cast. It is the weight of the shooting front taper and belly that pulls the cast and the length of its shoot. The back taper is like the tail of a kite, helping to keep the shooting head riding true. Beyond such obvious factors, it is line velocity that generates distance, and that velocity is entirely a function of tip speed.

Such tip-speed effects mean that an eight-foot rod throwing its proper line weight at a high enough velocity will equal the distances achieved with a nine-foot stick delivering a heavier line at slower speeds.

Tip speed is limited by casting skills and timing, the character of the rod action, wind velocity, and atmospheric friction that varies with temperature. The principal resistance a caster must slice through is atmosphere and wind, the drag factors that dampen the velocity of both rod and line. Basic physics describes inertia in terms of both static objects and objects in motion. Rod flexure is a result of the dynamic inertia imparted by the caster, plus its bending to overcome the static inertia of the atmosphere. The dynamic inertia of the wind contributes still more bending under stress. Casting simply overcomes atmospheric inertia and wind, and its rhythms are quickly converted to the dynamics of inertial acceleration. When peak acceleration is reached, the rod is loading at optimum tip speed. Skilled casters are able to deliver their shots at that maximum tip speed, and stressing the rod with a double haul just before that velocity is reached works to exaggerate both the tip acceleration and the distance the rod tip travels in unloading the cast.

The cast should always be delivered when line velocity and tip speed are identical. The catapulting spring of the rod adds virtually nothing to distance, and during the millisecond the flexing rod begins to straighten, it is no longer participating in line velocity. Its straightening is a form of rapid deceleration, and when tip speed drops behind, the line shoots out over the water fully separate from the rod. It flexes well past the horizontal direction of the cast, and its only effect on its velocity and distance at this point is negative, consisting of guide friction and line slap along the rod itself. Rod loading under the stress of casting is expressed in its resistance to bending and atmospheric drag, and it continues to resist flexure until its ability to fight these loads has reached equilibrium with its casting speed.

Translated in terms of your casting skills, you should not attempt to fish with rod weights and actions that you cannot bring to maximum tip speed. The lines you select should match your rods. The rods should pick up approximately forty feet of line and shoot fifteen or twenty for average fishing, and for distance work, should lift fifty-odd feet and shoot enough line to reach eighty. Any fly rod you can stress to its peak tip speed will also fit your physical skills at slower velocities. It will generate optimal distance in your fishing and result in less fatigue.

Properly designed line tapers matched to such rods will neither flutter nor sag in casting, and will float through the cushioning effect of the atmosphere smoothly. Such tapers will turn over gracefully, taking the balanced leader and fly along. The full weight will not drop to the surface until the cast has fully straightened, and it is that taper weight and its distribution that are the basic factors in line choice.

Raw line weight is the primary factor in a cast, once the rod has carried it to optimum speed. Weight is obviously effective when it is concentrated in a lead-head jig, but its efficiency and inertia decrease as its casting length increases in the form of a fly line. Its entire weight distributed along a seventy-five-foot cast is exposed to high ratios of skin friction in the atmosphere. Double tapers are designed for delicate presentation, fine leaders and tiny flies, roll casting, and casting distances of less than seventy-five feet. Weight-forward lines have been worked out to fish at ranges between fifty and one hundred feet, with accurate delivery of the fly and a subtle dry-fly presentation considerably diminished. Shooting heads were developed for the extreme ranges between seventy-five feet and as far past one hundred feet as individual casting skills permit, although neither accuracy nor fine presentation are possible with them, and even the precise control of fly speed is sacrificed.

Line length ahead of the front taper is critical in both double-taper and weight-forward types. When this level section connected to the leader is too long, the fly turns over completely out of control. It can fall at the mercy of the slightest wind or casting fault, dropping both right and left of its own leader butt and sometimes on the line itself. When the level head is too short, the fly and leader will roll over too hard, their inertia will carry over well past the horizontal, and strike the surface too hard. Several manufacturers now precut these level heads at the proper length, and you should not modify them without first checking their specifications.

Specific gravity is also a factor in line selection. The fisherman who fishes relatively shallow waters will need a floating line, designed to handle dry flies on the surface, and wet flies and nymphs immediately under its film. Fishing intermediate depths of water call for a slow-sinking line, and a medium-sinking line is suited to slightly deeper places. High-density lines are needed for deep lakes, sinking as much as thirty feet with patience, to reach down toward bottom-feeding fish in heavy currents. Compound sinking-tip lines have been designed to fish at moderate depths, with a running line that floats and strips from the surface smoothly in shooting. The fishing conditions of your favorite waters should dictate your selection of lines. Generally speaking, your equipment should begin with a floating double taper, and you should add a basic weight-forward sinking line to your gear as soon as possible. More specialized lines are optional for most conditions.

Charles Ritz has described a simple field test for checking rod action against optimal line loading. It is outlined in his book *A Fly Fisher's Life*, and begins by lengthening the line without false casting. Each successive length of line should be delivered easily, without particular effort, until the rod is finally loaded with too much line weight. Such overload is clearly evident when the backcast falls too low, the casting loop flutters and pauses, and the rod seems to collapse when pushed toward maximum bending stress. The forward casts also tend to belly low and drop too quickly toward the water. Approximately forty to forty-five feet should not overload a fly rod, if the line weight is proper for its action.

Ritz has also developed a good method of trying out a fly line in actual casting dynamics. It is best if a knowledgeable friend is observing from the side to study the motions of the line. His observations should provide a lateral appraisal of your casting, while you can evaluate the longitudinal behavior of the working line yourself.

The first series of trial casts should reach out approximately thirty to forty-five feet. Such lengths are sufficient to give the observer a viable picture of line behavior and extension, the casting oscillations in the line, any ragged casting flow and loss of speed, if the water is being struck on either backcasts or forward casts, and the relative smoothness of leader rollover and delivery.

Vertical casting oscillations in the backward and forward extensions of the line can have several causes. Such oscillations usually result from poor hand movements and timing, and mean the smooth rhythm between backcasts and forward extensions is being broken. The resulting drop in line speed causes the cast to oscillate and waver in midflight. Sometimes these erratic line waves indicate a rod taper too soft for the line weight and specifications.

Sloppy hand movements that vary from open- to closed-loop rotation can also affect the smoothness of line flow. Casting oscillations can also result from a line too heavy for the tip calibrations of the rod, although it may seem to match its general bamboo weight and length. Tip calibrations that are too heavy for the line and for the lower rod tapers result in so much line speed for the rod weight that casting flow is rough and jerky. Both backcasts and forward extensions that are completely free of oscillations and flutter are quite rare, even among highly skilled casters, and are the hallmark of perfect timing and technique.

Oscillation and flutter can also result from a level head in front of the forward taper that is either too short or too long. Both conditions can affect the smoothness of your casting as well as leader turnover.

Line flutter is also caused by shooting heads that are too thick for your rod, and running lines that are too light in diameter to stabilize the fly line in flight. Trial casts of sixty to seventy feet with a moderate left-hand haul and an observer watching the line flow are quite useful. Running lines that are too light will usually flutter badly and lose their equilibrium in the shoot, and in extreme cases such lines can even tangle in themselves under the accelerating cast. Forward tapers too thick for a specific rod can be pinpointed with a series of slow false casts that work the fly rather close to the water, since thick line belly and front tapers that are too long will fold and wobble clumsily at such line speeds. It should be remembered that some rods may have performance envelopes that lie precisely between standard line tapers and weights, and in such cases a skilled fisherman will invariably choose the lighter line. Its weight can be magnified with left-hand work, stressing the rod perfectly with line speed instead of weight, and a lighter fly line will fish with greater subtlety.

Many anglers seem quite unaware that our evolving line technology was perhaps the most remarkable development in tackle since the six-strip bamboo rod. Fly lines were a relatively simple problem only thirty years ago, when all types were oil-finished nylon and silk, but the introduction of polyvinyl chlorides has permitted us to control specific gravity. Precise manipulation of line density and weight has created a complex spectrum of tapers designed to float and sink at varying speeds. Proper choice of fly lines and the techniques of fishing them have become infinitely more complicated since midcentury. Detailed knowledge of these lines and their varied performance specifications is sometimes critical to success on our hard-fished waters.

But technology is merely a tool of fishing, and we should not lose sight of that fact in our preoccupation with fly lines, entomology, and tactics. Our technical skills must ultimately be focused on the selective fish of some difficult stream, and those rare days when the myriad pieces of the puzzle fall into place are worth all the discipline and study.

Perhaps the best stretch of fly water left in the United States is the classic Henry's Fork of the Snake in eastern Idaho. It is formed in a series of mammoth springs, rich in alkalinity and remarkably clear water and incredible fly hatches.

It was a warm September twilight on the huge flats of the Railroad Ranch. The evening sky was rich with color behind the gentle mountains across the river, and although the bright sun had made the trout shy through the midday hours, they were starting to work greedily now. No flies were visible on the smooth currents, and the gentle porpoise rolls of the nymphing fish seemed to promise a coming hatch.

The subtle rise forms were coming regularly along a bed of undulating weeds, and I searched my fly book for a delicate little pheasant tail or olive-bodied nymph. There was a rough olive dressed with a filmy wing case of nylon stocking, and I briefly held it soaking in my mouth while I studied the fish that seemed the largest. It was working in a small indentation in the weeds, and I quickly realized that a dry-fly float was virtually impossible in spite of the 6X tippet.

The Henry's Fork is demanding water in the sense that its fish are tippet-shy and sometimes lie at considerable distances from the angler. It calls for a difficult mix of requirements in both tackle and fishing skills. Eighty-foot casts are not unusual in themselves, but working at such distances with tiny flies and tippets as fine as .005 is rare, and the casts must be made with both softness and accuracy. Anticipating this set of problems, my baggage roll of rods included a superb eight-and-a-half-foot Leonard packed just for the Henry's Fork on its windless evenings. It is lighter than most eight-and-a-half-foot Leonards, weighing only four and a quarter ounces with tip calibrations so delicate that it takes only a five-weight line. Since relatively long casts seemed likely, I had selected a reel with a weight-forward WF5F and a long-belly taper to mute the hard delivery typical of multiple-diameter lines. It is an unusual outfit, but the Henry's Fork is an unusual river.

Let's try them, I whispered to myself.

The Leonard worked smoothly, false casting the little hatching-nymph imitation with the lengthening line, and my fly settled above the rising fish. It entered the current imperceptibly and I teased the nymph as its swing passed across the trout; it porpoised eagerly and I tightened even before the darting leader signalled that it had taken. The fish wallowed in surprise, and then it bolted downstream and jumped.

Good fish! I thought. *Two or three pounds!*

The Hardy Princess was whining again as the rainbow stripped another twenty feet of line. It jumped again in the twilight, and when it finally surrendered I admired its richly colored sides and gill covers in the meshes. It rested next to my waders when it was released, and finally it melted into the weedy currents.

It was a night when everything worked.

There were several good fish from twelve to sixteen inches in the hour that followed, and then the little nymph strangely stopped working. The trout were feeding more heavily, but the fly was refused consistently by fish after fish.

Maybe they've started feeding on top, I muttered.

There was little light remaining, but I studied the smooth current carefully for hatching flies. It was virtually covered with tiny pale-olive duns and spent-wing spinners, and while it was still possible to see, I selected a Blue-winged Olive and was surprised when the tippet threaded easily through its eye. It was lightly sprayed with silicone, and I dried it with a series of impatient false casts.

Downstream in the twilight there was a huge rise in the reflections on the current. It was not a rise form that threw spray or seemed spectacular, except that its deep sucking sound caught my attention, and the undulating disturbance that followed the rise was impressive.

Pretty far! I thought. *Maybe ninety feet.*

It was getting dark now and I was not familiar with the bottom, so it was unwise to wade out closer. It was more than eighty feet across the smooth current. The Leonard quickly lengthened the cast, and only a few turns of line remained on the spool when it settled across the river. The tiny dry fly cocked perfectly in the afterglow, and the fish came up again still farther out. It looked large.

The second cast was almost ninety feet, and I was happy to have the full eight-and-a-half-foot rod and the long-belly taper to reach that distance. It fell right, and it was impossible to see the fly on the water, but I tightened anyway when the fish rose softly. It threshed angrily and the reel protested in the gathering darkness as the fish ran upstream and jumped. It looked huge in the dying light, and its threshing cartwheels were too much for the fragile tippet. Suddenly the fish was gone.

It's a good ending, I smiled happily.

It was not really a failure, since reaching that big rainbow with such fine terminal tackle and hooking it with a tiny dry fly was a minor triumph at almost ninety feet. It was an example of the right tackle married to the right fly pattern, and it would have been impossible before the development of the modern polyvinyl line and the new long-belly tapers.

For even more recent developments, see Appendix: Notes on New Equipment.

3. Problems in Leaders, Knots, and Backing

The morning star glittered brightly, and just after daylight the air was cold and still. The station wagon was silver with its crystalline coating of frost, and I shivered a little outside the cabin. The sun already looked warm on the mountains, but it was still almost dark on the valley floor, and there was a faint dust of snow on the high peaks lying west of the river. It would be gone after breakfast. The cold air tasted sweet in my lungs. Mist still rose steaming from the currents, and a heron flew ponderously downstream, its wing beats working slowly in the morning light. My breath plumed in surprising clouds on the first stirrings of the wind, and I shivered again as I walked down to the Yellowstone below the outbuildings.

The trees across the river were shedding their leaves. The dark currents of the river worked and whispered through the log-cribbing foundations of the bridge. Except for a milk truck and two railroad workers from the switchyard, and a drunk cowboy just sober enough to find his way back to the boarding house beyond the tracks, the streets of the town were silent. The morning wind stirred again in the cottonwoods and poplars. The neon signs of the saloons were no longer pulsing their blatant promises, and the jukeboxes and pinball machines inside stood quiet.

October mornings are like that in Montana, and after breakfast we drove upstream toward Armstrong's Creek. It was still chill and clear, and the somnolent music of the cattle across the river carried crisply in the slowly warming air.

The station wagon rattled across the kingpost hay-wagon bridge, and several pintails exploded from the shallows as I walked lazily downstream. The sprig ducks climbed north and wheeled back along the Yellowstone bottoms and were gone. No flies were hatching yet. The smooth current was riffled with the wind that blew steadily now. It ebbed and sighed in the willows and cottonwoods above the watercress sloughs, stripping them of the last of their bright yellow leaves, and sail-boated them almost playfully across the current.

The sun grew steadily warmer and it started a few flies hatching. The tiny duns that had the temerity to emerge were quickly scuttled or foundered against the weeds. Finally a few good rainbows began to feed.

They're finding something, I thought.

The trout in these Yellowstone spring creeks are justly famous for their shyness and selectivity. Daily hatches of minute flies have made them diffident about their feeding activity, and suspicious of large imitations and naturals alike. These rise forms were only soft porpoise rolls that barely disturbed the wind-riffled currents. My little dry-fly imitations, patterns that usually worked on these late-season hatches of small mayfly species, were all refused without any sign of interest or inspection.

Several good fish were working steadily now, lying mostly along a thick bed of elodea about eighty feet across the current. The rises there were quiet swirls and lazy porpoise rolls, punctuated with an occasional showy splash that looked like a fish after a swimming natural about to hatch.

They're nymphing, I concluded.

The smaller fish working in the open currents at midstream quickly took my dark little olive nymph, but the fish along the elodea were another matter. The best position for fishing my nymph over them placed me opposite a break in the cottonwoods, and facing almost directly into the wind. It took an eighty-foot cast with a delicate tippet, and the leader balked at turning over into the wind at that range.

I was using a standard knotless leader of limp nylon, because hooked fish are often lost when a series of blood-knots collect pieces of floating weed in such spring creeks, but it simply refused to deliver the fly properly. Several times the leader butt collapsed and fell clumsily back on itself when I punched it out hard, and when I tried to force it with a left-hand haul, it simply tangled around the nail knot on the line. Slowing my casting rhythms and letting the line develop less velocity unfolded the leader and fly properly, but it lacked the line speed to reach out the eighty feet necessary to cover the fish along the weeds.

Stiffer butt diameters, I thought aloud.

There were several spools of stiff nylon in my duffel, and I walked back to the station wagon. The commercial leader I was using had a butt diameter of .017 inches, too much drop from the .033 polyvinyl tip of the fly line for the wind I was facing, and it was too limp to transfer casting power smoothly from line to leader. The tippet was the .005 that I use for most work on selective fish these days, dropping finer on the stream as needed. The stock knotless taper was nine feet, and I added a foot of .017 hard nylon to make the transition from the limper German material. Another foot of .019 was followed with .021, and I nail-knotted a short length of .023

to the line. It worked rather well, although a little more than four feet of hard nylon might have gone better, with a little less limp material than the nine feet of the original knotless taper.

The modified leader punched the cast cleanly into the wind, and I finally got my little nymph over the larger fish working at the bottom of the weeds. It settled into its swing, and the riffling current humped almost imperceptibly. The water exploded when I raised the rod and tightened, and the two-pound rainbow tail-walked downstream from its friends. It jumped several more times, spending its energy in the open water downstream, and when it tried to regain its weedy sanctuary it was too late. My gentle side-pressure stopped it short, and I turned the rod low along the water, forcing the fish toward me. Finally it circled weakly in the shallows and came to my net.

The little nymph took five more rainbows between fifteen and eighteen inches, deep-bellied fish completely unlike the smaller rainbows feeding in the open shallows, and I admired their bright markings while they recovered in my hands. It was fast sport, and the last fish was a rainbow of about four pounds that quickly submarined and broke me in the moss.

My fly worked well, until the wind dropped in the early afternoon, and the fish stopped taking. The little spring creek eddied again in its weedy growth, its currents silken and difficult in character.

Maybe it's too stiff, I thought. *Maybe it's coming down too hard, and it's not fishing limp enough.*

I removed most of the hard-nylon butt and replaced it with limp .0186 and .0239 German nylon. The results were better in terms of presentation, rolling out smoothly and settling softly enough for the more difficult conditions, but the fish still refused the nymph. Checking the current briefly, I found the hatch had not changed and continued with the nymph. It still failed and I stopped to watch the fish. The rise forms were clearly different, but I had become overconfident with several hours of success and had missed the obvious clues.

They're feeding on top, I thought sheepishly.

The lack of wind had changed everything, and now the tiny mayflies were drifting normally down the current tongues, riding the feeding lanes that regularly carried them over the trout. It was obviously dry-fly time.

But the dry flies failed too.

There was a good rainbow lying in plain sight just twenty feet above my position, and a few feet farther out over the weeds. It studied each tiny imitation with enough interest to cock under the fly for a brief moment, but then drifted back to its feeding station. The hatching flies had still not changed, so I decided to reduce the tippet diameter to .005 and keep fishing my tiny *Pseudocloeon* imitation. The first good float produced a positive reaction. The rainbow drifted back with the fly, coming closer and closer, and darted back so late that its movements created a spreading false rise behind its drift.

Fausse montée, I smiled.

The 6X tippet was clipped back to only twelve inches, and I added a sixteen-inch length of .004 limp nylon. The tiny Blue-winged Olive settled above the fish and was taken without hesitation. It is impossible to know if the rainbow was fooled because the thinner nylon made a better float possible, or because the fish could not see it. However, it is an episode that clearly demonstrates many of the problems and solutions in modern leader design and performance.

Curiously, the concept of the leader is relatively new in the history of angling. The separate leader connecting the line with the fly did not exist in the Chinese beginnings of our sport, in which only a delicate line of woven silk was used, and a horsehair line connected fly with rod in third century Macedonia. Similar tackle is described in the *Treatyse of Fysshynge wyth an Angle*, although Dame Juliana Berners did discuss dying the horsehair to camouflage it in streams of different background color and character. Charles Cotton did not advocate the separate leader in *Being Instructions How to Angle for Trout and Grayling in a Clear Stream*, but his philosophy did understand the relationship between light tackle and selective trout, and the need for playing fish skillfully:

> But he that cannot kill a trout of twenty inches long with only two
> hairs, in a river clear of wood and weeds, as this and some others
> of ours are, deserves not the name of angler.

Samuel Pepys records in his *Diary* that a varnished filament of gut string made a superb tippet at the fly, much stronger and smaller than horsehair. Pepys was fishing in the same years that found Walton and Cotton fishing together on the Dove in Derbyshire, and yet Cotton strangely made no mention of gut in his writings. Cotton was remarkably innovative, and its use cannot have been widely known in the seventeenth century if Cotton was ignorant of its properties.

The secret of silkworm filaments was obviously out a century later, and leaders tapered of Spanish silkworm gut were common long before the American Revolution. Such tapered designs are always better than the level leaders that persisted on some American waters as late as the threshold of the Second World War. Tapered leaders are necessary to transmit the energy of casting, delicately and progressively, from the fly line to the fly. Such leaders were relatively expensive, and during the Great Depression, level leaders of Japanese synthetic gut enjoyed a brief vogue. Such leader material was the first synthetic fiber available.

Many fishermen are so fascinated with learning to cast a fly past seventy-five feet that they forget most fish are taken at thirty feet or less. The cast that splashes down at thirty yards will catch far less trout than a good presentation at thirty feet, and many men who can cast ninety feet often forget that truth, preferring the exhilaration of their skills to the taking of fish. Such casting skills are eagerly sought by every fisherman, but much closer work should not be forgotten.

Leader specifications and performance are often more important than casting ability, and poor leader behavior is often a problem in butt diameter, taper, or tippet size. The leader is not only used to suggest an invisible connection between the fly and its caster, but its tapers also should deliver that fly as delicately as possible. Such performance means correct diameters and design. The weight and wind resistance and taper of the leader are critical in both good presentation and fishing technique.

The two principal components of a properly tapered leader are its tippet, the terminal section connected to the fly, and its butt section connected to the line.

Most polyvinyl fly lines found on American trout waters are from .030 to .037 in their tip calibrations, and to transmit their power smoothly we need leader butts from .023 to .028 diameter. Micrometers are invaluable in determining actual thickness of both lines and leader materials. Breaking-strain ratings are inadequate information for designing and tapering your own leaders since the difference in diameter between two leader strands is critical in knot strength and can override any other factors. Many commercial leader spools are carelessly labelled, and most experienced anglers are familiar with the tapering mistakes that are possible with unverified diameters.

Two common errors in commercial leader design prevail: most are too thin in their butt diameters, and many are too short in their heavier butt tapers. Commercially tapered leaders are often incorrectly made, because it is easier to construct them of strands having an equal length. It is still possible to purchase stock tapered leaders with butt tapers that begin as fine as .014, which is an unthinking echo of silkworm gut behavior and the .025 tip diameters of oil-finished silk lines. Gut strands were costly and trimming them was wasteful. The typical 3X or 4X trout point diameter was not possible in a length of nine-foot leader, since fifteen-inch strands stepping only .001 at each barrel knot soon reached .014 calibrations, unless the butt stopped there. The silkworm-gut tapered leader was typically a prisoner of its material, and its variables of length and breaking strain and diameter. Such leaders were filled with knots, but the limitations of silkworm gut are no longer a factor in leader design. Its fragile breaking strains were perhaps its most serious flaw, and even its finest expensive grades were relatively impractical in the diameters finer than .006, as the following table demonstrates:

SPECIFICATIONS OF SILKWORM GUT MATERIAL

TYPE	GAUGE	METRIC	ENGLISH	TEST
Drawn	7X	.10	.004	.3
Drawn	6X	.125	.005	.5
Drawn	5X	.15	.006	.8
Drawn	4X	.175	.007	1.2
Drawn	3X	.20	.008	1.6
Drawn	2X	.225	.009	1.8

SPECIFICATIONS OF SILKWORM GUT MATERIAL
(continued)

TYPE	GAUGE	METRIC	ENGLISH	TEST
Refina	1X	.25	.010	2.2
Refina	0X	.275	.011	2.8
Fina	10/5	.30	.012	3.2
Fina	9/5	.325	.013	3.5
Regular	8/5	.35	.014	4.5
Regular	7/5	.375	.015	7.0
Padron	6/5	.40	.016	8.7
Padron	5/5	.425	.017	10.2
Marana	4/5	.45	.018	12.5
Marana	3/5	.475	.019	15.2
Imperial	2/5	.40	.020	19.0
Hebra	1/5	.525	.021	23.5

It is clear from these specifications that a fisherman working our modern tippet-shy trout would be in trouble with silkworm gut in spite of its poetic synergies when matched with a line of oil-finished silk. The breaking strain of .010 gut is virtually identical to the strength of .005 tippets in the modern nylons exactly half the diameter. Many hard-fished streams cannot be fished successfully with tippets heavier than .007, and still finer tippets of .006 and .005 are better. My own fishing over selective trout is concentrated in these sizes, with an occasional .004 tippet under particularly difficult conditions. None of these diameters tested much over three-quarters of a pound in the finest Murcia silkworm gut, hardly workable for the average fishing we enjoy with such diameters.

Silkworm gut was commonly called catgut in my boyhood years, but this was a colloquial mistake heard everywhere on trout water. It actually consists of the silk that a mature silkworm has not yet extruded from its glandular sacs. The silkworm itself is the larva of the Asiatic moth classified *Bombyx mori*, and its domestic cultivation began in China many centuries ago. The species has been transplanted virtually everywhere that mulberry trees are found thriving, and perhaps their most successful introduction occurred in the southern Spanish province of Murcia. British tackle manufacturers purchased vast quantities of the most select silkworm gut from the Murcia growers for more than a century.

The life cycle of the silkworm begins in late winter, and it takes six weeks to reach maturity. It then starts a curious series of brief hibernations, in which it lies dormant for two or three days, after which it suddenly returns to its ravenous diet of mulberry leaves. Cultivation of the larvae occurs in small buildings, where they are kept on fragile feeding racks. Mulberry leaves are distributed across each rack several times each day, and they are quickly consumed by the larvae. The silk glands of these larvae consist of two long thin-walled sacs lying inside the abdominal structure, and feeding a single spinning orifice. When the silkworm reaches maturity its sacs are gorged with a clear fluid of considerable viscosity. The fluid quickly congeals and hardens on contact with the atmosphere, and the fully mature larva spins itself a pupal cocoon of raw silk.

Larvae destined for silkworm gut must be killed just before they spin their pupal enclosures. Six weeks of heavy feeding on mulberry leaves are ended in killing tubs filled with water and acetic acid. The silkworms remain for several hours in this brine, which congeals their glandular sacs into a consistency that may be stretched into gut strands. Their quality, thickness, and length vary radically with the chemistry of the brine, temperature, humidity, the size and health of the worms, and the skill of the hand strippers. The freshly drawn strands are dried in the sun, and their surface film dissolved and rubbed off.

The most difficult phase in the process is sizing and sorting for quality. Skilled hands discriminate endlessly between lengths, diameters, relative straightness, and general filament quality. Proper sorting requires exceptional skill and experience. Silkworm-gut quality was always critical and elusive. Its selection was possible only through experts, since even a highly skilled fisherman found that most top grades of raw gut looked pretty much alike. His criteria were usually resolved on the stream, since a Select tippet of .007 diameter held his fish, and a poorer grade simply broke. Competition for the finest silkworm gut was fierce in the early years of this century, and the prices spiralled after the First World War.

Earlier prices were high enough, and well over a century ago there was a large-scale effort to develop an American silk-growing industry in South Carolina. Huge mulberry groves were planted, and organized cultivation of the *Cecropia* moth was started. The *Cecropia* moth is closely related to the Asiatic silkworm species. These American insects have unusually large glandular sacs in their larval stages, sacs capable of stretching into strands of more than six feet. The economic collapse that followed the Civil War abruptly ended the American experiments.

Strength and quality were the grail in silkworm gut leaders, and there was both competition for supplies and marketing subterfuge. Hardy took pride in its dominance over other European firms as importers of the finest Murcia gut. Their drawn gut was made only from the best quality, and extruded through precise jeweled dies. It had a high reputation for its strength, but that reputation was the result of a clever stratagem—Hardy 4X tippets calibrated a full .008 inches, while their competitors commonly used the standard .007 diameters.

Japanese gut was the first synthetic fiber available to American fishermen, and its performance was so marginal that the subsequent response of American anglers to the introduction of nylon was lukewarm. The synthetic Japanese gut was really twisted silk saturated with a hard waterproofing gum, and when the gum binder washed out, the leaders often unwrapped and quickly frayed. It was a poor substitute.

Nylon was a totally synthetic material developed in the United States shortly before the Second World War. It is primarily derived from coal, water, and atmospheric components. It can be readily shaped into filaments, and it is characterized by its singular qualities of strength, elasticity, chemical and abrasive resistance, and its limited absorbency of moisture. It can be permanently formed with thermal setting, and it was first introduced in bristles and hosiery. Its chemistry consists of a series of linear polymeric amides with repetitive amide groups and is produced by the controlled polymerization of dibasic acids, diamines, and amino compounds. Literally thousands of such potential polymer structures exist, and the radical improvement of nylon leader materials in recent years is an example of these variables.

Primitive nylon leader material became available just after the Second World War, and since the production of Spanish gut had been seriously truncated during the conflict, many fishermen were forced to use nylon before it was really perfected. Du Pont nylon leader material was manufactured with the following specifications until well after midcentury.

DU PONT STANDARD NYLON LEADER MATERIAL

GAUGE	METRIC	ENGLISH	TEST
5X	.15	.006	1.00
4X	.175	.007	1.25
3X	.20	.008	1.75
2X	.225	.009	2.25
1X	.25	.010	3.00
0X	.275	.011	3.50
10/5	.30	.012	4.50
9/5	.325	.013	5.00
8/5	.35	.014	6.00
7/5	.375	.015	8.00
6/5	.40	.016	9.00
5/5	.425	.017	10.00
4/5	.45	.018	11.50
3/5	.475	.019	12.00
2/5	.50	.020	13.00
1/5	.525	.021	15.80

Knowledgeable anglers will quickly see that these calibrations and breaking strains are quite inferior to the nylon leaders we now have twenty-odd years later, but it is obvious that their strength then was slightly superior to the finest silkworm gut. It was about the time that *Matching the Hatch* was being written that the modern German nylons first appeared on the American market, and they were a remarkable advance over the nylon leader materials I had first used on European rivers earlier.

Advanced polymeric combinations have evolved several excellent types of these European nylons. Their limpness and elasticity and knotting qualities are striking, and their capabilities are a fly-fishing revolution fully equal to the development of the polyvinyl fly lines a few years later. Some comparative specifications are interesting:

GERMAN PLATYL NYLON MATERIAL SPECIFICATIONS

GAUGE	METRIC	ENGLISH	TEST
7X	.10	.0041	1.2
6X	.123	.0047	2.1
5X	.15	.0061	3.3
4X	.175	.0071	4.3
3X	.20	.0081	5.2
2X	.225	.0091	6.3
1X	.25	.0098	7.2
0X	.275	.0111	9.1
8/5	.325	.0129	12.6
7/5	.35	.0145	15.2
5/5	.40	.0159	17.8
3/5	.45	.0177	21.5
2/5	.475	.0186	25.7
0/5	.60	.0239	34.8

These German filaments were a revelation when they first became available to American fly-fishermen, particularly on eastern streams where the tippet-shy fish were getting wary enough to reject the 4X material we had used for years.

It was John Crowe, the author of *The Book of Trout Lore*, who gave me the first spools of German nylon more than twenty years ago on Spring Creek in Pennsylvania. Crowe had watched me fishing over several particularly selective trout without much success. The fish were lying in plain sight, and it was frustrating to watch them come to my dry flies, inspect them for a few inches of drift, and turn away without taking. These were all brown trout that had been caught and released before, and had obviously learned from the experience. Crowe became interested in the stalemate and stopped to watch.

It was embarrassing to have an audience.

The fish rejected my carefully tied imitations of the hatch for almost an hour before Crowe introduced himself, and I waded out of the water to talk. *These fish are picky,* I said sheepishly.

Yes, Crowe said. *They've seen flies many times.*

My fly pattern should be right. I showed him the specimens of the hatch I had collected. *It usually works on these insects.*

It looks fine, Crowe agreed.

The fish still dimpled and sipped the hatching duns in the swift run along the bank. The fluttering mayflies were still the same species. *Something's wrong,* I said unhappily.

Maybe they're tippet-shy, he said.

Tippet-shy? I asked. *I'm fishing 4X now.*

4X? Crowe chuckled softly. *Tippets that heavy look like ropes to these selective limestone trout.*

It's the finest material I've got, I said.

Try this nylon, he offered.

Crowe had two spools of German nylon and I studied them closely. The plastic .0061 spool was marked with a breaking strain of more than three pounds, and the still finer .0047 spool was surprisingly listed at slightly over two-pound test.

It's fantastically thin and strong! I gasped.

Crowe smiled. *Give it a try.*

The delicate .0061 material was twice as strong as my conventional nylon tippet, and Crowe gave me enough strands to build a taper from .0081 to .0047. It was a quick taper in twelve-inch lengths with a twenty-inch tippet, and I finally blood-knotted it to my regular leader.

The selective fish became surprisingly easy, and I took a fourteen-inch brown on the first cast. The delicate little nylon fooled every trout that had been feeding under the trees, the same fish that had humiliated me consistently for an hour.

That's pretty convincing, I admitted. *Those fish really are tippet-shy, and this stuff really works!*

It works well, Crowe nodded.

Since those early years, such remarkable European leader material has been widely imported into the United States, and its unique specifications have proved a revolution fully equal to the introduction of polyvinyl fly lines. Their calibrations and strengths have been a fishing breakthrough, and it is doubtful that we could fish many of our hard-pressed rivers successfully without these new nylons. Certainly the eastern streams and western spring creeks would prove difficult with silkworm-gut tippets no finer than .007, and the brittle postwar nylon that calibrated .006. Such leaders would test at a pound or less, while it would take a tippet of .009 gut to match the breaking strain of our modern 6X leaders. Our selective trout would collapse in hysterical laughter at such 1X tippets these days, although such clumsy point diameters were common thirty years ago.

Bergman made a number of recommendations concerning leaders in *Trout,* although in his chapters fishing a fine tippet meant carrying leaders tapered to .008. His book also suggested carrying a few coiled gut tippets of .007, adding these to his leaders under difficult low-water conditions or bright weather. Many fishermen fail to realize the magnitude of our recent revolution in leader materials, which make practical tippets as fine as .004 and .003 readily available.

Perhaps the comparative specifications and breaking strains of several other modern European nylons are worth studying; types commonly available are manufactured as follows:

GERMAN MAXIMA CHAMELEON SPECIFICATIONS

GAUGE	METRIC	ENGLISH	TEST
7X	.10	.004	1
6X	.125	.005	2
5X	.15	.006	3
4X	.175	.007	4
3X	.20	.008	5
2X	.225	.009	6
1X	.25	.010	8
0X	.275	.011	9
10/5	.30	.012	10
9/5	.325	.013	12
7/5	.375	.015	15
5/5	.425	.017	20
2/5	.50	.020	25
1/5	.55	.022	30
0/5	.60	.024	40

Maxima is a superb nylon leader material of the limp type, and although it has not been available as long as other German and French materials, it has a chorus of vocal advocates on widespread rivers. It has superb fishing and knot-making capabilities, qualities that also distinguish the Luxor nylon produced in France by Pezon & Michel:

PEZON & MICHEL LUXOR NYLON SPECIFICATIONS

GAUGE	METRIC	ENGLISH	TEST
7X	.10	.004	1.1
6X	.125	.005	1.4
5X	.15	.006	2.4
4X	.175	.007	3.2
3X	.20	.008	3.8
2X	.225	.009	4.5
1X	.25	.010	5.5
0X	.275	.011	6.4
10/5	.30	.012	7.5
9/5	.325	.013	8.6
7/5	.375	.015	11.6
3/5	.475	.019	19.2
1/5	.525	.021	23.7

Luxor is not quite as strong in its breaking strains as some of the more recent polymer variations, but it is a material that combines the elasticity and knot-making behavior of the finest limp nylons with slightly more stiffness. Tortue is another French nylon that is made in still finer diameters of fishable strength. Its .0039 diameter has a breaking strain of one pound, and its .0031 tests a remarkable three-quarter pound. Knowledgeable anglers add both diameters to their 7X tippets, not because there is much difference in breaking strain between .004 or .0041 and the .0039 Tortue but because of the critical character of knots between different diameters in such delicate nylons. However, only the most delicate rod calibrations designed for three- and four-weight lines are fully capable of fishing such fragile leaders in practical terms.

American manufacturers have recently been working to produce similar leader material. Gladding, Cortland, Berkeley, and Mason are making exceptionally fine nylon for fly-fishing, although the Mason product is a hard polymer for anglers who prefer a relatively stiff leader. It is also excellent for making compound leaders of hard-nylon butts with limp-nylon tippets and tapers. The Mason leader materials are available in the following diameters, and Leonard is fabricating knotless leaders of this hard nylon in a full range of sizes and tapers:

MASON HARD-TYPE NYLON SPECIFICATIONS

GAUGE	METRIC	ENGLISH	TEST
8X	.075	.003	0.5
7X	.10	.004	1.0
6X	.125	.005	2.0
5X	.15	.006	3.0
4X	.175	.007	4.0
3X	.20	.008	5.0
2X	.225	.009	6.0
1X	.25	.010	7.0
0X	.275	.011	8.0
10/5	.30	.012	10.0
9/5	.325	.013	12.0
7/5	.375	.015	14.0
5/5	.425	.017	18.0
3/5	.475	.019	20.0
1/5	.525	.021	22.0
0/5	.575	.023	25.0

Cortland is packaging its knotless tapers with two tippet strands of limp nylon for attachment to a seven-and-a-half-foot leader of stiffer material. It is convenient and workable and is proving popular with many fishermen. The specifications for the Cortland nylon leader materials are found in the following table:

CORTLAND CROWN NYLON SPECIFICATIONS

GAUGE	METRIC	ENGLISH	TEST
6X	.125	.005	1.5
5X	.15	.006	2.0
4X	.175	.007	3.5
3X	.20	.008	4.5
2X	.225	.009	6.0
1X	.25	.010	7.0
0X	.275	.011	9.0
9/5	.325	.013	12.0
7/5	.375	.015	15.0
5/5	.425	.017	18.0
3/5	.475	.019	21.0
1/5	.525	.021	23.0
0/5	.575	.023	25.0

It is interesting that these diameters are not quite as strong in the extremely fine sizes, yet are demonstrably strong in several intermediate sizes suited to average fishing. Cortland knotless tapers are also available in butt weights from .025 to .029, and are therefore extremely useful as prefabricated foundations for compound tapers based on your particular streamside needs. Their standard butt diameter of .029 is the heaviest now available in a machinemade knotless taper. Cortland is making a flat monofilament material originally intended as running line for shooting heads, but many fishermen have also been using it in the twenty-five-pound calibration for distance leader-butt nylon. Since it is a relatively flat oval in cross section, it unfolds and rolls out in a self-enforcing plane of delivery, and must be mounted carefully on the fly line to insure that its flat axis lies horizontal in normal casting. Like a good split-cane rod, which flexes only through its flat axis and fights poor casting habits, the Cobra flat monofilament will deliver cleanly in a vertical plane. It is an intriguing development that can provide a little better accuracy in making very long casts and is worth trying on your waters.

Berkeley is also making a so-called Magnum butt leader of modern nylon with a quick-taper design and .028 butt diameter similar to the Cortland .029 in performance. However, Cortland provides its .029 butt diameter in only a nine-foot leader tapered to fifteen-pound test, while the Berkeley tapers are available from ten-pound to 4X diameters. Berkeley is also treating its nylon with a special nontoxic compound to lubricate and increase the wetting qualities of its leader material. This wetting agent lasts as long as you would normally fish the leader without risk of casting-knot damage or molecular fatigue, and it seems far superior to the etch-tipped experiments tried by several manufacturers in recent years. However, it is probably not desirable to have your entire leader sink unless you are fishing wet flies, nymphs, or streamers. Specifications for these Berkeley leaders are from the following nylon diameters:

BERKELEY SINKING NYLON SPECIFICATIONS

GAUGE	METRIC	ENGLISH	TEST
6X	.125	.005	1.75
5X	.15	.006	2.0
4X	.175	.007	2.5
3X	.20	.008	3.0
2X	.225	.009	4.0
1X	.25	.010	5.0
0X	.275	.011	6.0
9/5	.325	.013	8.0
7/5	.375	.015	10.0
5/5	.425	.017	12.0
3/5	.475	.019	14.0
1/5	.525	.021	17.0
0/5	.575	.123	20.0

Berkeley is also introducing a line of unusual knotless leaders, which are a flattened oval in cross section and become round when they reach the tippet diameters. Field experiments indicate that these developments have a remarkable future, and Berkeley is testing some new nylons that could provide greater strength-to-diameter ratios than our best modern filaments, perhaps making tippets finer than .003 possible.

Gladding was perhaps the pioneer in importing the European nylon to the United States, and it obtained the exclusive rights to the German Platyl material twenty-odd years ago. The company still manufactures and sells nylon leader material made with the specifications outlined earlier in this chapter. It is packaged on color-coded plastic spools, and it is now treated with a modern process designed to stabilize its elasticity. Standard knotless tapers are available in heavier butt diameters than were manufactured in the past, and the nine-foot types tapered from butts of .0239 and .0275 are excellent foundations for building an all-limp leader tapered as fine as .004. Such ready-made leaders should be quick tapers starting with their tips of .009 and .013, using short, ten-inch strands to the final diameter. The ultimate leader tippet should be about twenty inches in length, until you are working below .005, and then it should be progressively shortened because its fine diameter simply will not extend properly when cast.

Tippet diameter is not only a function of delivering the fly softly and providing the illusion of an unattached insect, but also related to fly weight and wind resistance. Many fishermen still use the traditional rule of thumb which multiplies the tippet ratings below 0X times four to determine average fly size for each diameter. The Rule of Four holds that a 3X tippet is perfectly suited for a size twelve fly, since three times four equals twelve.

Many European fishermen recommend tippets as heavy as 2X for size twelve flies, and suggest a relatively coarse 0X for size ten. Such diameters are indicative of the private trout fishing found on most European rivers, where there are fish that see only a few anglers, compared with the large numbers found on public waters within a few hours of most American cities. There is no question that a 2X or 3X tippet will cast a size twelve fly perfectly, but it is equally clear that it will frequently put down the leader-shy fish on most eastern and many western streams. The following table is designed for such hard-fished waters, although the tippets might be shortened to insure proper turnover, perhaps to as little as twelve inches if necessary in a wind:

LEADER DIAMETERS AND HOOK SIZES

GAUGE	HOOK SIZE	GAUGE	HOOK SIZE	GAUGE	HOOK SIZE
8X	24-26-28	5X	14-16-18	2X	6-8-10
7X	20-22-24	4X	10-12-14	1X	4-6-8
6X	16-18-20	3X	8-10-12	0X	2-4-6

These ratios are valid for conventionally dressed flies on average-weight hooks. Windy conditions or particularly bushy hackles mean heavier tippet diameters, and really big nymphs or streamers need point sizes heavier than .011 nylon. Heavy-duty hooks commonly used on big western nymphs and steelhead patterns also demand leaders with more muscle, and fishing a long-hackled skater without the stiffness of a 1X or 2X point is futile. Conditions and your casting will tell you when your tippet is too light for the fly you are punching out, and when it refuses to deliver cleanly, you should try heavier diameters.

Leader shyness is also related to observation time. Trout have more time to inspect a fly floating or swinging in relatively slow currents and are much less tippet-shy in fast runs and pockets. Flies that are fished fast, like streamers and long-hackled skaters, move too quickly to give the fish a careful look. Such conditions and tactics will permit the successful use of heavier tippets.

Therefore, leader selection and design vary widely with the condition of the river, the character of its fish population, and the techniques employed. Dry-fly leaders are generally longer to insure both a delicate delivery and drag-free float, and similar leader performance is needed to fish wet flies and nymphs just under the surface or in the film itself. Leaders fished with a sink-tip or full sinking lines should be relatively short, since their buoyant character will tend to cancel out the sinking qualities of the polyvinyl high-density lines. Butt diameters should still have sufficient thickness to match the tip diameter of the lines.

Standard ready-made leaders were once seldom available in lengths over seven-and-a-half feet, although nine-foot designs are common now, and several manufacturers are also making twelve-foot tapers in both knotted and knotless types. Many experts regularly use leaders much longer than twelve feet, although iconoclasts like Charles Ritz and Polly Rosborough disdain such refinements, arguing that any fish can be taken with tapers of six-and-a-half to ten feet. Rosborough and Ritz are probably correct, except that their fishing seldom calls for the extreme cobweb-size tippets in common use on many particularly difficult or hard-fished American streams. It is not so much the length that the long-leader fanatics are after, but a leader working in relatively sophisticated compound tapers from butt diameters above .023 to ultrafine tippets under .005. It is difficult to make a workable leader under twelve feet that will meet these specifications, and fifteen feet is easier.

However, breaking strains are less important than diameter in fishing selective trout, both because of reduced visibility and the flexibility of a fine tippet. The average trout on most eastern streams will weigh something under a pound. Our famous western rivers hold a higher percentage of big fish, but their average is perhaps only a pound or slightly better.

Such fish are easily handled on .005 and .006 tippets, and with proper rods, even the finer .004 and .003 nylons are workable. Much heavier trout can be handled with gentle striking and playing skills. Such fine diameters are a problem with really big trout, especially in moss-filled spring creeks, but they are often the only tippet sizes that will coax them into taking the fly. There are few rivers where three- and four-pound trout are found in good numbers, except perhaps in Chile, Argentina, and the Antipodes. Such fishing calls for leaders from 4X to 0X, although dropping back to 5X and 6X may prove necessary at times. Skilled anglers can successfully take big trout, fish weighing eight and ten pounds, with leaders testing only two or three pounds of breaking strain. However, it is wise to select leaders that match your skills rather than fish too fine and lose the fish of a lifetime.

Edward Ringwood Hewitt insisted that silkworm gut stained with silver nitrate in a patented Hewitt process was the only effective color for a leader. His patent covered the gut with a crystalline structure of microscopic metal, which undoubtedly helped it sink readily. It also muted its natural glitter and flash in certain kinds of light, which was probably its chief virtue. Certainly the shine of a tippet can cancel out the benefits of its otherwise cobweblike diameter. Preston Jennings insisted that trout could not see a leader dyed his special shade of purple. Leader color has been the subject of countless arguments in trout-fishing camps everywhere, although my own experience would indicate that color makes little difference in actual fishing. A. J. McClane makes a similar observation in his book *The Practical Fly Fisherman*, in the following paragraph:

> The color of leaders, and whether they should sink or float, are both debatable points. I have made dozens of leaders dyed with methylene blue, potassium hydroxide, malachite green, tea, coffee, iodine and Bismarck brown. Aside from messing up the sink, they left no other mark on fishing history.

McClane is probably right in arguing that a dull, mist-colored leader is least visible to the trout, and anyone who has spent any time under the surface of a swift-flowing stream is aware that it has more kaleidoscopic reflections than a carnival hall of mirrors. Leader glitter is often lost in this world of bubbles and refraction and dancing light, but it undoubtedly ranks with a stiff coiled-spring leader lying in the surface film as a warning to a skittish fish.

However, I still believe that a dull mist color is best for dry-fly work, and that a leader for fishing deeper should be dyed to match the background colors of the river bottom. Dull green would match a weedy river, dark gray for a river with a bed of slate-colored stones, brown for a still current of tea-colored detritus and algae, and rust color for a river of reddish ledges of lava and basalt.

Conventional wisdom also argues that a leader should sink in order to fool a difficult trout, but a fully sunk leader is also difficult to tighten with sufficient speed when a fish takes the fly. It can also be argued that the fish usually see the leader no matter what subterfuge we use to disguise its presence. The dry-fly leader should probably be dressed except for its final tippet, and even half the leader should probably be oiled with silicone to fish a nymph or wet fly near the surface. Sink-tip and full sinking lines demand a leader that sinks and sinks readily.

Charles Ritz makes the point in his *Fly Fisher's Life* that a well-tapered leader should deliver its final taper and the fly with precision on the first cast, and that its specifications should provide that kind of performance in both wind and weather. It should provide such complete harmony with the fly line and the rod that it faithfully transmits the caster's art through its tapers to the fly. Such synergy comes largely from casting skill, but it is impossible without perfectly balanced tackle.

It was undoubtedly Charles Ritz who first developed the basic concepts for our modern nylon tapers, since his indefatigable tenacity became focused on the potential of nylon leader material virtually from its introduction in 1939. It took only six months of experimenting with the first samples from Rhodiaceta to convince Ritz that silkworm gut was ultimately finished as a leader material. It took other fly-fishing experts another dozen years to accept nylon, and there are still diehards who argue for silkworm gut and its Golden Age.

The conventional silkworm-gut leaders had always been made in a uniform taper using strands of approximately equal length working from .014 to a tippet of .007 to .006. Such tapers took five or six strands, and worked well enough with oiled-silk lines that had tip diameters of only .025. Limp nylon and polyvinyl chloride lines with tip diameters of .033 to .035 soon changed such conventional wisdom. Ritz soon realized that nylon was not constrained by the average length of its strands, and that the length of any single diameter in his progressive tapers should be determined by performance alone. It was a radical concept well ahead of its time.

Ritz also worked out the basic principle that a nylon leader should be tapered with sixty percent in its heavier diameters, twenty percent in its forward taper, and about twenty percent in its terminal diameters. It is a formula that works quite well, although the considerations of manufacturing caused the original knotless tapers of nylon to resemble earlier designs in silkworm gut and their uniform tapers from butt to tippet. The result was a series of leaders based upon this relatively heavy butt diameter and quick-taper formula which Ritz called his Rafale Storm specification.

However, the basic leaders in the Ritz series of Parabolic Normale, Super-Precision, and Short P.P.P. tapers is based on tippets no finer than .010 to .007 nylon. His formulas also included a nymphing design with an exaggeratedly supple front taper designed to sink and fish the fly with a free and unencumbered drift. Ritz recommended nymph-fishing tippets of .007 and .006, and under many conditions his tapers are excellent.

Yet such specifications fail to meet either the high-wind conditions of our western mountains, or the ultralight tippet requirements of our hard-fished eastern rivers. The following tapers are better adapted to American problems, both for momentum into a wind and for delivering a fine tippet with precision.

These leaders have proved themselves under many conditions in many parts of the country, and their balance and performance are exceptional. Their feel and the behavior of the fly are telegraphed exquisitely to the fisherman through his tackle, giving him remarkable control of both casting and presentation. Casting rhythms have considerable effect on leader dynamics, and leader tapers of these specifications work equally well when a cast is lengthening and has reached optimal line load for the rod. This means the leader must accommodate both the rapid flick-flick timing of the cast at close ranges, the more deliberate rhythms between thirty and forty-odd feet, and the slow rhythms beyond sixty feet. It must also transmit the varied patterns of delivery and line speed for the several basic casts.

Backing material is important too, far more critical than many writers have indicated in past books. Few trout fishermen have much experience in playing really strong fish that carry them regularly into the backing, and such lessons are truly learned on steelhead water, shallow bonefish and tarpon flats, and salmon rivers. Many anglers believe that backing strength and diameter are relatively unimportant, that the principal function of backing is merely in filling out the reel, and that its role in providing extra line for the rare fish strong enough to take the entire fly line is only a secondary factor.

Such truisms can cost you trophy-size fish, and it would be tragic to lose one of the few really big trout you will hook in a lifetime of fishing. Your tackle should be rigged to handle the solitary six-pound rainbow lurking in your home river, not the foot-long fish you usually take.

Modern fly reels are often machined from ultralight aluminum alloys, and the silk and nylon backing line we once used is no longer practical. Silk line like the old bait-casting type was too vulnerable to mildew and rot, and its weight tended to spin a light-alloy spool with too much inertia when a fish started running. Its weight also caused enough static inertia that a bolting fish could sheer a 6X or 7X tippet before the reel spool could respond. Nylon backing has too much stretch for backing performance. During a strong fight with a good fish, as much as a hundred yards of backing can be stripped from the reel. The strength of the fish added to the pull of a heavy current can stretch nylon enough that it can damage the spool. It is recovered grudgingly in its stretched condition, and is layered tightly as it is recovered on the reel. The elasticity of the nylon can literally distort a light-alloy spool, causing it to warp and bind. Its freezing means a lost fish when things go well, and such a reel malfunction could result in a shattered rod if your luck goes badly.

Dacron has solved these problems of elasticity in the backing line, and it has become quite popular in recent years. However, many fishermen are using it in diameters that are too thin for good backing performance, perhaps because they have no need for fifteen- and twenty-pound breaking strain in their fishing. Such misguided sportsmanship has cost many a well-meaning fisherman the best trout of his career. It is not the breaking strain of their backing that matters, but an equilibrium between its maximum reel capacity and its elastic behavior in coming off the spool under stress.

Obviously, the smaller diameters of backing provide optimum footage on any size reel. Such fine diameters can also bite deeply into themselves when a strong fish bolts suddenly, jamming tightly into its underlying layers. It is a bitter lesson I first learned on big rainbows in Patagonia. Although careful rewinding during a fight can reduce the possibility of such a backing jam, it requires a fisherman to pay too much attention to his reel while fishing, and too little to the fish and their fighting behavior. It is better to use backing of heavier diameters, since even the heavier synthetic lines are lighter than the older lines of linen or silk.

My preference is fifteen-pound dacron for light trout fishing, twenty-pound test for average work, and thirty-pound breaking strain for big-fish water. It is not strength that matters in selecting such lines, but their diameters and behavior under stress.

Several manufacturers produce dacron backing line of excellent quality. It is braided with a smooth finish, has only minimal elasticity, and is dimensionally stable either wet or dry. It is available in connected spools of as much as 300 yards, as well as bulk spools of 1,000 yards. Ashaway makes dacron lines in twenty- and thirty-pound test. Gudebrod has an excellent fifteen- and twenty-pound type, and Cortland Micron includes a superb thirty-pound line. Orvis also offers dacron backing line in the optimum twenty- and thirty-pound breaking strains. Such lines are all workable as backing.

Proper knots for modern leaders, lines, and backing are as critical as these pieces of tackle themselves, since knots are often the weak link in our equipment. It is not possible to become a really skilled fly-fisherman without a proficiency in knotmaking. Many of the finest trout fishermen are

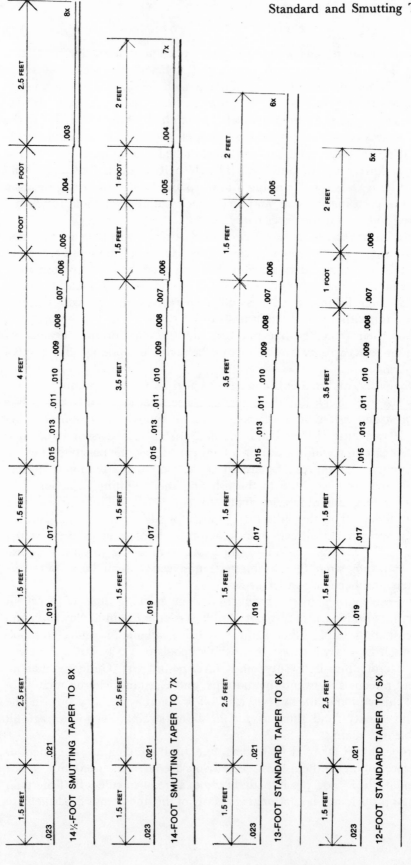

14½-FOOT SMUTTING TAPER TO 8X

14-FOOT SMUTTING TAPER TO 7X

13-FOOT STANDARD TAPER TO 6X

12-FOOT STANDARD TAPER TO 5X

Nymph Leader Tapers

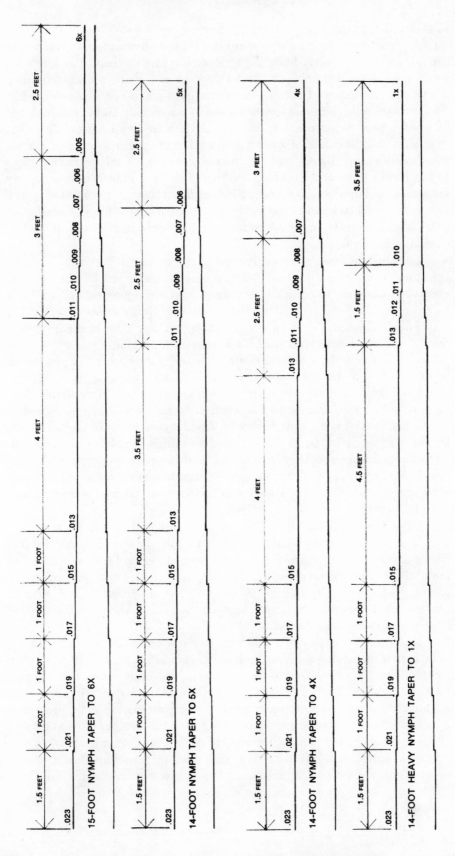

so aware that faulty knots are the primary cause of lost fish that they insist on tying their own knots and making up their own equipment. Such men are not austere or overly fussy. Experience has taught them that knots are more than mere connections, and that bad knots are an abomination. There are no universal fishing knots that will serve every possible need. Modern synthetic lines and leader materials have made all the fishing knots of my boyhood years obsolete, or relegated them to an extremely minor role, since silk lines and silkworm gut are largely gone. We no longer use the thread-wrapped loops at both ends of our lines, or the perfection loops in our leader butts and backing, and the Turle-type knot is now used only for attaching big flies and skaters. Modern fishermen are confronted with a galaxy of knots based on modern synthetic leaders and lines. Knowledgeable fishermen make it their business to know what knot to use and when that knot is needed.

Poor fishing knots are usually configurations that weaken the ambient breaking strain of the material used, filaments damaged by the thermal effects of tightening too quickly, and knots that are tightened too carelessly or have been incorrectly and sloppily trimmed. Bulky knots that will not travel freely through the rod guides will cost you fish. Your knots are poorly tied if you habitually must add an overhand knot in the end of your material, or touch the free monofilament tip with a cigarette, to prevent its slipping through and coming free under the strain of a fish.

Good knots will not slip when freshly tied. All knots in modern nylons slip just before they fail, but a knowledgeable angler will either discard or reseat his knots before that happens. Good knots must be equal to the breaking strain required in the situation for which they have been chosen. Such knots are neat, correctly trimmed, and have adequate strength. The best knots are those that deliver most of the unknotted breaking strain of their materials, since a poor knot can reduce that original strength more than fifty percent.

Good knots will part far below the rated breaking strain of the nylon, and it is best to use the knots described in this chapter for trout fishing. There are still stronger knots that have been developed for taking marlin and sailfish and tarpon with fly tackle, but such knots are relatively complex and their strength is unnecessary in our sport. It is foolish to employ complicated knots simply because they exist, when a less elaborate knot will perform adequately.

Knots should be learned and tied when you are not actually fishing, since expert knot tying requires both patience and practice. Some knots are more difficult than others. Concentrate on a few basic knots and attempt the more difficult types when you have mastered the primary types. Relatively few knots are actually needed, and your skill in executing them is infinitely more important in your fishing than the number of fishing knots in your full lexicon of skills. Practice will permit you to tie fresh knots in a fishing situation without problems and anxiety. Complex knots should never be attempted on the stream until you can execute them easily. It is infinitely better to execute a marginally acceptable knot expertly, than tie the best knot badly.

Popular knowledge clings happily to the myth that modern synthetic leaders, fly lines, and backing last virtually forever. It is simply not true. Humidity and temperature and light all play a role in their gradual denigration. Tippets listed at two-pound test might actually have weakened to fifty percent of their original breaking strain. Frayed leaders and lines are seriously damaged, will cost you fish, and should always be changed. Such fraying can result from badly worn and abrasive guides, tangling in the canoe or under stones, being stepped on, and raking over sharp ledges and boulders during the fight. Badly frayed lines should be discarded, and a leader should be jettisoned at any sign of deterioration.

Leader nylon should always be inspected for any brittle or stiff character, since it loses its lubricants and wetting agents with time. Such nylon has a wiry, springlike behavior. Comparison with fresh nylon of the same type will quickly dispel any doubts in your mind. Expert fly-fishermen will change lines regularly, and new leader material is inexpensive insurance against tackle failures. Most will change leaders after a single prolonged fight with a heavy fish if they think it may have touched a sharp ledge or stone or has been stretched too much during the struggle. Losing good fish is more costly than changing leaders.

Knots should be replaced as well. Freshly tied knots will lose about ten percent of their breaking strength in the first twenty-four hours. Some of this loss results from drying, since the knots were at their tightest while fighting your fish, and some results from nylon memory behavior. Such memory behavior means the nylon tries to find the earlier configuration of its storage spool, and its homing instinct causes its knots to stretch and open slightly. Slippage and weakening are often the result. Experienced fishermen will retighten their knots regularly to offset this tendency, and any knot that tightens too much should also be replaced. Big fish can also subject the fly knot to exceptional stress, and I always replace the fly after fighting a particularly large trout, making sure its knot is fresh and sound. The fly should be freshly attached after a few average-size fish are taken. It is perhaps wise to change all knots several times a season, and on major trips in big-fish country, knots should be replaced regularly.

The strength of nylon leader material is also affected by humidity and temperature and light, even when it has never been fished. High temperatures exceeding about 120 degrees for extended periods of time are trouble, although temperatures of as much as 200 degrees occur with a fly line sawing back and forth over the tip guide during a double haul. Nylons melt at about 500 degrees, but they lose much strength at considerably lower thermal readings. Storage in a hot automobile trunk is unwise, and leaving a reel lying in the sun inside a locked car can easily damage both leaders and lines. Many synthetics are weakened by exposure to both infrared and ultraviolet radiation in sunlight, and modern line and leader synthetics are no exception.

Nylon Wind Tapers

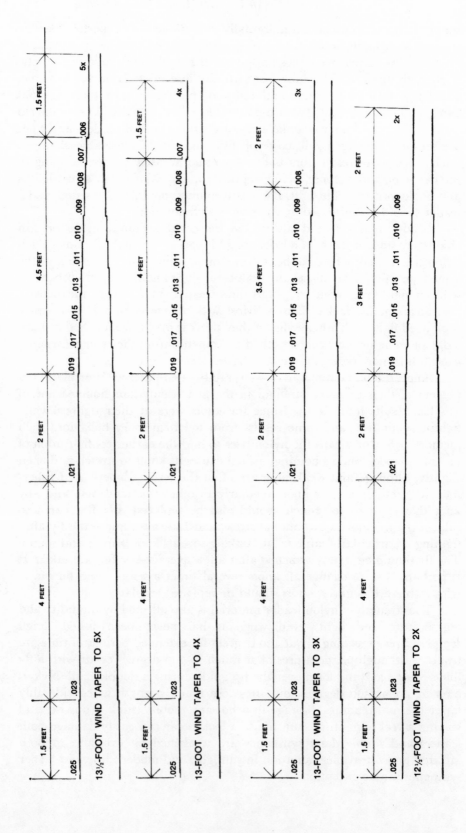

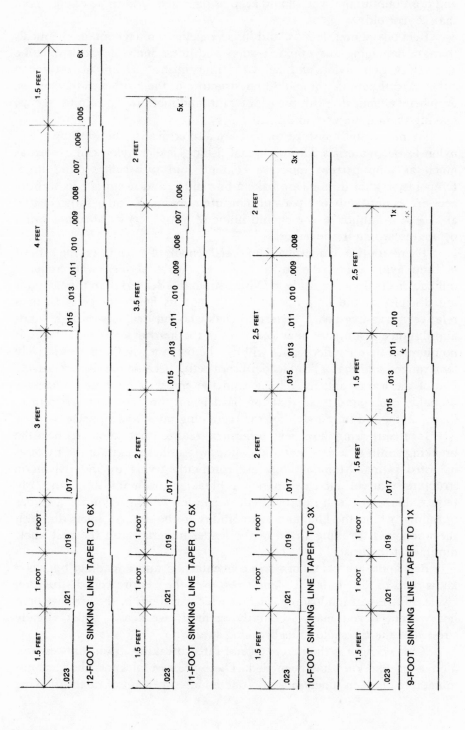

12-FOOT SINKING LINE TAPER TO 6X

11-FOOT SINKING LINE TAPER TO 5X

10-FOOT SINKING LINE TAPER TO 3X

9-FOOT SINKING LINE TAPER TO 1X

Such radiation exists in smaller amounts in normal levels of light, as well as some artificial sources of illumination. Nylon leader material should never be exposed to fluorescent lighting. Such factors in the shelf life of leader material mean a loss of strength before it is sold to the fisherman, and it is doubtful that you should keep using leaders and tippet spools more than a year old.

Reel oils, suntan lotions, and insect repellents often contain chemicals that are damaging to synthetic leaders and lines. Such chemicals must be kept away from nylon and polyvinyl line finishes. Their chemistry can either directly attack the molecular structure of the synthetics themselves, or quarrel chemically with their lubricants and moisture-entraining agents, making them quite wiry and brittle.

Humidity and moisture content are also critical to the working life of nylon leader materials. During actual fishing, leader nylon can absorb as much as nine percent moisture content, and it becomes quite limp. Evaporation after fishing can make a line stiffer, and in storage its stiffness accelerates until only one percent moisture remains. Nylon is rather brittle at this point, although you should immerse it and test its breaking strain before discarding it altogether.

There are two diametrically opposed schools of thought on the subject of limp nylon versus the stiffer types. Eastern fishermen who frequent difficult rivers from the Brule in Wisconsin to the Beaverkill in the Catskills are disciples of the limp-nylon school, since its flexibility gives them a relatively drag-free float. Western anglers who must cope with high winds and distance casting are often partisans of the hard-nylon school. There is no question that a stiffer leader will cast better in a wind and at relatively long ranges, and that a limp leader fishes better because the fly is relatively free of the leader and its influences in the current. The best leaders are probably compound types that use hard nylon through eighty percent of their length, and limp nylon for the remaining taper and tippet.

It is surprising how few fishermen realize that knots reduce the breaking strain of leader material. The raw tensile strength of the nylon is its listed rating. Manufacturers are constantly trying to find polymeric structures that will increase unknotted breaking strain and simultaneously reduce diameter. Such improvements mean less wind friction for a leader unrolling behind the line, and less visibility to the fish. All knots diminish the unknotted breaking strain of the leader material, and the best knots diminish it the least.

Bad knots are points of stress concentration under loading, but good knots tend to distribute the same stress over their entire coiled structure. Cycles of stress and unloading, such as wide variations in the pressure on a heavy trout if you play it clumsily, seriously weaken a tippet already stressed at the threshold of its breaking strain.

Knot strength is the percentage of rated breaking strain that remains after a specific knot has been tied. There are several knots that achieve something between ninety-five and one hundred percent of rated breaking strain, provided they are tightened slowly and moistened to minimize friction and prevent thermal damage.

Exceptionally limp nylon often has poor knotting qualities. It deforms under knotting pressures, creating a weak minimal diameter where stress is concentrated. The simple overhand knot that forms itself while you are casting is perhaps the worst for leader nylon, since each loop in the knot is deforming the other. Such casting knots can weaken a leader to less than forty percent of its rated breaking strain. Extremely stiff nylon can pose other knotting problems. Its wiry qualities can refuse to coil and seat tightly enough to provide a sound knot, and later failure can result.

Impact loading is another common problem. Watching a delicate-looking saleslady break strong wrapping twine during a Christmas rush, snapping it with a sharp application of strength, is a way to understand the difference between a simple breaking strain under steady pressure and the instantaneous effect of impact loads. The breaking strain of a line is based on static testing, and has little relationship to the physical deformation and molecular displacement of an impact-type stress. Such stress dynamics are related to material length and the duration of loading. Such performance under impact-type stress has important lessons for our fishing techniques. Heavy-handed striking subjects our tippets to similar dynamic loads, and too much reel palming or rod pressure during the fight can focus similar stresses to the failure point.

The elasticity of modern synthetics and the calibrations of the rod are our safety valves against such impact loads. Few anglers are aware of the full elasticity of their lines and leaders until they try to break off a fouled fly. Generally speaking, there is more elasticity in limp nylon than hard nylon. Too much elasticity means poor hooking qualities and erratic variations in tension while you are fighting a fish. Too little stretch in a stiff-nylon leader makes it difficult to shield a tippet against impact loads. Elastic behavior is clearly a two-sided coin.

The ability of lines and leaders to resist the normal abrasion of fishing is important too. Nylon leader material is remarkably resistant to abrasion, and its limpness or stiffness has surprisingly little influence on these qualities. Limp nylon is slightly better in its ability to resist cuts and scuffing, since its elasticity recoils slightly from objects that are hard and sharp. Some abrasion of lines and leaders comes from contact with ledges and stones in the river, but most occurs from worn guides and rough places on the reel itself.

Nylons are also surprisingly responsive to atmospheric variations in moisture. High humidity can result in wide variations of moisture content and breaking strain. Fully saturated leaders containing nine percent entrained moisture are about fifteen percent weaker than the same nylon when dry. Saturation is a function of diameter and duration of immersion in the water, but it takes from twenty-four to forty-eight hours to achieve full absorption of water. Such water absorption can vary with the reel you are using. Older closed-frame and spool designs like the Hardy Perfect

DOUBLE NAIL KNOT

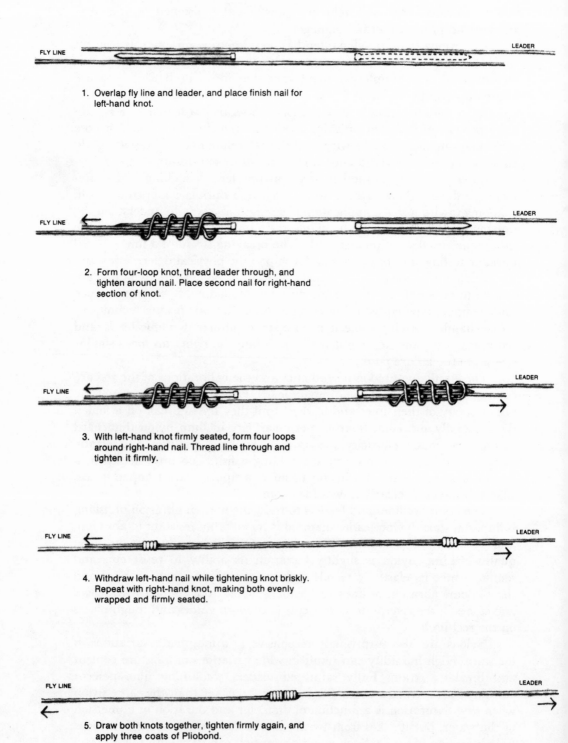

FLY LINE   LEADER

1. Overlap fly line and leader, and place finish nail for left-hand knot.

FLY LINE   LEADER

2. Form four-loop knot, thread leader through, and tighten around nail. Place second nail for right-hand section of knot.

FLY LINE   LEADER

3. With left-hand knot firmly seated, form four loops around right-hand nail. Thread line through and tighten it firmly.

FLY LINE   LEADER

4. Withdraw left-hand nail while tightening knot briskly. Repeat with right-hand knot, making both evenly wrapped and firmly seated.

FLY LINE   LEADER

5. Draw both knots together, tighten firmly again, and apply three coats of Pliobond.

OFFSET NAIL KNOT

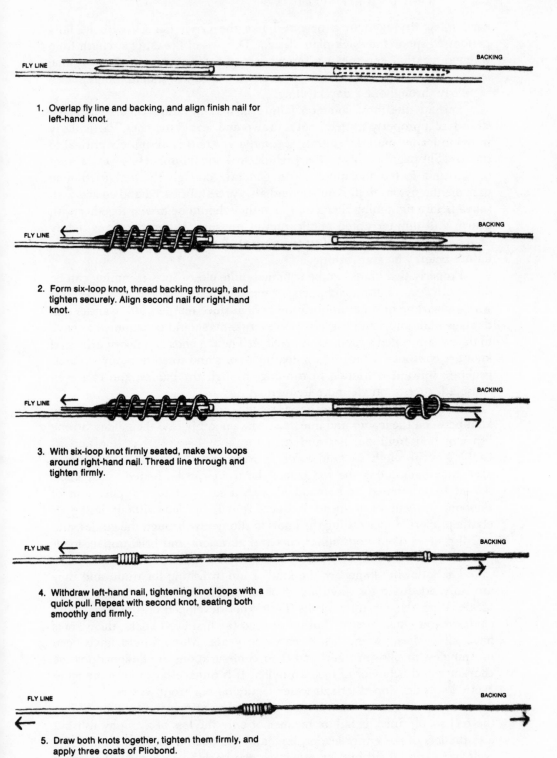

1. Overlap fly line and backing, and align finish nail for left-hand knot.

2. Form six-loop knot, thread backing through, and tighten securely. Align second nail for right-hand knot.

3. With six-loop knot firmly seated, make two loops around right-hand nail. Thread line through and tighten firmly.

4. Withdraw left-hand nail, tightening knot loops with a quick pull. Repeat with second knot, seating both smoothly and firmly.

5. Draw both knots together, tighten them firmly, and apply three coats of Pliobond.

permit less drying than a new reel like the Orvis C.F.O. with its fully perforated spool and back-plate design. The loss of breaking strength from water saturation can mean a serious loss of performance in the very fine leader diameters, and such delicate nylon strands should be replaced regularly throughout a day's fishing.

Perhaps the most common failure in making knots occurs when the strands of a properly started knot is drawn and seated together. Particularly in nylon leader material, tightly seating your knots is absolutely critical to success. Slippage is always the prelude to knot failure. However, a knot drawn and seated too quickly can generate enough thermal friction to damage the nylon itself. Knots should always be lubricated and cooled with saliva before tightening them, and then they should be drawn together with a firm and uninterrupted application of pressure. When a knot is tightly seated, test it with a series of strong pulls. It is far better to experience knot failure before you start fishing.

Properly tied knots can be trimmed quite close. Such trimming can be done with scissors, fishing clippers, or scissor pliers. It should never be done with a cigarette or other application of heat since temperature transfer can damage both knots and leaders. However, knots should be trimmed as close to their main coiled structures as possible. The tag ends of a poorly trimmed knot are continually picking up floating debris and weed in many streams, generate unwanted friction in running through the guides, and can even cause a leader to tangle more frequently.

Extralong leaders mean that at some point in the fight the connecting knot between the leader and line must pass smoothly into the guides. Strong fish can bolt from the net and strip the knot between the line and its backing out through the guides at surprising velocities, and that knot must also come back along the rod before the trout can be netted. Such knots should be laminated and smoothed with a series of thin applications of Pliobond cement or fly-head lacquer. It will harden without losing its elastic properties, permitting the knots to slip freely through the guides, and it will protect them from minor cuts and abrasions and brief impact loads when they catch along the rod.

The following knots are the kinds I use in fishing for trout, and they are fully adequate for anything short of taking billfish or tarpon on fly tackle. With the exception of the Turle knot developed on the Hampshire chalkstreams when Henry Hall introduced the first eyed hooks, these knots have all evolved in the last twenty-five years. Many would have been meaningless in silkworm gut, and their configurations are designed for the character and behavior of modern nylon. It is unnecessary to use the more exotic knots developed for salt-water tactics on our trout waters.

Perhaps the most basic knot is designed to attach the backing line to the reel spool, since its failure means not only the loss of a trophy fish but also the loss of the entire leader, line, and the dacron backing itself. Some reels have special fittings for attaching the backing line, but others have completely smooth spindles. Such reels demand a special backing knot. My favorite consists of looping the dacron around the spool, feeding it both in and out through the proper opening in the reel frame or its line guard. The backing is then secured with a simple overhand knot around itself, with a secondary overhand knot seated in its end. Seat the terminal knot and tighten the primary knot around the line. Pull both knots slowly until they tighten down flush with the reel spool and do not trim the excess line. Both knots and excess line should then be seated under a thin strip of electrician's tape. It will secure the knots and provide a mildly adhesive foundation under the first layer of backing.

Both modern nylon and polyvinyl chloride lines have resulted in a number of knots that would have proved worthless twenty-odd years ago. Our familiar nail and tube knots would have been ineffective with gut leaders and oil-finished silk lines, since the gut was not supple enough and nylon would have simply cut through the silk. Yet the knots are perfect for our more modern mix of synthetic lines and finishes, and the more tension applied, the tighter these nylon knots become. Our old clinch or jam knots, which joined our knotted leader loops to silk fly lines, are totally obsolete. It is not simply a question of their catching in the guides when a fish came in close and you were fishing a leader longer than your rod; with the development of ultralight nylon tippet materials smaller than .005, connecting knots.between leaders and lines became a critical problem, and the nail knots were perfected. Properly tied, they will seat smoothly and pass through the guides without trouble, since even the lightest impact can shear a .003 tippet. Nail knots were originally tied using a finish nail as the armature for forming them, so the name is still used even though a small tube or pair of scissors is perhaps a better tool.

Two basic knots are useful for joining your backing to a fly line, depending on your tackle, and the character of the river and its fish. Small rivers with moderate-size trout mean light backing lines and relatively light fly lines, and in recent seasons I have been using the double nail knot with such tackle. Since big fish and strong currents mean distance casting and somewhat heavier gear, joining your backing to a fly line of much greater diameter is the problem. The offset nail knot is the solution that I prefer. Both knots result in relatively small splices that do not deteriorate like the old silk-whip type and offer much less bulk than the rolling splice popular on salt water.

The double nail knot is formed in separate operations. It consists of lapping the materials being spliced with the backing material and reel on the left and the fly line at the right. The backing is knotted first, holding both lines together along a small ten-gauge aluminum or brass tube with the left hand. The backing is started into a right-hand nail knot by looping it back over itself, around the fly line and tubing, in a series of three turns. These turns should be held firmly in place with the index finger of the left hand, and the free end of the dacron is then inserted into the left end of the tubing and pushed through it with the right hand. Make sure the three loops around the tubing and lines are not permitted to slip, and draw both

SPEED NEEDLE KNOT

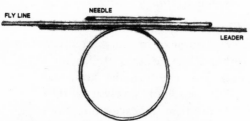

1. Lay needle along fly line and form loop of leader material, holding loop open with thumb and index finger.

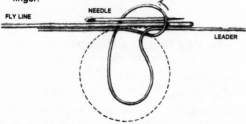

2. Warp loop upward, wrapping it over fly line and needle in a clockwise motion, and secure under the fingers.

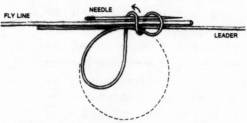

3. Wrap loop over again, tightening each succeeding loop against the last, until six turns are complete.

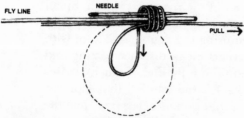

4. Holding the coiled loops in alignment, draw the leader itself to the right until the knot is seated tightly.

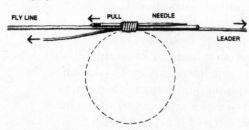

5. Tighten both ends of leader and withdraw needle.

6. Trim line and leader ends, and coat with three applications of Pliobond.

TUBE KNOT

1. Lap fly line and leader, leaving a foot of leader material to form knot. Lay tube in position shown.

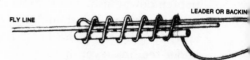

2. Hold line, starting loop and tube firmly in left hand. Make six complete wraps of leader, working from left to right.

3. Hold all six wraps securely and insert leader material back through the forming tube.

4. Seat coils carefully, still holding them in the left fingers, by pulling at the leader material.

5. Pull both tube and leader material through briskly, simultaneously tightening leader to right.

6. Pull slowly and firmly at both ends of leader to tighten and seat knot into finish of fly line.

7. Tighten with leader and line pressure, finishing with three coats of Pliobond.

NEEDLE KNOT

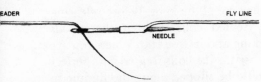

LEADER   FLY LINE

NEEDLE

. Use fresh razor blade to shape leader butt into
hair-fine point and insert into small needle.
Force needle into lower quarter-inch of fly line, and
work out through side.

LEADER   FLY LINE

NEEDLE

. Hold fly line and needle in left hand.
Grip needle point with pliers, and pull both needle
and leader through line completely.

LEADER   FLY LINE

NEEDLE

. Trim delicate leader point off and draw enough nylon
through to shape a four-loop nail knot.

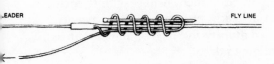

LEADER   FLY LINE

. Form four nail-knot loops around finish nail and tighten.

LEADER   FLY LINE

5. Withdraw nail, seat and trim knot, and coat with
Pliobond.

SIMPLE NAIL KNOT

FLY LINE   LEADER

1. Lap fly line and leader, and align forming nail.

FLY LINE   LEADER

2. Wrap five loops and thread leader through along
nail.

FLY LINE   LEADER

3. Withdraw forming nail and seat knot firmly with
tension at ends of leader material.

FLY LINE   LEADER

4. Test knot and apply three coats of Pliobond.

REEL SPOOL KNOTS

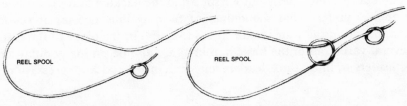

REEL SPOOL

1. Loop backing around reel spool
and form overhand knot in end.

REEL SPOOL

2. Form second overhand knot around
backing, close tip knot, and tighten on
spool.

the tubing and backing carefully from the core of the knot. Before releasing the fingers still holding the partially seated coils, tighten these coils carefully, pulling gently on both the backing and its free end. When you are certain the knot is formed perfectly, with its coils seated in perfect alignment but not fully tightened, it should be slipped along the fly line to make room for the left-hand nail knot in the line itself that completes the operation. With ultrafine tackle, joining twenty-pound backing to lines finer than a DT5F, some fishermen are content to seat this right-hand nail knot tightly into the line finish, and coat it with Pliobond. It is sufficient for small fish and fine tippets. Other anglers like to remove the polyvinyl chloride finish from the line and complete the rest of their double nail knots using only its dacron or nylon braided core. It is usually possible to form the knot between the fingers without the tubing when you are using only the core of the line. Otherwise the left-hand nail knot formed around the backing with the core of the line is simple enough. It is started with the line, backing, and tubing (or without the tubing if your dexterity is good) held in the right hand. Four turns of the line are worked back toward the right, the free end is inserted in the right end of the tubing, and pushed through toward the left. The knot should be seated slowly until it is completely formed but not fully tightened. The double nail knot is then two-thirds finished, with two knots formed around the opposite material. Pull the four ends of the knot tight. It is complete when a careful tightening on both line and backing draws the two knots together, seats them firmly against each other, and tightens them securely with a steady pressure of about twenty pounds. The knot ends should be trimmed at forty-five degree angles with a razor blade. Coat with Pliobond and allow to dry.

The offset nail knot is better for joining a heavier fly line to dacron backing of about thirty-pound test. It is shaped exactly like the double nail knot, except that the heavier material is started first and is tied with only two turns before it is worked back through the knotting tube. Then it is partially tightened around the backing. The backing is then formed around the fly line by shaping eight turns and holding them in place with the fingers. It is then threaded through the tubing from right to left. Slip the tubing out carefully and close the knot. Completing the full offset knot involves pulling the untrimmed ends tight, and then tightening the lines with a strong tension until the knot is fully secure.

Similar knots are used to join shooting-head lines to backing and their running lines. The special running lines of the Aircel-type measure about .029 in diameter and join easily with a double nail knot to thirty-pound dacron backing material. The offset nail knot is fine for joining this running line to the back taper of the shooting head too, and I also use it with flat monofilament running lines, both for splices to the backing and the fly line. Many anglers prefer a flat monofilament running line, because it resists tangles and coils in the water and it tends to unroll in the plane of the cast.

Several variations of the basic nail knot are also becoming popular for joining leaders to lines, since leaders longer than the rod are necessary on many hard-fished rivers. Nail knots must be particularly tight and neatly formed and must pass effortlessly through the guides if a fish suddenly bolts with the leader inside the tip guide. Salt-water nail knots involve seating a loop of fly line inside the coiled leader material, and provide a relatively symmetrical exit for the leader from the centerline of the knot. The simple nail knot relies on its tightening and friction alone, omitting the internal loop altogether, and projects asymmetrically from the end of the line. The speed nail knot is similar in its configuration, but has been worked out for execution at streamside. Each of these knots is excellent, although they all display the tendency to crack through the adjacent polyvinyl finish, creating a hinge action in the line.

The needle knot was developed to provide a system of joining the leader butt to the line, with both leader and line on the same longitudinal axis. It also is a superb knot that resists hinging and provides a smooth continuity of casting power. The development of the needle knot on the salt-water flats off Florida soon led to experimenting with a simpler version of its construction that secured the leader inside the fly line with epoxy. George Keough worked out the pioneering epoxy knots on steelheads along the beautiful North Fork of the Stillaguamish, and they are unquestionably the best type for running freely through the rod guides, and providing a hinge-free transition of casting power. Dave Whitlock has worked out a similar knot which adds a short length of bright-colored plastic or fly line over the leader, both for visibility in nymph fishing and to prevent hinging and provide smooth power transfer in casting. Such knots both involve threading through the core of the line, and its diameter obviously limits the diameter of the leader worked inside. Elasticity and diameter in the line are the controlling factors in the calibrations of your leader butt, making some of the magnum-butt tapers impractical. However, for fishing relatively light tackle the Keough and Whitlock knots are superb.

The original nail knots evolved on salt water where fishermen were desperately searching for methods of using the full strength of the remarkable modern nylons. Their knotting behavior did not resemble silkworm gut or even the more primitive nylons, and knots worked out for these older materials failed miserably on tarpon. Big salt-water fish were so explosive with their infighting near the boat that knot performance in the guides became critical. Poor knots or tangles that jammed when a strong fish bolted could strip guides from a rod like popcorn, and the salt-water nail knot was the result. It is also useful on really large trout in heavy currents, like steelheads or the big rainbows in Argentina and Chile.

Tying the salt-water nail knot involves holding the line, leader, and knotting tube in the left hand, with the leader material lying on the right. The fly line should be turned back in a loop and held between the fingertips. The leader material is passed inside the loop, rolled back outside, and coiled three to five times around the entire system. Its free end is then inserted from the left and threaded back through the tube toward the right. Draw the tube free carefully, tightening the free end of the leader at the

SALTWATER NAIL KNOT

FLY LINE

NAIL

1. Lap finish nail with fly line.

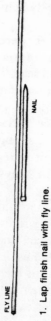

FLY LINE

LEADER

2. Loop fly line back along nail and thread leader through.

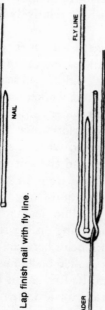

FLY LINE

LEADER

3. Wrap leader six times around nail and folded line.

FLY LINE

LEADER

4. Withdraw nail and thread leader through entire knot.

FLY LINE

LEADER

5. Tighten knot and coat with Pliobond.

BLOOD KNOT

3x   4x

1. Overlap leader material to be joined.

3x   4x

4x

2. Twist left-hand tippet five turns and fold back carefully.

3x   4x

4x

3x

3. Thread tippet through and hold firmly in place.

3x   4x

4x

3x

4. Twist right-hand tippet five wraps, fold back smoothly, and insert through center loop.

3x   4x

5. Moisten knot, seat with gradual tension, and trim.

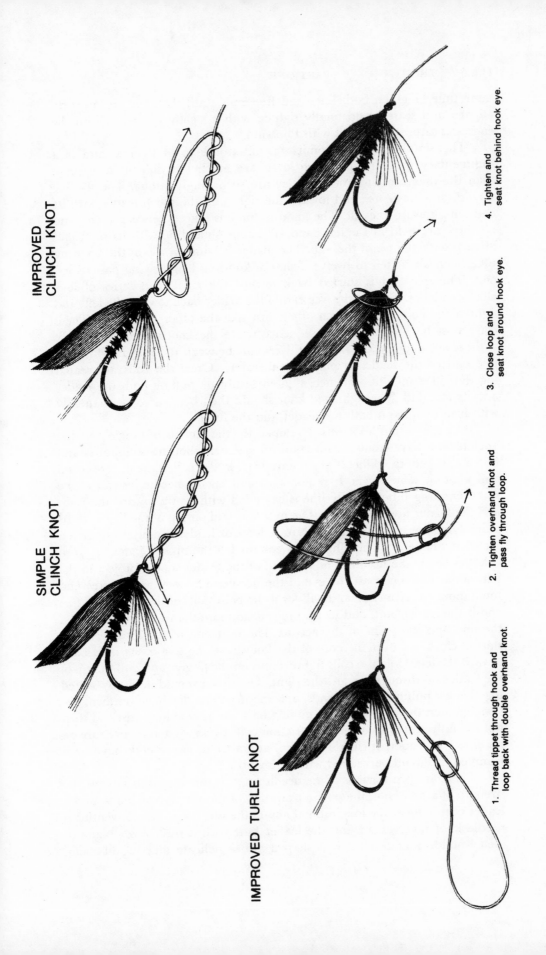

IMPROVED
CLINCH KNOT

SIMPLE
CLINCH KNOT

IMPROVED TURLE KNOT

1. Thread tippet through hook and loop back with double overhand knot.

2. Tighten overhand knot and pass fly through loop.

3. Close loop and seat knot around hook eye.

4. Tighten and seat knot behind hook eye.

same time. Tighten both lines and free ends until the coils are properly aligned and seated, and finally tighten with a steady pressure. Trim the ends and saturate the knot with Pliobond.

The simple nail knot omits the interior loop of fly line and is a rudimentary friction type. Such knots are much less difficult to execute than the diagrams suggest and they are surprisingly strong. The fly line should lie with its free end toward the right and the nylon leader with its end lying toward the left. The knotting tube is placed between them, and all three are held in the left hand. The tube should lie with its right end aligned with the tip of the line. The leader is lying on top of the knotting tube, with about ten to twelve inches of knotting length lying past its left end. The free end is started back toward the right in a series of four clockwise loops. Thread the free end of the leader back toward the left, and tighten the coils against each other, just like the other nail knots. These coils must be held tightly in sequence while the knotting tube is slowly withdrawn, and the coils must still remain between the fingers while the free end of the leader is pulled deliberately. Once the coils are seated together in a smooth sequence, tighten firmly by pulling both the leader and its free end. The tightened knot should then be secured permanently with firm tension on both the leader and the fly line.

The speed nail knot was developed for the legions of tangle-fingered anglers who have trouble with conventional nail-knotting techniques and find a nail knot too difficult at streamside. It is also called the thirty-second nail knot on some rivers. It requires a small sewing needle instead of the small knotting tube. The fly line is extended with its tip toward the right and the leader toward the left. The needle is laid on top of the line with its point lying toward the right. Form a loop of leader material about ten inches in diameter by holding it between the left thumb and index finger so it hangs below the needle. The free end of the leader should project to the left, about one inch past the eye of the needle. The loop and its free end total about thirty inches, and will form the belly coils of the knot. The free end is the leader butt, and its tip projects no more than one-half inch past the line and the point of the needle. The butt end of the leader is then started clockwise over the core of the knot, working five or six coils back toward the left. Hold the coils tightly between the fingers and pull the tip of the leader on through toward the right. The nylon should be firmly seated together by pulling on both ends, and the needle is slowly withdrawn, eye first. Tighten the knot again by pulling hard on both nylon ends, and then test the fully seated security of its friction coils by strong tensile pressure on the line and leader. It should not slip, and after its excess ends have been trimmed, it should be secured with Pliobond.

There are two versions of the needle knot. It is designed to provide the strength of a nail knot, the power transition of the epoxy-type knots, and a leader butt lying at the longitudinal axis of the line itself. The conventional needle knot involves shaving the leader butt with a fresh razor blade or model-building knife until it is shaped into a delicate tapering filament.

The tapered filament is threaded through the eye of a small sewing needle, and the needle is worked into the core of the line from its tip. Penetration should last about one-half inch before the needle is angled out through the side. Grasp the half-inch section of line penetrated by the needle with the left thumb and forefinger, with the shaved nylon threaded tightly into its eye. Grip the needle firmly with a pair of point-nosed pliers and draw both needle and leader nylon smoothly through the core of the fly line. Continue pulling the nylon through until enough length is strung beyond its exit from the line. Complete with a conventional four-coil nail knot, and coat smoothly with Pliobond.

The Bates needle knot involves pliers and moderate heat. The needle is carefully forced into the tip of the line along its core, and out the side, skewering about one-half inch of line on its steel shaft. The needle is held with the pliers and heated briefly with a match until the polyvinyl finish of the line begins smoking faintly at its tip. Push the line toward the heated eye-end of the needle. Now you strike a second match and heat the point of the needle until its exiting point from the line smokes slightly too. Overheating the polyvinyl chloride finish can seriously weaken the fly line, so heat must be applied with caution. The heat cauterizes the rim of the needle's entry and exit points in the plastic finish, keeping them open when the needle is withdrawn. The open core is then threaded with a knotless tapered leader, inserted tippet first into the side of the line, and drawn out through its tip until about twelve inches of its butt diameters remain. This length is then worked into a conventional nail knot of four coils, tightly seated and trimmed and coated with Pliobond.

The Keough epoxy knot is similar to the standard needle knot in its beginnings. The leader butt is carefully shaved to a slender filamentlike point, and the line is penetrated about one-half inch with a needle, entering at its tip. The needle point is allowed to exit at the side of the fly line. The shaved nylon is threaded through the needle's eye, along with a two-inch length of cotton darning thread saturated in epoxy. Both the nylon leader material and the epoxy-soaked thread are then drawn through the fly line with pliers until the leader is inside the line along with the epoxy-saturated darning cotton. The shaved nylon is carefully trimmed, along with the excess lengths of epoxy thread. Finally, the side exit-point is coated with epoxy, and epoxy is also applied to the leader and line tip. Such epoxy knots are exceptionally strong when properly executed and cured, but since their strength depends solely on the thin internal coating of the adhesive, the Keough-type knots should be tested vigorously before fishing them.

The Whitlock epoxy knot is essentially the same in its execution, except for the addition of a sleevelike length of line on the leader before the knot is started. The sleeve is usually one-half inch of fire-orange fly line or fine plastic tubing provided by the line manufacturer. It is hollowed out with a needle, and the shaved nylon butt is drawn through its full length. The sleeve is then slipped down the leader several inches. The entire sequence of the Keough-type knot is followed through, and once it is completed, approximately one-half inch of the leader below the line is coated with additional epoxy. The sleeve is slipped back up the leader and seated tightly against the line. Epoxy is also used to seal the point between the leader and the free end of the sleeve. It is my experience that the Whitlock knot is slightly more secure than the Keough type, and better transmits the dynamics of a cast from the line into the leader. Both epoxy knots limit the butt diameter of the leader material, but otherwise these knots are superb for trout fishing.

The blood knot is the only configuration that passes unchanged from the silkworm-gut years into our era of modern polymeric nylons. It is used to attach a fresh leader to the butt strand that has been permanently attached to the line. It is also used to join leader strands together in building specially tapered leaders, or adding fresh tippets. The blood knot is the strongest possible method of joining two leader strands together, delivering ninety-five percent of rated breaking strain when the diameter change between strands is only .001 inch. It is started with the two strands overlapping and held between the thumb and index finger of both hands. Approximately four to six inches of overlapping ends are needed in forming blood knots of trout-size leader materials. Holding the right-hand strands firmly, twist the left end around the main tippet with a rolling motion of the fingertips for five to six turns. Bend the free end back, lay it in the slot between the leader and right end, and hold its position firmly in the left hand. The right strand is then twisted about the main leader an equal number of turns. Its free end is then bent back and inserted through the same loop holding the first tippet. Holding both free ends to keep them from slipping, tighten the knot carefully with a steady pressure. Then trim the knot carefully. Less pressure is obviously required to seat blood knots in the fine diameters below .009 inches. The blood knot is perhaps the most basic knot in fly-fishing.

The extension blood knot is used to provide dropper tippets for fishing wet flies and nymphs. It is executed in exactly the same manner as the standard blood knot, except that its heavier strand is exaggeratedly long and remains untrimmed once the knot is fully seated. The knotting angle of the extended strand and its thickness tend to hold the attached fly away from the leader in both casting and fishing.

Turle knots were developed on the British chalkstreams in the late nineteenth century, and although the development of modern nylon has made them virtually obsolete, a modified version is useful. Our nylons slip too easily for use in the conventional Turle knot. However, it is useful when you wish to have a relatively rigid connection between the leader and the fly for such tactics as skittering a variant or skater. It must be seated carefully to prevent its slipping. The original Turle works on hook sizes below fourteen, but larger sizes demand an improved Turle knot, with its better friction and control. The Turle knots deliver about seventy-five percent of rated breaking strain.

The original Turle knot is formed by threading the tippet through the hook eye, looping it back on itself behind the eye, and closing it with a simple overhand knot. This loop is shaped below the hook with the down-eye type, and above it with a turned-up eye. The loop is opened and slipped over the hook, wings, and hackles until it can be tightened and seated behind the eye. It should be pulled firmly to make sure all slipping is stopped. Such knots insure enough rigidity to hold a skater or variant high on its hackles, and are still extremely useful in such tactics when carefully and firmly executed.

The double Turle knot is a modification based on the character of our modern synthetic leaders. Both their limpness and their smooth finish cause traditional knots to creep and work and slip free. Many fishermen have completely abandoned the original Turle knot to use the double type, except in very small tippets and hooks. The double Turle knot is formed exactly like the single Turle, except that the simple overhand knot is replaced with a two-twist slip knot. Three twists are sometimes used with heavier tippets and large flies.

The simple clinch knot is perhaps the best fly knot developed for attaching flies in trout sizes. The tippet is simply threaded through the hook eye, looped back along the leader, twisted four or five times, and inserted back into the loop at the hook eye again. Hold the leader tip and fly with your left hand, and then tighten and seat the coils with a steady tension. Properly tied, this knot delivers almost one hundred percent breaking strain, and is my favorite for trout flies smaller than size twelve.

The improved clinch was developed for larger hook sizes, and it is rated at ninety-five percent of breaking strain. The tippet is inserted through the hook eye, turned back along the leader itself, and twisted four to five turns. Its free end is inserted through the loop at the hook eye, as the fly is held with the left hand and the knot is worked toward its conclusion with the right. The final step is threading the free end back through the large loop remaining, and holding the half-finished knot firmly while it is tightened. There are endless arguments along trout water about the clinch knot versus the improved clinch, and except in cases of slippage with relatively light leaders and large hook eyes, my own preference lies with the ordinary clinch knot. Its fishability seems stronger to me in the ultrafine tippet diameters, and I use it regularly.

These are the several knots used in rigging my tackle, from seating the backing on the reel to attaching my flies. Although many readers may consider discussions of leader calibrations and breaking strains and knots excessively dull, these details are too often our Achilles' heel. It is impossible to give too much emphasis to the problems of terminal tackle.

The truth of this observation brings to mind the loss of a big fish on the Gunnison in Colorado. It was a heavy brown of seven or eight pounds that lay under a logjam in a side channel of the river. It had been hooked any number of times that summer, and it had smashed several leaders and rods. It was a fish that was becoming legendary.

Geronimo, my old friend Herb Salzbrenner shook his head and grinned. *He's getting some reputation!*

Geronimo was not taken that summer, and when I returned to the Gunnison that next year it seemed the big fish was still there downstream from the Cooper ranch. Several fishermen had broken off in a heavy brown.

You think it's still Geronimo? I asked.

It's possible, the ranch foreman nodded. *He's lying right under the logs where Geronimo always stayed.*

They think he's a big fish? I pressed.

Big enough! he said.

The first evening I fished the hole carefully, working so deep under the dead trees that I fouled and lost several big wet flies and nymphs. The only fish that took were several small rainbows and a brown of about two pounds. The cabin beside mine was occupied with a new party that had just arrived, and it included a surgeon from Denver who had been fishing only two or three seasons. The man was absolutely a fanatic on fly-fishing, building his own split-cane rods and tying flies and making his own tapered leaders. The table on the screen porch of his cabin was covered with English hook boxes and gamecock necks and fly-tying tools, and he was busily at work on a fresh twelve-foot leader tapered to a .006 tippet.

Like some coffee? he waved from the porch.

Yes, I said gratefully.

Making up some leaders! he explained and poured two mugs of black coffee, and pushed the sugar bowl across the table. *River looks a little low now.*

They're a little shy, I agreed.

Heard some talk in Gunnison, the doctor began. *Boys in the tackle shop were talking about a big fish below here.*

That crowd in the tackle shop? I asked.

Yes, he nodded. *Know anything about it?*

What did they say? I parried.

Something about a fish called Geronimo, he continued. *They said he's here on the Cooper stretch, just below the corrals.*

It's possible, I smiled. *We had a big brown called Geronimo last summer.*

But they talked about this year! the doctor said.

There's another big fish in the same pool, I said. *It might be Geronimo—and then again it might not.*

Where is he? the doctor asked eagerly.

Just below the corrals, I replied. *You'll see the logs jammed in along the willows.*

And he's under the logs? he asked.

Yes, I said. *He's there.*

The doctor finished his leader and tightened the final blood knot skillfully, but he tightened the knots almost too facilely, and failed to test them with a steady pull. It was obvious he was a good fisherman and had mastered an impressive catalogue of skills in a remarkably short time. But watching him swiftly rig leaders told me that his experience with big fish was lacking.

What flies should I use? he asked.

Big flies worked deep under the logs, I laughed. *Biggest you can find!*

The doctor nodded and got the coffee pot from the coal stove inside the cabin. *Like some more coffee?* he asked.

Please, I said.

We fished the Gunnison for more than a week, and there were good fly hatches each morning. The fish came readily when the flies were on the water. Fishing was excellent, and several two- to three-pound rainbows and browns were brought in almost every day. Several fishermen tried the big trout under the deadfalls below the ranch without luck.

Hey! the doctor waved from his cabin. *I've got something I'm going to try on Geronimo!* His fly-tying tools were out and he had gone into Gunnison that morning. He poured us both fresh mugs of coffee and handed me a box of big bait-fishing hooks.

They're 3/0 trolling hooks, he said.

Think they're big enough? I laughed. *Where'd you find hooks this size?*

Had them in the tackle store, he explained eagerly. *Found them in the back of a drawer.* He adjusted his vise to hold the hooks.

They're three inches long! I said.

They're perfect! The doctor was excited now. *I'm going to make the biggest bucktails you've ever seen!*

They're big all right, I smiled.

The next morning I took a fine brace of two-pound rainbows a mile below the ranch, and I was wading back slowly when I met a local character who was a living legend along the river. The old man offered me a pinch or two of his Copenhagen as we compared the morning's results.

Chew? The old man held out the can.

It was an old ritual between us. *No,* I shook my head. *Don't think I'm ready for your brand just yet.*

No? the old man cackled raucously.

Thanks anyway, I said.

We waded upstream through the shallows, following the side channel downstream from the corrals. Someone was fishing the deadfalls where the big fish stayed, and suddenly we heard him shout excitedly above the river sounds. It was the doctor and he was into a heavy fish at the throat of the pool. The old fisherman looked at me and I stared back.

Well, he spat a dark stream of tobacco. *I'll be damned!*

Geronimo! I said in disbelief.

We waded quickly upstream along the gravelly riffles and found the surgeon fearfully holding his straining rod. The man glanced at us in alarm as the great fish stripped thirty feet of line from the reel. It threatened to penetrate the logs, but finally it turned and the doctor forced it back. It fought deep for another ten minutes before it came to the surface.

That there's some brown trout! The old fisherman released another stream of tobacco for punctuation. *Biggest I seen this summer!*

How big? the doctor asked excitedly.

It's big enough, I said quietly.

The huge brown was a strong, hook-jawed male of six or seven pounds, and I did not want to excite him with an estimate of its size. The surgeon seemed nervous enough. The big fish threshed heavily on the surface, but its strength was ebbing now, and the doctor increased his rod pressure.

Suddenly the leader parted, and the doctor stared in shock. *He broke me!* he wailed. *He broke me!*

Geronimo's broke a lotta folks, the old man said softly.

What did I do wrong? the surgeon asked.

His freshly tied leader had broken in its heavier middle tapers where the strands were better than twelve-pound test, and its broken end had the little pigtail curl that spelled a poorly made knot that had slipped.

You didn't do anything wrong now. I showed the curled pigtail of nylon to the old man and shook my head.

What do you mean now? the doctor protested.

You played that fish jest fine. The old man tucked a fresh wad of tobacco high inside his cheek. *It's them leader knots you tied at breakfast.*

Dammit! the doctor shook his head angrily. *Surgeons tie knots every day that people's lives depend on.*

Doctor, the old man replied, *the patient jest died.*

For recent developments in tackle, see Appendix: Notes on New Equipment.

4. Random Thoughts
on Waders, Clothing,
and Other Equipment

Boyhood memories are a strange mixture of people and places and occurrences worth remembering. No odyssey of growing up is without its measure of pain and frustration, and thoughts of happy times are always mixed with less happy times. It is curious that many youthful memories are a scrapbook of sensory echoes, and such memories often become more intense as we grow older.

It is possible to remember the tastes and smells and sounds of boyhood with a sharpness that erases the intervening years, and I remember the house with its high ceilings and the huge porch across the entire front with its newelled railings and trellis of roses. The big house creaked and groaned during a storm, and sometimes its millwork and flooring cracked in hot weather. The bay window looked out from the library, and I often sat there on summer afternoons, reading in the leaf-flickering shade of a giant maple whose branches also sheltered my room upstairs. Robins nested regularly outside my window, and I watched them carrying worms to their babies in early summer. Their birdsongs had a lilting note heard only after a rain. Sometimes late at night, I can almost hear the freight trains whistling balefully on the long grade past Sager's Lake. There was an ineffable poetry in those steam-driven trains, and their melancholy music still echoes clearly in my mind.

The white-carbon street lamps of boyhood were always swarming with moths, each circling dizzily in its own mindless orbit, and katydids and crickets filled the night with their rich orchestrations. Other sounds and smells are remembered too. There was a fierce crackle of lightning that once shattered an oak across the street, and its terrible thunderclap rattled the windows and shook the entire house. Locusts filled the August doldrums with their droning chorus, and that was the summer I attended my first funeral. It was unbearably hot and the wind eddied through the cornfields. The locusts made it impossible to hear the services or the parched soil clattering across the coffin. Walking back from bluegill fishing the following summer, I took a shortcut through the country cemetery, and I will never forget the scent of the shrivelled roses that surrounded the tombstone of that boyhood playmate.

There are happier memories too.

There were ice wagons rattling through the streets on hot summer afternoons. We ran after them noisily, begging the iceman to chip off small pieces that we could suck like lollipops. The corner store had lollipops and licorice and jawbreakers in huge apothecary jars, and I can remember the rattle of the penny gumball machines.

My mother often stopped in another store where fresh coffee was ground, and I listened as the hard chocolate-colored beans spilled into the hopper, anticipating the rich smells that would soon fill the shop. The butcher shop was a different world, with the faint pine fragrance of fresh sawdust on its floor. Blue pike and whitefish and smoked shrimps lay in the freshly-cracked ice of the trays. Beef and sausages and lamb hung in the cooling chests behind the butcher-block counter. Freshly baked bread had its unforgettable fragrance too, and I remember the summer I first delivered the Chicago paper on my bicycle. The paper boys always stopped for fresh doughnuts that were almost too hot for our fingers when we sat on the bakery steps to eat them.

There was fishing tackle at the hardware store, along with a few small-calibre rifles and shotguns off in a corner, with red and green boxes of ammunition locked behind the glass-doored cabinets. The guns gleamed with oil and we were forbidden to touch them, and they stood neatly in the racks with a strange totemic power. There were several split-cane rods racked on a circular display stand, although these were factory rods without any particular pedigree. Bass plugs and a few flies shared a simple glass case with fly lines and leaders and small bottles of citronella.

There are similar memories of the huge sporting goods store in downtown Chicago, and I was totally unprepared for its riches the first time my father took me there. Its handsome interior was overwhelming.

What's this store called? I whispered softly.

It's Von Lengerke and Antoine. He smiled. *It's the best sporting goods store between New York and San Francisco.*

It's beautiful! I stood awestruck.

There were big-game trophies and beautifully mounted fish above the walnut cabinets, and rich wall-to-wall carpeting covered the aisles and fitting rooms. The gun room was lined with glass cases enclosing racks of gleaming rifles and finely engraved European shotguns. Its subtle odors were a delicate mixture of gun oil and Spanish leather cases and handsomely grained and tooled stocks, but they were nothing like the leathery smells of boots and fine English saddles and luggage in the other departments. The camping department was a trove of similar treasures, such as wicker baskets bursting with stainless plates and cups and tableware, costly down-filled sleeping bags, and the delicate paraffin smell of tenting. The racks of gleaming fly rods, with their bright varnish and beautifully machined ferrules and fittings, were intoxicating for a small boy, and several cases smelling faintly of moth crystals held tray-on-tray of exquisitely tied trout and salmon flies.

It's fantastic! I whispered reverently.

It was that afternoon that my father bought several dozen dry flies, and I used most of my allowance money to buy a copy of *Trout*, and on the trip home in the Oldsmobile it was impossible not to sneak a glance at the color plates in Bergman. There was also a copy of the Von Lengerke & Antoine catalogue, and poring over its pages of tackle and equipment and gadgets soon became a boyhood vice.

The celebrated Sparse Grey Hackle, in his commentary for *Great Fishing Tackle Catalogs of the Golden Age*, tells us that such fascination with tackle catalogues is not a particularly rare disease. Catalogues are unquestionably an addiction. My room was quickly filled with them, and sometimes I sat reading them with a flashlight under my blankets until late at night, wondering about these stores in distant cities I had never seen. The catalogues of Abercrombie & Fitch and the celebrated William Mills & Son, where the legendary Bergman once worked as a tackle salesman, were familiar to me many years before I first travelled to New York. The Orvis catalogues were old friends long before I had seen the forest-covered mountains above Manchester or fished the Battenkill River below the Orvis factory and store. Twenty years would pass before my rod collection included either an Orvis or a Leonard, but with their catalogues I was like the hungry boy outside a candy store, and I read them hopefully hundreds of times in those boyhood winters.

Fishing-tackle catalogues are still favorite reading matter when they arrive in the mail, and for most serious American anglers they are a primary source of equipment. Their pages are filled with a galaxy of temptations, although relatively few items included are absolutely essential. Perhaps the best frame of reference for discussing waders, clothing and other equipment might be to explore my own choices and preferences in everyday fishing gear.

Wading equipment is absolutely critical. Generally speaking, waterproof footgear is classified in two primary categories: boots or hip-length waders and the full chest-length waders. Most waders are constructed with rubber or rubberized feet, while the stocking or full-trouser parts are usually made from a rubberized cloth of various natural or synthetic fibers. The waterproof cloth is intended to reduce the weight and cumbersome effect found in all-rubber equipment.

Hip-length waders or hip boots are often adequate for brooks and small trout streams and the shallows of larger rivers. Their lightness and shorter length function perfectly and provide better comfort in extremely hot weather. Most hip boots are fitted only with cleated rubber soles that are best suited to marshy streams and open gravel-bottomed riffles, but always remember that such soles are dangerous on larger stones and ledges slippery with algal growth. Well-made boots will be equipped with cushioned insoles, reinforced arches, and strongly serrated cleats. Reinforced toes and sides are found in the better quality footgear, and some hip boots are also available with felt soles, which are vital when wading among ledges and slippery rocks. Hip-length waders are rather dangerous when a fisherman becomes preoccupied with his sport and works into swift currents too deep for his boot length. Such boots fill quickly and completely, and can have a dangerous sea-anchor effect in a heavy current.

Chest-high waders obviously permit wading in much deeper water. These waders are absolutely essential on big streams, and they also provide surprising tactical mobility on average water. Full-length waders are obviously warmer and drier in cold or rainy weather. They come in two styles: waders fabricated with regular cleat-soled boot feet, and waders with stocking-type feet intended for wear with separate wading shoes called brogues. Both styles have their partisans. Boot-foot waders are more commonly stocked in most sporting-goods stores and are much easier to pull on and strip off, but most expert anglers still use brogues with stocking-foot wader construction. One distinct advantage lies in their better protection for the feet and their tighter fit at the ankle and along the lower legs. Stocking-foot waders can more easily be turned inside out for drying after a day's condensation. Although the stocking-foot waders are comparatively light in themselves, and pack compactly in a duffel bag, their brogues are bulky and cumbersome. Since the brogues are separate from the waders, they may be packed at the ends of such travel bags, forming a durable shield for the more fragile items lying in between.

Boot-foot waders are more clumsy for travelling but have their advantages too. They are clearly preferable on marshy bottoms and for silt-type wading, since the tangle of mud weeds that gathers in wading socks is an unpleasant mess. Their wading shoes need not be removed for drying after each day's fishing. Many boot-foot waders are fitted with a heavy ankle material that reaches halfway up the lower leg, protecting it from deadfalls and stones. It is more snag-proof too. Some fishermen find it difficult to dry the condensation inside a pair of boot-foot waders, but it is possible to turn them down as far as their ankles, drying them in the sun or in the heat rising from a radiator or fireplace. The small hair driers popular in recent years are perfect for drying boots too, and one manufacturer actually makes an electric boot drier.

Both from a sense of tradition and because I thoroughly believe in the foot protection and traction possible only with British wading brogues, I have used nothing but stocking-foot waders for years. There are many fishermen who still use hip-length boots for their fishing, particularly on shallow streams in hot weather, but I prefer full waders even under those conditions. It is important on all types of water to have the capability of wading and crossing the current as freely as possible. Such freedom of movement is useful both in terms of convenience and in searching out effective casting angles and positions for fishing difficult currents. Hot weather usually means relatively low water, and waders also permit crawling infantry-style to stalk the fish and cast from your knees. Such mobility is important on low or hard-fished water.

The quality of waders has sadly declined in recent years, and many plastic finishes and synthetic fabrics simply have not worked out. Like some fly lines woven of synthetic fibers that proved incompatible with their finishes and cracked badly after relatively minor use, many synthetic wader fabrics stretched too readily for their waterproofing. Tiny checks and layered cracking occurred along primary seams and stretch-points. Poor workmanship has become unacceptably common with even the well-known manufacturers at the same time that prices have spiralled higher and higher. It is only prudent to purchase your waders today from a major sporting-goods house or a well-known tackle shop, since these stores are more likely to replace defective waders as a matter of course.

Some fishermen have been turning to industrial types of waders in the hope that their heavy-duty materials might last. It is an understandable choice. However, industrial wading equipment is not designed for the movement and agility involved in fishing a trout stream, its workmanship and materials being specified for wear rather than mobility. In spite of these obvious problems, heavy-duty waders have developed loyal fans.

Why, one argued enthusiastically in a group of fly-fishermen not long ago, *they'll even withstand hydrochloric acid!*

That's pretty strong, I admitted.

Hydrochloric acid! somebody repeated waggishly. *How long's it been since you saw a good hatch of mayflies on a riffle of hydrochloric acid?*

You're right, the man said sheepishly.

The perfect fishing waders must have several qualities. Their fabric and waterproofing must be strong enough to resist a lot of hard wear, including the abrasive effects of bottom sand and volcanic materials in some waters. The seams must be strong enough to withstand the twisting involved in climbing a steep bank and the constant stretching caused by pulling waders on and off. Both the fabric and its waterproofing must be tough enough to resist snagging on briars and brambles and to retard penetration by sharp beaver sticks in the shallows. The waders must also be heavy enough to provide a degree of thermal insulation in extremely cold water. However, with all of these qualities the waders must still provide enough mobility to permit easy movement along the stream and be light enough that on a hot midsummer afternoon fishing in them is cooler than a Finnish sauna.

Modern wader construction employs basic materials far better than the British waterproof fabrics that evolved in the nineteenth century. Rubberized cotton and linen were common when I began trout fishing just before the Second World War. My father rented waders at a tackle shop in

Baldwin, near the famous Pere Marquette of Lower Michigan, and I can remember how even the smallest pair in the rental rack accordioned comically down my legs. Such waders were a rubberized cotton with rubber-boot feet. The wader-rental business subjected those waders to unbelievable amounts of relatively steady wear, although the sand- and gravel-bottomed trout streams of Michigan cannot equal the rocky streams farther east or western volcanic rivers, with their abrasive sands and razor-sharp ledges of fractured lava, in wear-and-tear on waders. Yet the workmanship in the seams was far better than anything we seem able to produce today, since the crotch seam and the seam between the upper waders and their feet are obviously the Achilles' heel in most modern wading products.

The best waders I have worn in recent years were fashioned of synthetic materials. Orvis is using a new three-layer fabric of rubber pancaked between layers of nylon. Marathon is sandwiching industrial nylon cloth between an outer layer of natural rubber and an inner layer of neoprene. These fabrics have proven themselves both light and strong in recent years, resisting as many as 30,000 machine abrasion tests without showing unacceptable wear.

Both fabrics are light enough to provide boot-foot waders across the full range of men's sizes weighing between five and eight pounds. Synthetic fibers are highly resistant to rot and mildew, unlike the waders of English manufacture we used in our boyhood years. Their outer finishes will readily accept temporary patching with either Pliobond or the new heat-stick adhesives designed for temporary repairs. Orvis is using excellent soft-rubber soles of the Vibram cleated type, and Marathon specifies gum-rubber cleats of a deep-lug design. Both makers reinforce their arches with steel shanks. The felt soles provided by both companies are relatively good. Orvis is using a new woven felt highly praised for its durability, while Marathon is using the dense, hard felt popular with fishermen over the years. It should be remembered that wading felt wears well in the river, and poorly when you are walking along the streamside roads and paths. Four belt loops are provided for cinching the waders securely around the waist, and I prefer a sturdy, perforated leather belt with a strong two- or three-tongue buckle. The perforations allow it to dry quickly after deep wading. Inner chest pockets and drawstrings are also important; drawstring cords around your wader tops that are too long should always be trimmed to prevent their tangling in the reel while you are playing a fish.

There should be at least eight suspender buttons on your waders to distribute the strain of twisting, stooping, and climbing. Mills-type wading suspenders of solid nylon webbing reinforced with leather are preferable. Such suspenders have an H-shaped yoke across the back which prevents the tangling, rolling, and slipping common with the cheaper criss-cross pattern. Like the older British-design suspenders, the Mills type are mounted with two-loop elastic cords or button straps at either end. Hip boots are usually supported by belt-loop straps, although a shoulder harness is preferable.

Experienced fishermen trim off the extra length of the boot-harness straps, since they often loop and tangle the fly line in a casting shoot or the slack accumulated in fighting a hooked trout. All good waders provide such thoughtful details.

Some fishermen have been using the less expensive stocking-foot waders of pure gum rubber in recent years. They are relatively light and quite elastic, easily permitting you to stoop, climb steep paths, bend and refasten the laces of your brogues, or sit and kneel in the current. Their cost is about sixty percent less than the price of regular waders. The feet are seamless and fit well without wrinkling, and the gum rubber is easily patched. Chest-length, waist-, and hip-type waders are available in a full range of sizes. But the still cheaper vinyl waders found on the market cannot really be recommended. They are manufactured in both waist- and chest-high types, using both lightweight and heavy-duty vinyls. The seams often tear out, particularly when extremely cold water has made the plastic much too brittle. It also punctures and tears easily, its thickness offering little thermal protection against a bone-chilling current, yet it is so airtight that it is extremely hot and uncomfortable in warm weather. Such waders might prove acceptable as a backup in emergencies, but their durability is so limited that they are expensive in the long run, in spite of their undeniably low first costs.

Canvas wading shoes with felt soles are marginally acceptable, but only the true British brogues really offer the advantages of such footgear. British-made wading shoes are typically shaped from expensive chrome-tanned leather throughout. The box-type reinforced toes and rigid soles provide the superior foot protection that only a wading brogue can give your feet. Drainage grommets are found along both sides of the instep, and strong grommets hold the laces. The best models provide a back-strap pull and reinforced heel, and perhaps the most important advantage lies in the shoe bottoms themselves. Soles and heels of the finest hard felt are one option. The combination a felt sole with a leather heel, its wearing surface studded with eight soft-iron hobs, is highly practical and popular. It provides both the ability of felt to hold on very smooth surfaces and the bite of iron hobnails through thick layers of algae and moss. Rivers where these latter conditions prevail and slippery patches of marl or clay are perhaps negotiated best with brogues having an all-leather sole and heel, both studded with soft iron caulks. It should be understood that hobnails do make sharp sounds on the rocks, which are readily transmitted underwater, but are not as noisy as other metal studs.

The American wading shoes manufactured with combination uppers of leather and canvas are usually more easily purchased in the United States, and they have performed equally well in the past few seasons, although they are available only in a felt sole and heel. These Russell brogues have strong canvas uppers and a full bellows tongue. The lacing eyelets and sides are reinforced with dark brown shoe leather, and four weep grommets drain the shoe. The reinforced box toes and heels are covered in extremely heavy leather, and the soles are made of the finest hard white felt. Hopefully, American manufacturers will also provide the option of caulked leather heels in the future.

Wading underwear and socks are important too. Some fishermen like goosedown and nylon-fleece undergarments for cold weather, while others use waders manufactured with insulated feet and thick fabric uppers. Both solutions to cold water wading are bulky, and the insulation of down is clearly diminished when the water pressure forces it tight against the legs. Pure silk underwear is possibly the finest cold-weather solution for warmth without bulk or weight, and experienced skiers have long used silk for their basic next-to-skin layer of clothing. Silk undershirts and socks are also highly recommended. Really cold conditions find me wearing Norwegian mesh longjohns under a layer of silk, and when the water pressure forces my pants tight around my legs, the mesh traps a layer of body heat between the silk and my skin. Such string-type underwear is extremely elastic, but you should buy a size larger than your normal measurements since mesh underwear that is too tight can bind you like a suit of armor—and its patterns can wrinkle your skin like a waffle.

Brogue socks worn under a stocking-foot or boot-foot wader cushion the foot and give it some warmth. Some fishermen have come to like the German slipperlike wading socks in recent years, and they have a fleece layer quilted between nylon stretch cloth. Such construction permits condensation to pass through the fleece and form on the outer lining. Norwegian boot socks are readily available, and are a fine combination of eighty percent wool and twenty percent nylon and Spandex. Silk underneath will multiply their warmth and protect those who are allergic to wool. Wading brogues also require a sock between the stocking-foot wader and the brogues themselves. These socks are used to prevent chafing, and the abrasive effects of volcanic sands and ash in many rivers. They are most effective in a thickly woven wool or wool mixed with nylon and a similar synthetic. Because I believe a dark-colored wading sock is less visible to the fish, and I like a bright spot of color too, I have been using the fine Thermo socks woven entirely from virgin wool. These socks have a three-dimensional stitch across both the instep and the full twelve-inch ankle, with bright red trim at the ankles. Since fish are more startled by value in colors, their relative lightness or darkness, rather than the hue itself when lateral visibility underwater is involved, the red border around the ankles does not disturb the trout and I like the color accent of its happy chroma.

Brogue and wader sizes are figured by the combination of your shoe size plus your sock requirements. Brogue sizes are controlled by water temperature, as well as the sock layers inside the stocking-foot waders. The brogue must fit around a silk sock and a thick wool-and-nylon sock on your foot, the wader foot itself, and another wading sock that goes on between the brogue and the wader material. Proper cold-weather footgear thus includes a brogue approximately two or even three sizes larger than normal shoe size. Its fit must accommodate the three layers of sock, plus the wader thickness. It should also be remembered that water pressure and the factors involved in downstream wading subject the toes to wedging problems not unlike those found when backpacking down a mountain trail. Wading shoes should fit firmly without pressure while dry, since the softening in the river will probably be neutralized by water pressure. The fit must not cramp the toes; it must allow enough room for the feet to flex and move properly. Fishermen who seldom work a really cold river can omit heavy socks inside their waders, and can perhaps use brogues only one or two sizes larger than normal shoe size.

Stocking-foot waders must be identical with shoe size when only light socks are worn underneath, and a size larger with a heavy wading sock inside. Boot-foot waders should match shoe size for a summer trout fisherman, and should be a size larger with cold-water socks layered underneath. Some manufacturers make only full-size shoes on their waders, and if you take a half size, you should perhaps go a size larger. However, foot size is not the only factor in wader fit. Chest measurement is important too, and should be taken under the armpits with the lungs relaxed. The inseam measurement is taken between the floor and crotch and should be made wearing shoes. The outseam is also taken with shoes on and runs from the floor to the wader tops. The seat dimensions should be made at the widest measurement around the hips. Standard wader size-tolerances are approximately as follows, and if your measurements lie within the chart, you should not require custom-made waders to achieve a proper fit:

CHEST-LENGTH WADER MEASUREMENTS

SIZE	CHEST	INSEAM	OUTSEAM	SEAT
5	36–40	29–30	50	40–44
6	37–41	29–30	51	41–45
7	38–42	30–31	51	42–46
8	39–43	30–31	51	43–47
9	40–44	30–31	52	44–48
10	41–45	31–32	53	45–49
11	42–46	31–32	54	46–50
12	43–47	32–33	55	47–51
13	44–48	33–34	56	48–52

The principal wader manufacturers all provide wader repair kits with adhesives and patching fabrics compatible with their own products. Pliobond cement can also be used as a temporary patching compound for seepage holes and seams that have started to leak slightly. It must be applied each night for the next day's fishing. Punctures, snags, and small tears can be temporarily repaired with the flexible patches made with a thermal repair stick. It can be used along the stream while you are still in your damaged waders; it requires roughing the surface with the sandpaper on the repair stick itself, and melting the adhesive with a match. It softens and spreads like old-fashioned ferrule cement, seals the leak, and remains as flexible as the rubber itself when it dries.

Fishermen who prefer ordinary boot-foot waders with cleated soles, or who cannot afford the more expensive stocking-foot waders and felt-sole brogues, can still improve the gripping qualities of their equipment with several types of wading sandals. Leonard provides a superb wading-chain sandal that can make a dangerous rubber sole as secure as wading with hobnails. Leather sides secure the four chains below the ball of the foot and lace across the instep, and a buckle-strap sling loops back around the heel. Felt wading sandals with half-inch woven-felt soles are also available, and the Mills-type with two instep straps and a heel strap is excellent. Umpqua-type sandals are popular on western steelhead rivers, and there is no better test of wading gear. These sandals have felt soles that fit under both the foot and the heel, with leather side panels reaching over the toes and in front of the ankle. These side panels lace with four grommets across the instep and two at the ankle, and the felt soles are studded with twenty-eight carboloy studs under the foot, plus eleven steel caulks under the heel. Steelhead fishermen also developed the aluminum-grid wading sandals popular on some rivers, and they are extremely good. Flexible aluminum plates form an interlocking grid under the ball of the foot, as they are strapped over the toes and around the ankles securely. There are expert big-river fishermen who swear by grid-type wading sandals.

After the expense of a first-rate rod and reel, proper wading equipment is the most important part of our gear, and a fisherman should spend that money carefully. His wading jacket is perhaps the next item in terms of its importance.

Lee Wulff is certainly the man who conceived the first tackle vest for deep wading, and his design has since been the prototype for a veritable blizzard of copies and mutations. Since its development, the Wulff wading vest has become a kind of uniform for fly-fishermen, rivalling the pin-stripe suit for bankers and corporate lawyers. The original tackle pack had two sheepskin fly patches high on the shoulder blades, with two small pockets just below. Three small pockets were next, lying like cartridge loops on either side of the chest. Two zipper pockets on either side of the belt buckle parallel the bottom of the vest, with matching zipper pockets inside. Two small pockets were located under each armpit, and a huge zipper pocket reached across the back, large enough for an extra reel, rain jacket, and lunch. Wulff also added a net ring behind the neck, and a loop and snap holder to secure the rod when you need both arms. There was also a small nylon-mesh creel that zippered along the left side of the vest, although most fishermen soon left it behind.

Orvis has modified the original Wulff design since it appeared more than twenty-five years ago, and there are now two basic models. One is designed for normal fishing and waist-deep work, and the other is for really deep wading.

LEE WULFF

Both are still made from the tan cotton poplin with the water-repellent sizing that Wulff specified years ago. The fabric is now machine washable, and the pocket flaps have abandoned the old-fashioned snap closers for Velcro fasteners. The sheepskin fly patches are now removable, and I firmly believe they should be left off. Flies allowed to dry there are flattened and hopelessly bent out of shape, and some fall off and are lost. Others are blown off in high winds, or frequently stripped off in casting when the hooks snag on a sleeve or catch in the shooting line.

The regular Orvis waist-length fishing vest is practically identical otherwise. It has abandoned the small pockets under the armpits, since it was virtually impossible to use them without taking the vest off completely. There are more small changes inside the new jackets. The sunglasses pocket now has a zipper closure, which prevents a costly pair of prescription Polaroids or tempered shooting glasses from wedging upward due to casting rhythms until they are lost. Opposite the glasses pocket is a square Velcro-flap pocket for packaged leaders, and each bellows pocket inside has a flap pocket designed for eight tippet spools. The material is impregnated with silicone to waterproof the lower pockets and protect your costly flies. There are also permanent loops for clippers and scissor pliers. It is a superbly designed piece of clothing, and it performs its function perfectly, simultaneously carrying and organizing tackle on the stream.

The Orvis modification for deep-wading tactics is virtually the same except it is made about six inches shorter, and it omits the middle row of small pockets to make the bottom that much higher. The vests can now be purchased in a fabric of sixty-five percent Dacron and thirty-five percent cotton. Older fishermen and men with physical problems affecting their wading skills will welcome the flotation vest available from Orvis now. It is made in a handsome dark tan material, and has almost as many pockets as the standard vests. It has a surprising lack of bulkiness, and will float almost as well as an inflated life jacket. All three Orvis jackets are fitted with a detachable creel that clips onto the bottom hemline.

There is a Japanese copy of this Wulff fishing vest in a dark tan cotton poplin that has been waterproofed. It has an incredible fourteen small pockets with Velcro flaps. Four large horizontal zipper pockets are provided in front, with eight smaller pockets mounted on them in turn. It has all of the other features too, along with chrome-plated rings inside for connecting scissor pliers or clippers. The rod-holder flap is matched with a ring system below, and front closure is accomplished with a nylon zipper. These Japanese vests are available from a number of small fly-fishing shops, and the imitation has some worthwhile features the more expensive originals might copy.

Western steelhead fishermen have also evolved some valuable mutations of the Wulff-type vest. The North Umpqua design is fashioned of fifty percent nylon and fifty percent rayon in a deep moss green. The fly-box pockets are zippered inside and out, with big bellows pockets both places, and smaller zip pockets on the larger outside faces. Two rings are provided under each small chest pocket, and the entire back is a roomy rucksack-sized pocket that zippers horizontally just below the net ring at the neckline. The Kalama deep-wading style is similar, but about eight inches shorter, barely covering the wader tops. The inner pockets are zipper-closed at a steep angle, with the zipper secure in the high position. Steelhead fishermen carry much less equipment and flies, like most Atlantic salmon anglers, and this fact has some influence on the relatively simple design of these vests. Both have some original features.

Perhaps the best fishing jacket I have used is the new wading vest designed by my good friend André Puyans and manufactured for his California tackle shop in Hong Kong. It is also featured by Dan Bailey in Montana. It is made of fifty-two percent polyester and forty-eight percent cotton poplin in antelope tan, with a strong fabric reinforcement along its edges. The regular length model is my current wading vest. It has two small Velcro pockets high on the chest that are fitted with metal rings for attaching clippers or surgical forceps or scissor pliers. Two larger pockets are located against the ribcage, and are sized to accept the Wheatley-type fly boxes, like the zippered bellows pockets at the waist. The left-hand bellows pocket has another Wheatley-size pouch fitted on its face, with two generous leader-size pockets on the face of the right-hand bellows. There are two Wheatley snap pockets inside the vest at waist level, plus two zippered pockets inside the upper vest, with a large bellows pouch across the back for extra reels and a rain jacket. The deep wading variation on this Puyans design is five inches shorter and lacks the two Wheatley-size pockets in front, raising the two larger zippered pockets against the ribcage. Both vest designs include a rod-holding snap loop and butt attachment. Interestingly, they both omit an attached creel and sheepskin fly-holder patches—André Puyans obviously shares some of my prejudices about killing trout and manhandling fine flies.

All fishing vests are worn over bulky clothing and are usually filled with fly boxes and other equipment. Experienced fishermen always choose a vest one or two sizes too large in order to have a roomy fit for easy casting. There are three unique pieces of equipment designed for fishing deep water safely. The small life preservers that firmly clip to your vest and inflate when pressed hard with the fingers are good insurance. Although I have never triggered one in actual fishing, sailboating friends tell me they work beautifully when you get too tired in difficult situations. Although I own a handsome split-cane wading staff, which Orvis salvaged and converted from a surplus of their impregnated ski poles manufactured during the Second World War, it is seldom used. Several times when I was using my staff on a difficult salmon river, it became tangled in my legs or the loose loops of fly line that hung downstream in the current. Other times the sense of security the staff provided led me to wade too deeply into currents I might otherwise have shunned, and I almost never carry it these days. Perhaps it will come out of my tackle closet in my geriatric years, if my health survives a life of too much fishing. The third piece of equipment is a floating tube, and although I have never used one, such tubes are becoming popular on high lakes and back-country ponds and marshy spring-fed streams like Silver Creek in Idaho. The method has become so common there that it has led to strange-sounding conversations in the restaurants and bars at nearby Sun Valley.

Hey! It was a young man sitting at the bar in the Ore House. *You guys finally finished with my tubes?*

Yeah, came the reply. *They worked fine.*

That's good. The young man took a long pull at his beer mug. *Where'd you leave my tubes?*

They're in your jeep, they answered. *Thanks.*

Okay, the young man nodded.

The fishing tubes are similar to the inner tubes we played with at the beach as children, except that they are fitted with a strong canvas seat and a heavy webbing strap. The tube itself is a standard truck-tire inner tube capable of supporting two hundred fifty pounds. Its canvas cover is silicone treated, providing both a seat system and a pair of zippered equipment pouches. The webbing crotch strap has a simple release buckle that readily allows an angler to mount and disengage himself from the tube. It is worn with full-length waders, of course, and a pair of ingenious aluminum fins. The fins strap around the heels firmly, and are designed to flip out on the swimming stroke, folding cleverly to reduce water friction on the back stroke. Having seen them used expertly during the *Tricorythodes* hatches in the Yellowstone country, and on the sloughs of Silver Creek at Sun Valley, I can testify to their practicality and worth. The tubes are useful both for safety in potentially dangerous wading, and to reach fish in still currents too deep to wade. Yet they are not infallible, and one tube fisherman was drowned on Silver Creek this past season.

Foul-weather gear is also important. My own rain jacket folds virtually to handkerchief size and stows perfectly in the bellows pocket across the back of my fishing vest. It both sheds the rain and breaks the wind. It is an ultralight Austrian product designed for mountain climbers and alpine hunters, and is made of forest green featherweight nylon. It has a light nylon zipper and a hood with a drawstring. It also has a clever back vent with a nylon mesh closure; its covering flap is designed to ventilate with a bellows action as you move. It has served me faithfully for more than ten seasons, and until the past year its equal was not available here.

However, both Orvis and Marathon are marketing a product that is perhaps better suited to fishing. The Orvis jacket is made in both parka and wading lengths, with matching foul-weather pants. It is fabricated of soft, high-count nylon so light that even the ankle-length raincoat will fold compactly enough to slip into the back pocket of a wading vest. It has a drawstring hood, lightweight zipper, and nylon-mesh venting under the armpits and across the back. It is also a deep forest green. The hood is cut to keep the rain off your fishing glasses. There are tape closures at the wrists, and generous raglan-cut shoulders. Orvis has added two front pockets with

Velcro-flap closers, a feature missing in my Austrian cape. The Marathon wading-length rain jacket is quite similar in its detailing, except for its elastic wrists and zipper pockets. These rain jackets are both relatively expensive, but their comfort, lightness, and performance over years of fishing are well worth their additional cost.

These past few years I have fished extensively in some climates notorious for their cold weather and wind. Norway, Iceland, and the subarctic latitudes of the Labrador are legendary for their foul weather, as are Patagonia and Tierra del Fuego. Norwegian sweaters and the soft knitted sweaters from Iceland, with their rain-shedding unwashed wools, are superb cold-weather garments. The traditional folk patterns are worked in intricate mixtures of black and gray and white in Norway, and in interlocking patterns of black and brown and gray and white in Iceland. Over the years I have acquired matching pullovers and button-front cardigans that I wear in raw winds and subarctic temperatures. The outer cardigan is easily removed if the weather improves, and it is a system that has worked for me. These sweaters are beautiful and practical.

Extremely cold weather demands other measures. Silk undershirts and mesh underwear are useful, and a lightweight goosedown shirt has no equal for such conditions. The best I have used is made from a tightly woven waterproof nylon, with its insulation quilting more than an inch thick. The fabric is a pale sand color that matches the poplin fishing pants and shirts I commonly use. The front zippers shut and there are two muff-style pockets for warming the fingers from the chill of evaporation and wind. Such down vests and shirts are compact and weigh less than two pounds.

My preference in fabric for fishing shirts and trousers is the cotton poplin material commonly found in safari-type clothing. The well-known Abercrombie & Fitch poplin trousers and front-pocket shirts are excellent, providing durability, warmth without the thickness that can prevent hot-weather ventilation, and absorption of perspiration or condensation inside your waders. Orvis makes a similar cloth in a safari-tan color and tailors it into trousers and shirts specially designed for fishing. Their cut is generous to facilitate wading and casting. The shirts have four button-pockets in front, sized to take the smallest Wheatley boxes, and another button-pocket on the left sleeve. The sleeves are cut full for the motions of casting and the left-hand haul, and there is even a butt loop and snap loop for a rod in shirtsleeve weather, when you might fish without a wading vest. Woolrich makes matching tan poplin trousers and military-type shirts that are fine summer gear. Leonard has designed a finely crafted leather belt box for really hot weather when even a wading vest feels like an overcoat. It has two large compartments for fly boxes and two small pockets out front, and is perfect in hot weather with a multipocketed shirt. Some fishing pants are also fitted with snap-fastening tabs that hold them tightly rolled at the ankles, and keep them from riding up inside your waders. Such clothing is practical and well designed.

Foul-weather protection for the head and hands is important in fishing too. Headgear has several primary functions. It protects us from both heat and cold, from precipitation, and from too much sun. It must be shaped to keep the rain off your fishing glasses and outside your collar. It must be waterproof or water-resistant enough to keep your head dry. Its brim should shade both glasses and eyes. It should also have enough weight to stay on in high winds, and enough thickness to protect your head from a misguided double-haul cast with a really big bucktail. Light poplin hats meet all these criteria, except stay-put performance in strong winds and protection from a fly travelling at considerable speed. The years spent in Germany after the Second World War fishing the mountain rivers and hunting the forests with the *Jaegermeisters* and their beaters taught me respect for their loden hats and shooting capes. Loden is a material originally made for the damp cold encountered in the mountains while stalking red stag and chamois at considerable altitudes. Hats made from loden are excellent for fishing, virtually waterproof, heavy enough to stay put in a wind, warm, and enough like a helmet to protect your head from a fly that comes screaming off the tip speed that shoots a hundred feet of line. Some fishermen have adopted the Scottish tweed deerstalker, since its front and rear brims protect your glasses and neck from rain in a traditional foul-weather design. The traditional Irish tweed hats from Donegal and Connemara are excellent fishing hats too, meeting each of the criteria well, since they were designed for fishing rain-swept mountains and moors. The ordinary sailor hat of cotton poplin or denim is good in hot weather with little or no wind, although it offers minimal protection from casting. However, fishing in the fierce midsummer winds of Patagonia is impractical in normal hats, and there we soon bought the head-clinging Basque berets worn by the sheepherders in the hills around Junin de los Andes. Their berets were not waterproof, and they were too soft to offer much protection from a clumsy cast, until we discovered that an application of silicone dry-fly spray added some of these qualities.

Cold hands are a serious problem in marginal weather. Raw temperatures are trouble in themselves, and handling a wet line or fish simply adds evaporation to the problem. Some fishermen like full gloves of the supple shooting-type, and often wear tight silk gloves under them. The leather can also be treated with silicone spray. Other fishermen find that actual gloves are too confining and hamper their dexterity. British fishermen have solved the problem with wool-knit mittens treated with silicone, the fingertips left uncovered and free.

Raw winds are also a problem for the throat as well as the head itself. The past few seasons I have learned to use silicone-treated turtlenecks of stretch nylon or Merino wool. Their high collars keep the neck warm and protect it from the wind, although there are still times when only a wool scarf is warm enough. Traditional red bandanna handkerchiefs are also useful around the neck in hot weather or insect country.

No discussion of fishing clothes would be complete without some comment on the effect of color on fish. It is perhaps safe to argue that the ability of a color to reflect or intensify light, like the proverbial white shirt or shocking yellow rain slicker, makes it the most obvious to the fish. Color technicians call this quality value, describing a color hue totally in terms of its relative darkness or lightness. Hue itself is simply a color in abstract terms, without any consideration for its paleness or darkness, let alone its chromatic intensity. Schiaparelli coined the term shocking pink to describe the intensity of the Bangkok silks used in her superb couture, and many of the modern synthetic fibers also glow with an inner fire that is the very soul of a technical color word like chroma.

Fishing talk is often trapped in some alarming axioms, typically based on local experience. There are fishermen who argue for camouflage fabrics, which were originally developed for jungle tactics and work well in forests, yet a figure in jungle camouflage is comically visible in the pale straw-colored grass along a western river like the Firehole or Silver Creek. Forest green wading vests and shirts are popular among many steelhead addicts, whose rivers tumble toward the sea in dense rain forests, sliding past slate-colored boulders made leaden with autumn rains. The color makes sense on those rivers. But a dark green figure makes little sense in the bright ochre canyon of the Yellowstone, or silhouetted against the October cottonwoods and pale sagebrush hills along the Big Wood in Idaho. Bright red shirts and the soft chamoislike yellow shirts have been popular in recent years. Such colors certainly provide a chromatic focal point to photographs, and that is why you see so many of them in fishing magazines, but they are too visible to the fish. Bright red is probably better than bright yellow, since it is darker in a light-to-dark scale and bounces far less reflective light. Weather and the variables in light on a given day provide almost infinite patterns of change even against a background of dense foliage, and trying to imitate such a spectrum of colors with a piece of clothing is futile.

Which brings our ruminations full circle, to the conclusion that good fishing clothes are neither too pale and light-reflecting nor too dark against a pale background. In fact, they should never present too much of a contrast against any background or too much chromatic intensity. The grayish tan of our traditional poplin meets each of these criteria.

Before we leave talk of fishing clothes for a discussion of the equipment we carry on the stream within or attached to our fishing vests, perhaps we should discuss the problems of packing our gear for travel. Fishing pressure on the rivers near our cities, the technical revolution in air travel that has occurred since midcentury, and our relative affluence have all combined to allow us to travel more widely than our ancestors dreamed. It is possible to fish the rivers in Argentina and Chile, six thousand miles on the other side of the earth, in less time than our grandfathers took to reach the rivers of Maine or the Adirondacks from New York, or the forest-dark rivers of Michigan and Wisconsin from Chicago or Detroit. It is a climate of remarkable change.

Travelling with fly rods and reels has some special considerations, and fishing travel is a happy by-product of writing about the sport. Some years I have totalled as much as 50,000 miles in search of trout and salmon, and that much travel teaches a footloose angler something about packing his gear. The lessons are useful, since much of our fishing equipment is relatively fragile.

Shipping expensive rods in the baggage holds of aircraft frightens me even when they are fully protected by aluminum tubing. Years of airline travel have convinced me that the mechanical engineers who design baggage-handling equipment have a standard performance specification: their equipment automatically damages one suitcase in every twenty-five pieces of luggage. Skis tagged for Switzerland arrive uncannily in San Juan each winter, and I once wandered in shock in New York when a canvas roll containing six expensive split-cane rods failed to arrive from Denver. The airline located them only hours later in Detroit, and they were happily returned undamaged the following day. It might have been worse.

When I travel with one or two rods, their aluminum cases are not really enough protection either separately or taped together. For such trips I have come to like the fine saddle leather rod cases available from makers like Orvis and Leonard, although some airlines will not permit them as cabin baggage. These cases are made with a high-strength aluminum tube inside the stitched leather cover. The cases have leather caps and adjustable carrying straps that make them convenient to carry on your flight as a handsome piece of hand luggage.

Sometimes an extended trip can mean several rods to match varied fishing conditions, as well as provide a spare rod or two in case of breakage. My favorite method of packing several rods is the lightweight canvas rod roll that combines the strength of three or four cases. Three aluminum tubes pack into a triangular shape of considerable strength, and four are even stronger. Orvis has made a superb canvas carrying roll for some twenty years, and I have worn out three of them with air travel. It is made of heavy-duty tan canvas. It is designed to hold a standard aluminum rod case in a deep bellows pocket at the butt, with two wide canvas loops at its third points, and a generous flap that folds down over the caps. When the entire case is rolled up, the top flap is firmly wrapped inside, and three leather straps tightly bind the roll together. There is a leather strap for carrying the roll when it is packed and secure. The roll will carry four aluminum cases two inches in diameter and is long enough for a two-piece rod measuring nine-and-a-half feet. The loop beside the rolling spline will accept only one two-inch case, but each of the others will take two rod cases of the normal diameter. Packed this way, the roll will hold seven rods. However, I have purchased four two-inch diameter cases especially for packing in the canvas roll. It is possible to pack eight trout-size rods in them, with the butt of one in the bottom of each case and the other slipped in carefully with its butt under the machined cap. The second rod should be worked in cautiously to prevent damage to both tip sections and guides that might catch together. Leonard is now making a beautiful leather rod carrier in lengths of forty, forty-eight, and fifty-six inches. It has a zipper closure and carries as many as eight standard diameter cases.

Fly reels are expensive and fragile too, and should not be packed loose in a suitcase or duffel bag. Several times I have watched men unpack their equipment thousands of miles from home to find a reel has unhappily travelled as well, working its way through layers of clothing to rest against the outside of a suitcase. Sometimes in the rough-and-tumble of baggage handling such a reel can receive a blow that shatters its frame or bends its spool. Such tragedies can ruin a costly trip, and can easily be avoided. Good packing can prevent some damage, but a good reel case is also important. Hardy once made excellent saddle-leather cases lined with chamois skin, and later used exquisite plum-colored velvet linings. The early reel cases were buckled, and later versions used a spring-loaded catch. These cases were superb protection for an expensive reel, providing an equilibrium between rigidity and softness, and someone should resurrect them. They pack well either lid-down in a suitcase or with the reel-shaped bottoms down in the center of a duffel. Some fishermen pack them lid-to-lid in their luggage for greater stability. Two weeks ago I was examining several century-old Hardy reel cases that once belonged to the famous Arthur N. E. Wood, who developed low-water fishing for salmon on the Dee. Like most well-made things, these leather cases grow more beautiful with time.

Modern reelmakers are using vinyl zipper-cases with white foam linings that cushion the reels perfectly, and hold them in place with a hole cut into the plastic foam for the handle. Such cases would be better if the manufacturers exercised the taste and restraint to stop disfiguring them with gaudy trademarks and colors. Many fishermen like the suede and vinyl cases that zipper around the perimeter and are lined with sheepskin. These cases are inexpensive and adequately protect a reel from abrasion, but it is doubtful that they could protect it from a damaging impact in the baggage hold of an aircraft. Buckskin reel bags are also handsome, but provide little protection from sustained weight or an impact load. Cowhide backs offer a little more protection, but not enough for a really sharp blow. The handsome vinyl cases also available from two or three reel manufacturers have the same failing, but they do omit the sheepskin lining, which has the nasty habit of shedding and working deep into the finely machined entrails of an expensive reel it is supposed to protect—ask the men who make and repair reels how they feel about sheepskin cases.

Fishing tackle luggage is another problem. Tackle boxes are useful filing cabinets for the myriad small items and gadgets we all collect and use, but most tackle boxes have been designed for bait casting. Some open to reveal an astonishing number of aluminum trays, levering out from the depths of the box to improbable, cantilevered displays of glittering spoons and frog-colored baits and traditional red and white plugs, with treble hooks hanging like tinsel on a Christmas pine. The soft-rubber nightcrawlers and preserved pork rinds that really catch modern bass are concealed at the bottom, like the secret entrance to a bootlegger's cellar.

Both Orvis and Abercrombie & Fitch sold beautifully made tackle boxes of mahogany, with fitted wooden trays and mirror-bright finishes of clear lacquer. Canvas coverings are also made to slip over these cases to protect their finishes, but such cases are unable to withstand the rigors of shipment on airlines, with or without their covers. They are superb for filing and storing tackle, and for automobile travel to and from the stream. Mills once sold a saddle-leather tackle box that enclosed aluminum trays, and a full metal interior that came out for cleaning. It had heavy suitcase-type latches and a strong lock, with a generous leather handle and fittings. Such cases were superbly adapted to travelling, like the saddle-leather trunks especially fitted for tackle that British anglers once took to Scotland and Norway for salmon fishing, and some firm should make them again in a medium tackle-box size. Such boxes are perfect, both for organizing the sundry small items of tackle that wander around loose through a duffel bag, and for providing a rigid shell around a collection of expensive reels and fly boxes in transit.

However, the duffel bag is a superb piece of luggage for packing bulky rough-tackle items like waders, wading brogues, foul-weather gear, fishing vests, thermal underwear, and bulky sweaters. My trips have thoroughly proved the practicality and wearing qualities of the standard flat-bottom station-wagon bag. It is made of strong thirteen-ounce sailcloth that has been treated to shed water and resist mildew. There is an outside two-snap pouch which I seldom use, and a full-length zipper, modified with a grommet ring in its leather tab for a small combination padlock. Such bags come in three sizes, and the smallest twenty-four-inch type comfortably holds my brogues, waders, rain gear, fishing vest, two or three sweaters, and miscellaneous smaller equipment. It is usually packed sausage-tight on a trip, and I have two that have served me faithfully for more than a dozen years, although they are getting a little dog-eared. The end-loading duffel bags of the military type are not recommended, since they must be unpacked completely to find anything, and even the full-zipper round duffels are too limp for convenient handling when partially opened. The station-wagon type is easier to use in camp. Some fishermen like the lighter tote bags and duffels made of extremely light parachute nylon that are watertight and mildewproof. The round bag weighs an incredible six ounces, and measures twelve inches in diameter and a full thirty inches in length. The bag is reinforced with heavy nylon webbing and has two carrying straps. The full-length steel zipper provides convenient access and packing capability. Two brass buckle straps secure the opening and reduce strain on the zipper, and the entire bag is encircled with nylon webbing. There is a larger nylon tote made by the same manufacturer, except that it is fifteen inches square and thirty inches long. It has generous bellows pockets at either end and along one side, each closed with nylon zippers. Its capacity is unequalled for its surprising eight-ounce weight, and its zippers can be modified to take small combination padlocks. Both nylon bags are also available in sailcloth duck, but it is their incredibly light weight that makes them valuable on air trips, since excess baggage charges are prohibitive outside the country.

Leonard is making a round duffel bag of top grain cowhide as elegant as its fly rods. It is secured with two leather straps that work around the entire bag, which measures ten inches in diameter and twenty inches in length. The leather duffel easily fits under a plane seat and is designed for packing reels, cameras, clothing, and other small gear. Many anglers carry their film in their hand baggage to protect it from fogging, overexposure and other curious effects associated with electronic inspection of baggage. Leonard also makes a larger cowhide duffel with two leather handles and a shoulder strap, designed as a matching piece of tackle luggage. It is closed with a full leather flap and two buckle straps of leather wrapped completely around the bag. There is also a carrying handle at one end, and both bags have full-length zippers. These bags are a little heavy, but there is something beautiful about fine leather, and both are readily accessible without unpacking their entire contents.

Some thought should also be given to what the late John Alden Knight called his falling-in bag. It carried dry underwear and socks, clean shirt and trousers, sneakers, and an extra sweater in case you take a pratfall in some bucolic riffle. It should even provide a towel or two.

Several manufacturers recommend strapping rod cases under the handles or along the sides of their duffels, but my unhappy experience with air travel makes me wary, and I will not expose my fly rods to such risks. There are also combination duffels that pack normally through full-length zippers, and then hold three aluminum rod cases under a second flap on the outside. Unlike the canvas rod rolls, these canvas loops do not combine the three cases in a self-reinforcing triangle, and the rods are relatively vulnerable to loading impacts. Their safety is also threatened when the duffel itself is not tightly packed. Two years ago I witnessed the fracture of two split-cane rods on a trip to Buenos Aires, and the villain was a loosely packed bag. Apparently, the contents shifted in flight and formed a fulcrum across a hard lump of equipment. The trip was a little rough coming into Ezeiza Airport, with towering thunderheads over the pampas, and the weight of other baggage simply deformed both aluminum cases across the gear inside the duffel itself.

Creels are unfashionable these days, not because the classic wicker baskets of the past are at all ugly, but because killing a creelful of trout is in disfavor. Although the wicker creels are bulky and cumbersome when you are wading deep, their ventilation keeps fish fresh even in hot weather. The nylon-mesh creels attached to most fishing vests are also quite practical, in spite of their short length, which was obviously designed for catchable-size hatchery trout. The British-type flat bass of woven straw were much preferred by Edward Ringwood Hewitt, and he advocated them so persistently that the old Mills catalogues even called them Hewitt creels. Flat bags measure about twelve by fifteen inches, have a webbing-reinforced opening, and are carried on a simple clip harness. Filled with freshly picked mint or ferns, the straw bass keeps fish beautifully, and can be quickly cleaned with a hose. Ray Bergman recommended the Hewitt creel in *Trout*, and used nothing else in his fishing, although he recognized that they seldom lasted more than one or two seasons.

Stripping baskets are a creellike piece of equipment that evolved on our steelhead rivers to take full advantage of weight-forward lines, the technique of the left-hand haul, and the more recent shooting-head equipment. The baskets are canvas trays on a stainless wire frame, with several holes in the bottom to drain moisture carried on the fly line. Some are worn across the stomach, with an adjustable strap across the back. The basket is semicircular in shape, and about fifteen inches along its straight side. It functions a little like a spinning reel, since you retrieve your running line into the basket in precisely layered coils after a long shot with a sinking line or shooting head. The entire fly line or monofilament running line behind the sinking head can be coiled in the basket, and when a long cast powers out across the current, the running line leaps cleanly from the stripping basket and scurries after the heavier weight-forward belly and head. Hundred-foot casts are relatively easy with a stripping basket, since the line is freed of the water friction involved in shooting it free of the surface. Left-hand coils also tend to knot and tangle with the line velocity of a strong double-haul, sometimes jamming hard against the butt guide. Distance casting is easier with a stripping basket, although it is clumsy looking and a bother to wear. Some fishermen who are expert with a stripping basket have fabricated their own designs, wearing them along their left sides, and making them large enough to hold still more shooting line in generous loops.

Landing nets have become almost as unfashionable as creels in recent years, although it is paradoxical that releasing fish is the cause. Some anglers subscribe to a code that believes landing a trout without a net is more difficult, and therefore gives the fish an advantage that is more sporting. It may also make that fish more frightened and tired. It is harder to hold a trout to work the hook free without the friction of the net meshes, and you can easily press too hard into the gills or around the belly. Internal injuries, exhaustion, and shock kill more released fish than hook damage or fungus, and fishing without a landing net both extends the struggle and makes releasing a fish more difficult. Forget the arguments for fishing without a net, land your trout as mercifully and quickly as possible, and take advantage of a landing net to handle them gently. It is unfair to tire a fish unnecessarily and risk injuring it as it struggles in your hand when you ultimately intend to release it.

For most stream fishing I prefer the old-fashioned wood frame landing nets I have used since boyhood. Such nets are usually hung from a frame of laminated birch or hickory, with an ornamental walnut spacer in the handle. The net bag itself should be fashioned of a synthetic fiber like Dacron or nylon, since it is extremely strong and resists rot, although superb bags of heavy waterproofed cotton have long been used in Europe.

Some nets are made with double strands in their loops along the frame, and the mesh size should diminish progressively from the throat to the bottom of the bag. Such details provide both strength and sufficient current drag to blossom the meshes instantly. The dimensions of the net frames are often much larger than necessary in standard designs. Frame width of ten to twelve inches, and a throat length of fifteen to eighteen inches are common. Such nets are usually fitted with a bag about twenty inches deep, and in skilled hands, nets of these dimensions can easily handle fish of twelve to fifteen pounds. Some makers have added ornamental corded grips and leather trim to their nets, but I find them unattractive and unnecessary. Except for the tightly wound linen reinforcing where the laminated frame bows out from the walnut spacer in the handle, I believe a net should be free of embellishments. Its beauty lies simply in the character of its wood and its craftsmanship, like a fine fly rod or delicate violin.

These past years I have been using a little net built with great skill and simplicity by Joseph Swaluk, who later made similar landing nets for Leonard. Its frame is top-grade hickory with a handle of burled American walnut, and its gleaming lacquer finish is applied in the Leonard rod factory. It meets each of my specifications for landing-net design, and its frame is relatively small, measuring only eight inches across the throat. It has handled fish as large as ten pounds easily, and like all beautifully designed equipment, it is a pleasure to own and use. Guyrich is manufacturing similar nets made entirely of walnut with grip spacers of exotic hardwoods like Macassar ebony. Their design and craftsmanship are remarkable.

Some fishermen like the collapsible nets popular in Europe, and I have used both the Pezon & Michel model from France and the slightly more expensive British design. The French product is made in two handle lengths of a fixed type, while the British net has a handle that extends from seventeen to thirty-two inches. The extra length is clearly necessary on the chalkstreams of Normandy and Hampshire, where an angler is often on a high bank above the water, with a current too deep to wade. Last season I fished the Maigue in Ireland, a small limestone river below Limerick, where I soon learned the advantages of a borrowed net with an extension-type handle. This spring on the Abbots Worthy water of the Itchen, and the Kimbridge beats of the Test, it was obvious that such long-handled nets are valuable. The less expensive collapsible nets manufactured in Europe are made with oxidized brass handles and aluminum frames, while the better models are entirely aluminum alloy. Both types extend to a total length of forty-three inches, and the triangular frame has a fourteen-inch throat. These collapsible nets are snapped open and extended with a sharp flick of the wrist, and although I have never seen one fail, the collapsible net that refuses to open is one of my nightmares.

Anything that can go wrong, runs the now-familiar theorem of fallibility called Murphy's Law, *will!* And usually at a crucial moment.

Landing nets can be attached to the fisherman in several ways, and a swivel-clip lanyard of elastic was common on my boyhood rivers. It was simply looped over one shoulder and slung under the opposite arm, which worked perfectly well out in the river, but walking a brushy path could transfrom it into a lethal weapon. Its meshes would invariably catch in the branches, stretch the lanyard like a bowstring, and catapult the frame back into your kidneys. Eastern fishermen soon jettisoned the lanyard with its swivel connection, and replaced it with a French-type clip. The clip was connected to the net with a small split ring, and consists of a spring-actuated clamp. The clamp closes itself until finger pressure across the middle of the device opens its jaws. These clips were attached to the small ring that hangs down the back of most wading vests, although many fishermen found it difficult to unhook it there. Such understandable clumsiness soon led to the pin ring, a leather loop connecting a stainless ring with a strong industrial safety pin. It could be fastened anywhere on a fishing vest, depending on the preferences and dexterity of its user. However, many fishermen lost nets when they tried to disengage them while fighting a fish, and watched them tumble downstream into heavy water. Others who were more agile succeeded in bringing their nets into play, netted their fish and then released them. Having learned to fish in a time when nets were hung from the shoulder with a lanyard, they sometimes forgot and lost a net when they simply let it go.

It once happened to me in the excitement of a big fish on the Gunnison in Colorado years ago, and it soon led to the hybrid system I have now used for many seasons. My net eye is connected to the old-fashioned lanyard clip with a stainless split ring, and the elastic is looped to the jacket ring hanging behind my neck. The French clip is then permanently fastened to my fishing vest slightly behind my left armpit, and clamps around the split-ring connection. It can be located anywhere. The system has the advantages of a net that is secured with an elastic lanyard, and can be dropped when the fish gets a second wind that requires both hands. Yet its French-clip connection prevents the catapult effect when the net snags in the brush, and it is still easily reached and freed.

Fishing glasses are often overlooked, but they are quite important in several ways. Obviously, dark glasses reduce eye strain and glare in bright weather, and prescription lenses are a modern blessing. Polaroid filters allow us to see more readily into the water, and are invaluable in both observing and playing a fish, yet few fishermen have learned to use the yellow shooting glasses to magnify light. Such lenses are a surprising help on dark days and in evening fishing, although an angler who carries a camera will quickly discover that they distort his judgment for good filming light. Optometrists tell us that therapeutic use of dark glasses in bright sun will insure improved night-fishing vision later in the day. Clear glasses with tempered lenses are good eye protection in night fishing. Fishing glasses should always have tempered shatterproof lenses, since they also have the function of protecting the eyes from a poor double haul.

There are other optical devices a fisherman can find useful along the stream. Hardy manufactures the Wardle magnifier, which is designed to help a man with failing sight tie knots in delicate nylon, and to thread tippets of such nylon through the minuscule eye of a twenty-eight hook. It is a precision lens mounted in a sturdy black-oxidized frame which clips firmly to your clothing, leaving both hands free. There is a light cross brace that prevents twisting or rolling while you are using the lens, and the device folds flat when not in use. It stows easily in a small poplin shirt or fishing-vest pocket.

The British magnifying spectacles called the Bishop Harman glasses are a remarkable fishing tool. They are perfect for threading small flies on fine tippets. Since their lenses are not corrective, supplying only a remarkable magnification, no prescription is needed. The glasses are worn at the tip of the nose, in front of your prescription glasses. The Bishop Harman spectacles are expensive, but are invaluable at streamside.

Space technology has also perfected a remarkable monocular less than three inches long, weighing only two ounces, yet it has full eight-power magnification. It is useful for watching a rising fish. Fishermen who are dedicated to collecting and imitating the hatches and other diet forms on their rivers will find two other optical gadgets useful. The first is a kind of mini-microscope called a linen tester, and it consists of a folding anodized frame with a calibrated bottom, a half-inch lens of 9X power, and a focal length of slightly less than an inch. The second is a small hand magnifying glass two inches in diameter which does not require a flat surface like the linen tester, and swivels into its own attached leather case. The pocket magnifier can also be used to concentrate solar energy and start an emergency fire if both you and your matches are soaked. Both gadgets are quite compact when folded and are easily carried astream.

Other useful gadgets are available for the streamside study of trout foods. Common round-throat kitchen strainers or square aquarium nets can be stripped of their short handles and equipped with a twelve-inch basswood dowel handle. Such strainers make picking an insect from the water remarkably easy, and with a small stainless screw eye attached to the dowel, a hatch collector can easily be fastened to a belt loop on your waders with a small chain button. Catching a fluttering caddis or an egg-laying mayfly spinner in flight can prove frustratingly difficult, and biologists have long used a small butterfly net with a slender bamboo handle. Handles as long as twenty feet may be required for spinners that swarm high above the current. Such equipment is impossible to carry while fishing, although any serious student of fly hatches should fabricate one for his research. It is also possible to make a wire frame that will fit in the back bellows pocket of a wading vest, and attach to your rod to make a collecting net. Hardy made such gadgets just before the First World War, when the streamside entomology of Halford and Moseley was in vogue on British streams. Their collecting net had a bag of mosquito netting fastened to a circular rim of aluminum wire. Fine nylon mesh seems to damage flying specimens less than cotton material. The wire frame had two loops and a waterproof cotton cord attached to the center of the wire. After the two loops were slipped onto the rod, the cord was threaded through the tip guide. Then it was threaded between both wire loops, extended down the length of the rod, and held taut with the hand. It was both ingenious and effective, since mating aquatic insects are typically shy and difficult to capture, and I once saw a friend fall and almost smash a favorite rod trying to catch a dancing *Isonychia* spinner with his fishing hat.

Several manufacturers are selling a small nymph-collecting net these days. It consists of a fine nylon mesh seine measuring ten by twelve inches, and it rolls into a ten-inch package the thickness of two pencils. The free edges are reinforced, and the whole net is easily carried along the stream. It also has a white nylon center panel intended to make it easy to examine a captured nymph, but this white fabric is a well-intentioned mistake. Clambering and clinging nymphs are easily captured in spite of the white panel, but many swimming nymph species see it too easily and deftly avoid the net. You can make a fine pocket seine yourself, omitting the white panel and adjusting its length to your needs. One fisherman I know carries his rolled and secured with a rubber band, and hung from his belt loop with a screw eye and chain button. It can easily be disengaged for use. However, for serious nymph collecting you should construct a larger hand seine from fourteen-mesh metal or nylon window-screen material, and attach two three-quarter-inch dowels about thirty inches long to either end. The dowels should project about two inches below the seine. The seine area itself should measure about two by three feet. Small split-shot can be attached along the bottom of the seine to hold it along the river bed. The nymphs are then dislodged by disturbing the detritus and bottom trash and stones upstream from its meshes.

Burrowing nymphs that live in the bottom silts are most easily captured with a steel-frame scap net used in fish hatcheries. It consists of a relatively strong quarter-inch steel-wire frame that is virtually rigid and attached to a sturdy wooden handle. Its mesh bag should be strong enough to excavate and lift several pounds of bottom silts, and you will need a large white enamel hospital pan for sorting through the silts and organic detritus for your specimens.

Many swimming nymphs that inhabit open currents are as shy and quick-witted as baby trout, and are seldom captured with seines or scap nets. For them, fine nylon screening can be used on a heavy wire frame about twelve inches in diameter, attached to a sturdy wooden handle about six feet long, and used in the manner of a landing net to capture specimens. Eight-inch strainers attached to similar wooden handles are sometimes used to collect burrowing nymphs in deeper water, and can deftly capture specimens from surprisingly deep water when skillfully used.

Collecting freshly hatched and molting duns from the streamside foliage with the fingers is relatively easy for the larger species. Specimens of the tiny genera are more difficult, and such collecting must be done carefully to avoid damaging the insects. Mayflies are particularly fragile, and the slightest damage to their wings can make subsequent molting impossible. Some anglers have modified surgical tweezers for this purpose by rounding their points and fastening a thin surface of felt inside the jaws with modern adhesives. Others have constructed cube-shaped collecting traps of white bobbinet, leaving one flap open and illuminating them all night with electric torches from the inside. Many species are attracted to the light and gather on the netting. Specimens that land outside can be placed inside by hand. The collecting traps should be small enough to fit in a station wagon, since they can be used to transplant insects from one river to another while they are molting. The traps can be sited in a shady place where the newly hatched duns will feel secure and molt successfully to their imago stage. Sometimes you will find several species hatching together, and a number of outdoor molting cages may prove necessary to separate the specimens, making sure you will know which spinners hatched from which immature subimagoes. Such work is fascinating and rewarding.

Rearing live nymphs into their adult stages is difficult, but it is the only way we can be certain that a specific nymph hatches into a particular dun. Nymphs and duns are often more important to both fishermen and fish than the spinners, yet it is only the male spinners that are consistently described in the taxonomic tables that identify each species. Hatching nymphs evolve into duns in captivity, clearly establishing the identity of both stages, and when the subimagoes molt, the resulting spinner can be easily identified from the taxonomic keys.

Most nymphal forms can be reared and hatched in aquariums and photographed and observed through the glass walls. Constant water temperatures accelerate nymphal maturity, making a species hatch earlier than in its wild habitat. Some fast-water species adapt poorly to aquariums, needing both more oxygenation and current to thrive, although some success is possible with a striated board placed to receive a strong flow of cold water. Such species can also be raised and hatched in cylindrical wire cages, hung from a styrofoam raft that has been anchored in their natural habitat, using actual river stones laid on the bottom mesh. Portable vibrator aerators are required to furnish sufficient oxygen for many species in aquariums, and large beakers of the type used to incubate trout eggs are ideal mini-aquariums for isolating many carnivorous ecotypes. Water temperatures of sixty to sixty-five degrees are needed, and a few stones or plants from their original waters are advisable. Both tank aquariums and the beaker-size containers should be fitted with screened tops to trap the adult insects when they hatch, and a cylindrical cage fitted upside down is perfect for the beaker-type chamber. Fast-water nymphs are extremely interesting in aquarium conditions, and are often found clustered on the air hoses and beakers, holding tenaciously in the streaming bubbles.

Specimens can be preserved in glass lip-vials of the standard laboratory size. Ordinary corks are adequate stoppers for freshly collected material still under study, but rubber stoppers are mandatory for permanent storage. Strips of good paper should be carefully labelled with India ink from a fine-point pen like a 000 Rapidograph. Date, location, water character and other data are important. With nymphs reared in captivity, it is good practice to place the cast nymphal skins along with the hatched insects. Four parts ethyl alcohol to one part distilled water is a fine permanent preservative for the adult insects, with three parts alcohol to one part water for nymphs. Some technicians add a few drops of acetic acid to set the original color as much as possible, although it is difficult to preserve such color. Storage bottles must be full at all times or the specimens will incur breakage. Final storage should be cool and dark.

Collecting bottles carried on the stream are another problem, involving both easy handling and a relatively open throat that makes removing a specimen fairly simple. The killing-jar solution should be about ten parts distilled water, five parts ethyl alcohol, and one part acetic acid. This mixture is less expensive than the formulas outlined above, and much killing-jar fluid is lost in stream collection while fishing. The best collecting bottle I have found is the small Alka-Seltzer type, with its wide throat and smooth lip-free design. It is also important to carry one or two deep plastic boxes that fit into your wading-vest pockets, perhaps drilled with a few tiny ventilating holes. These are used to keep freshly hatched insects alive until they can be transferred to the molting cages.

Final identification of species is often based on wing venation in many aquatic insects. Experts mount the actual wings in microscope slides, but a wide-field binocular microscope would be much too costly for a fly-fishing entomologist. The wing venation can just as readily be studied by mounting the actual wings in a glass color-projector slide, projecting its image on a large sheet of paper, and tracing its outlines and venation for large-scale comparison. Other factors in identification of specific insect forms will be found in their physical structure, since the taxonomic keys are also based on abdominal morphology.

There are gadgets that can extract the contents of a trout's stomach without injuring the fish. Skues and others pioneered the use of a stainless marrow scoop for recovering stomach contents through the fish's throat. It took more than a little skill, both to penetrate the throat without hurting the fish and to withdraw the scoop without damaging the insects. Orvis is now offering a plastic suction device manufactured in England that is much safer and easier, and fishermen interested in what their fish have been eating can find out without killing them first by using the Aymidge extractor. It is a worthwhile development, I suppose, though it is also a somewhat insensitive violation of something as beautiful as a trout.

Stream thermometers are an important piece of equipment for a skilled angler. Hardy makes an excellent stream thermometer that resembles a fountain pen, its glass scale calibrated in both fahrenheit and centigrade. It is encased in a bright, temperature-sensitive metal shell. The thermometer and its casing are designed with a five-minute temperature lag to provide accurate water readings. Its top is fitted with both a keeper ring and fountain-pen clip, and I have used one for a number of years. Orvis is marketing a similar clip thermometer encased in a light metal case, with water perforations at its bulb. Its scale is not calibrated in centigrade readings. Both thermometers are quality products and easy to carry on the river, measuring only about six inches in length.

Vexilar manufactures a special thermometer designed for taking temperature readings in lakes and impoundments. It is lowered on a measuring line, allowed to remain for a few minutes, and quickly retrieved again. It has a built-in depth and thermal lag to provide accurate readings. Its information will pinpoint the thermocline temperature layers in a lake and help locate trout in hot weather.

Orvis is selling a field kit for testing water quality and chemistry. It will provide readings of dissolved oxygen, alkalinity and phosphates, carbon dioxide, nitrogen, hydrogen sulphide, and coliform counts. Such information will provide exceptional insights into the cycle of the season on your favorite waters, as well as monitor any denigration under the effects of pollution in the watershed. Armed with such information, you can actually trace the concentrations as well as the sources of that pollution, and function as a watchdog on your home waters. The kit has sufficient chemicals for approximately twenty-five tests, and each component is easily replaced. This pollution monitoring ability will unquestionably grow in importance in the years ahead.

My fishing friends Jim Ong and Roy Reinhardt originally designed the popular angler's log for William Mills & Son, but now this special diary is widely available from Leonard and other first-rate tackle shops. It is a thoughtfully designed item that can definitely catch you more fish in the future. It provides a two-page checklist for each day's fishing, and comes with twenty-five of these two-page fillers in a six-ring vinyl booklet. It is handsome and remarkably easy to use. Its checklist organizes all the necessary daily data in a series of brief entries that take most of the drudgery out of keeping an effective stream diary. Most entries merely involve checking a box or simply circling a number. The printed entries include fishing time, air and water temperatures, weather, barometer, wind, water conditions, and a galaxy of other relevant information. Refill pages are available. Having such a log before writing *Matching the Hatch* twenty years ago would have simplified my life.

Other gadgets are equally important. Fishing knives have always fascinated me since I first discovered a ring knife made just for dressing trout in a Von Lengerke & Antoine catalogue thirty years ago. The first really good basic fishing knife I owned was a Puma made in Solingen of beautiful German steel. It had a three-quarter-inch chromium steel priest opposite a razor-sharp blade and disgorger. The priest was heavy enough to dispatch a tarpon with authority. Its handles were handsomely grained Brazilian rosewood. The Puma knife was later stolen in Argentina, and since it had been a birthday gift, I have tried in vain to discover another place where it was sold.

There are two good fly-fishing knives available. One has a thirty-eight-inch tape in its handle, and it conceals a knife, file, small screwdriver, and a superbly machined pair of small scissors. Its entire length is slightly more than three inches, and it is made of fine nickel-alloy steel. Unfortunately, it does not have a clevis that can fasten it to a chain pin. Case made the ring-type trout knife years ago, and I have one of their stainless steel fly-fishing knives. Its handle is engraved with a three-inch rule. Its tools include a knife blade, stiletto, screwdriver, disgorger, and a small scissors precise enough to trim the wings and hackles of an overdressed fly. It has a clevis for clipping to a fishing vest, and totals four inches in length. Some fishermen like the occasional cold beer, though my preference leans toward a dry river-chilled Riesling or a fine bottle of Pouilly Fuissé. Such raffish tastes demand bottle openers and corkscrews, and I carry one of the incredible Swiss military knives that includes so many blades and attachments that it is literally a three-inch toolbox. Widely available, it is all stainless steel with a bright red handle. It has two sizes of knife blades, and two screwdrivers. It provides a can opener and a bottle-cap lever. One blade is both a nail file and a metal saw, and another is a combination of punch and reaming blade. The combination bottle opener and large screwdriver also has a wire-stripping slot, wire bender, and wire scraper. The disgorger has a fish-scaling edge, and a fine pair of scissors folds into the handle. The knife even has a toothpick and tweezers, a shackle is provided to attach it to your jacket, and its final triumph is a gleaming little corkscrew.

Most fly-fishermen use the standard angler's clipper that provides a stiletto, small blade, and disgorger on a strong woven lanyard. It is a fine little tool, useful for trimming off excess nylon protruding from a freshly tied knot. Hardy has a similar device in its small stainless scissor pliers, with finger holes thin enough to take the clip ring attached to a chain button inside your jacket. The jaws are useful for removing stubborn hooks from the fish—so long as they are not imbedded too deeply in the throat—and for seating lead shot on a leader. Both the scissors and the clipper must be closed when not in use, since any fly-line slack tangles easily in such gadgets in casting or playing fish.

Surgical forceps and hemostats are an essential component in the fishing vest of any skilled angler. Six inches long and exquisitely made with slender curving jaws, their ability to reach deep inside the throat of a fish, clamp a tiny fly with precision, and work its hook free with a simple push is unequalled. Forceps are also excellent for removing hooks from fishermen, breaking off hook shanks, and flattening barbs with precision. Their stainless steel workmanship is superb, and the locking device across the handles makes it possible to hang the forceps from the jaws outside your jacket—or use a pair as a streamside fly vise in emergencies.

It is surprising how long the fly retriever has been around. William Mills & Son illustrate an excellent version of this handy gadget in their catalogue of 1899. It was an even better design than the present type, with a rounded top for ready penetration into the foliage, and its cord pulled straight down from its cutting notch. It was seated on the fly rod with a rubber sleeve and raised over the twig where the flies were tangled. The rod was then slipped free and held away from danger, leaving the angler to pull hard on the cord and cut the offending foliage. Even when the branch was too thick to cut, you could often pull it within reach with the cord and free your leader. The Mills fly retriever came in a leather case. The modern version is a skeletal shape with a pin that slips into the tip guide, while the ten-foot cord held taut along the rod keeps it there until it is hooked over the intended branch. It is packed in a three-inch vinyl case.

Sharp hooks are far more important than many fishermen realize. Hook hones are not a recent fishing tool, but there are two types available today that are excellent. For streamside hook sharpening I use the miniature nickel-silver files with gem surfaces that have been developed in recent years. They are packaged in a thin vinyl case with a punched hole that can be attached to your vest. One is coarse-grained for big hooks, while the other is finely abrasive for tiny midge-sized flies. Orvis has recently introduced a new metal hone with a gem-surfaced groove, and a punched hole for attaching a lanyard. It comes highly recommended by skilled fishermen I respect. Pezon & Michel also make a fine French-designed carborundum hone that I keep in my fly-tying box. It is about two inches long, square in cross section, and tapered into a thin wedge. Hones should not be ignored in precise fishing.

Scales are something I seldom carried in the early years, when a two-pound brown looked like a broadbill swordfish, but on the rivers of Patagonia and our western mountains a lucky fisherman can often catch a fish worth weighing. Quality spring-loaded scales are usually built of nickel-plated brass. My equipment includes three scales. The smallest is an eight-pound balance manufactured by Hardy, and I carry it on most trips in the United States. The middle size is a thirty-pound scale that I bought the first time I went salmon fishing, and the largest is a fifty-pound scale purchased in Oslo after I had seen a forty-four pound salmon weighed in at Jøraholmen on the Alta. The following season it was a breathtaking thrill when that fifty-pound scale touched bottom with a Norwegian salmon of mine.

No tackle box is complete without a finely machined pair of needle-nose pliers. My pair is dual-chromium-plated to prevent corrosion, has lightly serrated jaws at the tips, and measures about eight inches in length. It includes a tempered wire cutter and is superb for removing hooks from people and fish.

Considerations of first aid and survival are also important in your tackle, particularly for fishing in frontier regions and back country. Cutter makes fishing first-aid kits and insect repellents. Their first-aid kit measures only five by eight inches, and contains medication for everything from a headache or minor hook prick in your finger to bleeding that must have a tourniquet or a rattlesnake bite. It is perfect for your tackle box, and Cutter also makes a letter-size pocket kit for a fishing vest. I also have no qualms about carrying prescription antihistamines, medication for diarrhea and dysentery, hyperacidity, muscle inflammation, and bursitis from too much casting. Fishing in our western mountains often means sun, very low humidity, and incessant wind. It can dry your skin until lips and fingers crack and split painfully. Your medicine kit should include healing cream for your hands and fingertips, chapsticks for your lips, and antisolar ointments if the sun broils your nose. Cutter also makes excellent insect repellents in both lotion and spray foam. Both types come in containers small enough to fit in a fishing-vest pocket easily. Western fishermen who fish in snake country, like the Big Wood Canyon below Magic Reservoir in Idaho or the Lower Deschutes in Oregon, commonly carry a separate Cutter snakebite kit on the stream. It includes a suction device, a surgical blade, antiseptic, and a one-hand lymph constrictor.

Survival presents some other equipment requirements. Waterproof matches are available, and in the back country I also carry a package of windproof matches wrapped and taped inside a vinyl sandwich bag. The two-ring cable saw consists of an eighteen-inch toothed wire, and when coiled it is smaller in diameter than a fly reel. The two rings can be used to stretch the saw taut like a bowstring by anchoring a bent limb between them. Since my trout fishing started in Michigan, I have carried a stainless two-piece drinking cup, purchased from the late Paul Young when I was only sixteen. It is a unique gadget made of two ovoid pieces of steel connected by a fixed pin that rides in a curved slot. The cup lies flat in your fly-box pocket, but warps and catches in a conical shape under pressure from the fingers. It has held everything from the icy water of snowmelt lakes in the Sangre de Cristo mountains of Colorado to exquisitely chilled Dom Perignon champagne, celebrating my first salmon in Norway. The so-called space blanket developed in recent years folds to pocket size, and is worth carrying in the back of your wading vest whenever you are in back country. It weighs only eleven ounces. It uses the principle of reflective insulation with its mylar lining, stays pliable at all temperatures, will not mildew or rot, and is completely windproof and watertight. Unfolded it measures fifty-six by eighty-four inches and, wrapped around your body, it functions as a temporary sleeping bag and tent combined. Wilderness fishermen should carry a compass like the fine little Silva Huntsman which folds flat in your pocket or the watch-size little German compass I carry. Military survival kits have given us another useful tool in the tiny one-ounce distress flares available in a three-flare vinyl pack. Each flare is about four inches long, and fires with a simple pull-chain. It will function in high winds and driving rain, shooting hundreds of feet above the water. The flare will burn with sufficient intensity to attract attention from miles around, in both darkness and daylight. Its casing is rustproof and floats. Like the pocket snakebite kit, this three-ounce watertight pack of flares could mean your survival in a crisis.

Many types of flashlights are used in fishing. Some anglers keep pencil-size lights in their pockets, and I have carried small conventional flashlights in my wader pocket. The flex-light type is designed for fishing, and will concentrate its beam exactly where it is needed, leaving both hands free to work. It is less than ten inches long. It consists of a barrel for the batteries, with a strong locking clip to anchor it firmly in the long inside pockets of a standard fishing vest. Its light is separate, attached to the battery case with a flexible gooseneck that will hold any position you choose. However, light should be used sparingly on the stream, since it can frighten the fish. Any time-consuming work should be done away from their principal holding lies, with your back turned to the trout.

Head nets are clumsy and annoying, but they are less annoying than the swarms of mosquitoes and biting blackflies along our north-country waters, particularly on a still evening in early summer. Orvis makes a head net attached to a cotton poplin hat with two layers of material, and a light ring at its brim. The net is a soft nylon mesh fitting with a second ring that hangs at about chin height, and enough length to fit down around the shoulders like a wrap-around muffler. Wearing such gear is far less troublesome than the insects—once I had both eyes almost swollen shut by blackflies on a river in the Labrador.

Your tackle box should also include a small tool kit with some reel lubricants. It ought to carry a small screwdriver and several assorted bits, a miniature adjustable wrench, small pliers, and oil in a handy pressure-needle applicator.

Reuben Cross used to like the story of the meticulous Wall Street investment banker who was a steady customer for the exquisite dry flies that made Cross a legend in the Catskills. The man had a battery of expensive fly rods that were sent back to their makers each winter for refinishing, his reels were impeccably cleaned and lubricated, the lines were British oiled silk which the man dressed and dried religiously, and he always wore a button-down shirt and silk challis tie when he was fishing.

But with my carefully tied flies, Cross paused and shook his head, *the man was a bloody barbarian!*

Cross would wince as he described the way the man clamped them tightly in his fist, and stuffed them into fly boxes already jammed with flies. It is tragic what such treatment can do to fine dry-fly hackles and tail fibers and perfectly cocked wings. Only putting flies away wet is worse.

Reuben Cross was certainly the robust Tintoretto of the Catskill school, and the perfect dry flies that came from his powerful hands were miraculous. Cross looked more like a rugged stevedore or lumberjack than an artist who worked in fur, feathers, and steel, but like all artists, there was something he gave of himself in everything he made. It was possible to buy his flies, but impossible to own them completely, and to treat such works of art with anything less than reverence is unacceptable. Only the trout should ultimately destroy them, since that fate is both their purpose and their destiny.

Dry flies should not be allowed to dry by themselves after fishing, and should never be hooked into those sheepskin pads that are ritually fastened on fishing vests. Such pads dry them beautifully, but flies become hopelessly bent out of shape against the wool. Knowledgeable fishermen carefully dry their flies before replacing them, both to prevent hook corrosion and its discoloration of a fly, and the matting of its delicate hackles. It can be done easily by carrying a piece of amadou, a dark European fungus once used by primitive surgeons for its remarkably absorbent qualities. Amadou quickly dries the fly and its hook, and a stubbornly matted hackle can sometimes be fully restored in the steam from a tea kettle. Silicote fly dressing can be applied to your dry flies before you fish with them, limiting the amount of water they will absorb. Some fishermen prefer to treat their flies in advance with a spray silicone rather than fully immerse them in silicote.

Deep wading often soaks into fly boxes and sheepskin hooks, and a fisherman should remove his flies to dry both their feathers and their containers. Cleaning and drying a fly on the stream when I was a boy usually consisted of washing it briefly in the current, drying it with a handkerchief, and dressing it with a homemade mixture of shaved paraffin and carbon tetrachloride. Bergman's *Trout* recommends a similar formula. Other anglers with more money and better sources of supply used the exotic amadou, which sounded like a palace in some Arabian fairytale in my boyhood years, and the liquid mucilin made by Aspinall in England. Its base is a mineral grease and its evaporative agent did not discolor the most delicately colored flies. Some fishermen preferred the paste mucilin, brushing the hackles of their flies lightly with a thin film of the dressing on their fingertips, and some purists like the late John Alden Knight, advocated using both liquid and paste mucilin on their flies.

Our modern silicone fly dressings are infinitely better than the traditional mineral- or paraffin-base ointments and oils. Their only fault is their cost. Silicote was the first of these modern fly dressings that became widely available after the Second World War, and it is still popular. Donald Du Bois is the author of the *Fly-Fisherman's Dictionary of Trout Flies*, and an old friend from past summers on the Letort Spring Run in Pennsylvania. Du Bois developed the fine dry-fly flotative called Up, which was the first pure silicone liquid for fishing. Unlike the earlier silicone oils, the Du Bois formula needs no drying immediately after application, and its restorative powers on the stream were a revelation. It is now available in a spray can for fishermen who prefer that method of application. Cortland and Orvis are both manufacturing a similar dry-fly oil in a small spray can, and I have used both with satisfaction. Charles Ritz is rapidly becoming the most famous tackle tinkerer in the history of the sport, and his contribution to dry-fly dressings is a remarkable silicone paste packaged in small plastic capsules. It is applied to the hackles in a fine film by the fingertips, and is a perfect solution for the fisherman who liked mucilin paste better than anything else. Pezon & Michel also makes a Siliflot dry-fly dressing packaged in a spray can, and a fly treated in their silicone-base spray plus a light application of paste on its hackles is virtually unsinkable. These new fly-floating products are superb.

Du Bois also developed a granular product for cleaning and drying the blood and fish slime from a fly. It is simply spilled into the palm, and the fly is rolled in it briefly. It dries such sinking dry flies, cleans their slimed and matted hackles almost instantly, and conditions their fibers like new. Du Bois called his formula Fly-Dry, and it solves a problem dry-fly fishermen have had since Pulman first described floating flies in 1841. Cortland is making a similar new compound that performs well, and Orvis is now selling a product which consists of a fine white powder. These fly-cleaning mixtures are not only useful at streamside, but also in maintaining a fine stock of flies.

Each line manufacturer makes a fly-line cleaner and conditioner for its products. Modern polyvinyl chloride lines are virtually indestructible in normal fishing, but they must be periodically cleaned of the microscopic aquatic residues that collect on their finishes. Plastic finishes must occasionally be conditioned and fed with a paste solvent to prevent hinging and cracking. Charles Ritz has developed a new Parabolic cleaner with Pezon & Michel that is among the finest available, and I use it regularly in my fishing. The best polyvinyl floating lines also need occasional dressing on the stream to function properly and float high. Mucilin and the red stag fat once sold by Hardy Brothers were long the finest line dressings available, but the appearance of the silicone pastes has ended their supremacy. Silicote is perhaps still the finest, and it should be lightly kneaded into the finish with the fingers along its final thirty feet only. Although there are handsome leather line dressers with felt linings, a line should probably be cleaned with a conditioner and handkerchief. It should be rubbed along its full length with your fingers twice, and then the excess paste should be removed with a clean handkerchief or felt pad. Such dressing is needed about once a week.

Modern nylon leaders also require much less maintenance than the silkworm-gut leaders of the past. Their relative specific gravity is higher than gut, and leader-sinking compounds became more important as the surprisingly tough, limp nylons began to make gut leaders obsolete. Various leader-sink formulas are available, and are usually detergents and other wetting agents. Such dressings are important in getting a wet-fly presentation on a high-density line to sink readily, for the buoyancy of the nylon can ride back toward the surface and neutralize the depth of swing achieved by the line. Many old-time fishermen used ordinary soap on their leaders, and it was the cantankerous Bob Carmichael who predictably discovered the most unusual leader sink.

Hang on! He growled and hobbled to a garbage can behind his fly counter. *You need some leader sink.*

I've already got some, I said.

Not like my secret compound! he wheezed theatrically. *It's the best damn leader sink in the world.*

What is it? I asked him innocently.

Carmichael's mud! he said.

Bob Carmichael loved his private jokes, and he laughed to himself as he filled two little boxes with a dark slate-colored clay. His leader-sink compound was excellent, but he never would tell me what it was. Carmichael always shrugged like some wry bulldog and called it Carmichael's mud. Twenty-five years later I discovered it was really bentonite, an unusual clay soil common in Wyoming that readily absorbs water and expands radically when wet.

Leader-sink compounds are widely used as a quick wetting agent for flies and nymphs, and bentonite is superb for that purpose too. However, saliva is also useful and the spectacle of an old-time fisherman with three snelled flies in his mouth was familiar on my boyhood rivers.

One minor problem with nylon is its memory, particularly in the hard, relatively stiff types. It twists and kinks badly, often spiralling off a fly reel like a coiled spring. Stretching it carefully will straighten a nylon leader in a few seconds, and many fishing writers have recommended carrying a piece of inner tubing to fold over the leader and draw firmly along its full length. This straightens a leader partially by stretching it and partially with heat generated by friction. Like bamboo in a fine rod, the molecular structure of nylon is essentially linear and parallel to the leader itself. Stretching a coiled or twisted leader with a little heat forces the molecules back into their linear alignment, pulling it straight again, but too much heat scrambles its molecules and seriously weakens its breaking strain. Thermal strain and its resulting molecular dislocation is the reason why a perfectly formed nylon knot sometimes breaks when it is too hastily drawn tight. Knots that are too quickly tightened can generate enough heat to destroy the tensile strength of their nylon. Donald Du Bois worked out a superb leather-backed rubber pad for stretching leader material, which he christened the Curl-A-Way, and a similar leader straightener is since available at Orvis.

Leader materials are often incorrectly marked, perhaps through careless sorting and spooling at the factory, and in making your own leaders or splicing fresh tippets the nylon strands should not drop more than .001 inch in the small diameters. New tippet spools should always be checked, and only a precision micrometer can provide accurate data. Such micrometers are also useful for checking line diameters and taper specifications. Orvis offers one that gives convenient dial readings, with a table of line and leader diameters on its back, although it is less precise than the small micrometers used in industrial work.

Many nymph fishermen have learned that a little split shot on the leader will get their flies on the bottom, and take fish that are seldom taken with conventional gear. Scissor pliers are needed to seat them on the leader, and there is a fine six-compartment rotary pack of assorted shot sizes made by Pezon & Michel. Some of these tiny shot seem virtually impossible to make, and are difficult to attach to anything but the finest tippets. Their delicacy makes it possible to cast with something approaching normal rhythms, because their smallness creates little atmospheric drag or eccentricity of concentrated weight. The reusable split shot are also effective under many conditions, and can be carried in several sizes.

There are a number of gadgets for forming blood knots for making tapered leaders, but I have always found it harder to master such knot-making devices than simply forming the knot with my fingers. The best blood-knot former is only an inch square, and there are fishermen who use it religiously. However, there is one important knot that cannot be shaped without a proper tool. Bud Lilly sells a nail-knot tool for attaching leaders and backing to line. It is a simple steel eye pin with a flattened and perforated tip and a lanyard for hanging it from a fishing vest. However, some weeks ago I was asked to demonstrate a simple nail knot in a friend's shop, and in searching for an adequate mandrel for shaping the knot, we discovered that a small Phillips-head screwdriver was perfect. The leader butt could be threaded effortlessly under the primary coils of the knot, and it seated cleanly when I pulled it from the bit with a gentle tug. Perhaps a nail-knot tool with a slotted tip would prove more effective.

Leader cases are another problem. Mine are fifteen years old, the elegant British type made years ago by Wheatley. The covers are light brown pigskin about five inches square and close with an intriguing German silver expansion hinge. The insides consist of six interlocking bellows pockets made of parchment. These leader books were expensive fifteen years ago, and it is unfortunate that they are no longer made. Many seasons ago, my father gave me a round leader box of aluminum. It was designed to store silkworm-gut leaders between felt pads moistened with glycerine and distilled water. When nylon became better, I continued to use the case out of mere habit, but eventually I came to dislike its rolling around in my inside bellows pockets. It invariably jammed awkwardly among my fly boxes or got hidden in a far corner. There are a number of snap-closure leader cases available in both leather and vinyl, with transparent envelopes sewn inside. Wheatley still makes a fine aluminum fly and leader box with separate compartments for leaders and flies. Its fly compartment provides seventy-five spring clips for several sizes of wet flies and nymphs. Its leader compartment has a snap cover with felt pads and a protecting flange to hold them in place.

Fly books have long been a weakness of mine, ever since I sat in the grass along the Platte in Michigan twenty-five years ago admiring the pigskin fly books of my father and his friends. Their books were literally bulging with huge numbers of English wet flies and streamer patterns from Maine, rich with feathers of junglecock and bright accents of kingfisher and blue chatterer and macaw.

Since that time I have preferred fly books for carrying streamers as well as wet flies or nymphs too small for the English clip boxes. Leather books lined with fine sheepskin are perfect for holding and carrying big streamers and bucktails so long as they are not so crammed with flies that the feathers are bent and crushed. The sheepskin dries the moisture and prevents hook corrosion, although wading too deep can play havoc with a leather fly book when it really gets soaked. Bucktails and streamers should be stroked into shape with the fingers while they are still damp, and then folded carefully between the covers of a fly book. Wet flies and nymphs smaller than about size fourteen are dressed on hooks of wire so fine that they will not clip firmly in a wet-fly box. Such small flies are perfectly suited to fly books, and there is an excellent leather-covered Reed fly book with a number of soft pressed-felt leaves. It is fine for carrying tiny wets and midge-size nymphs in large numbers.

Fly boxes have been another serious weakness of mine since that long-ago afternoon at Von Lengerke & Antoine in Chicago, when I first saw the English Wheatleys with their transparent spring-clip lids over each compartment. Such boxes are only three-quarters of an inch deep and should not be used for dry flies larger than about ten or twelve, since they will hold too few of each pattern without crushing their hackles. For larger patterns I still use the standard plastic boxes with twelve or sixteen compartments, depending on fly size. These transparent boxes are surprisingly strong and fitted with stainless hinges. Standard plastic boxes measure eight and one-quarter by four and one-quarter by one and one-quarter inches in the depths suited to large dry flies. Orvis is making a similar eighteen-compartment box with a white opaque bottom and clear plastic lid. They are also making a pair of slim plastic boxes measuring seven and a half by three and one-quarter by seven-eighths inches, with the same white bottoms and transparent lids. The eighteen-compartment design is excellent for small dry flies, and the six-compartment box has three-and-one-quarter-inch trays for bucktails and streamers.

The Richard Wheatley boxes offer something more than mere fly storage to a serious fisherman. They are like a fine split-cane rod or an exquisitely machined reel in the sense that their design and functional qualities and workmanship are combined into a character that can only be described as esthetic. That fine equilibrium between function and beauty has a primary role in the ethic of fly-fishing. Wheatley boxes are made of a heavy gauge aluminum alloy in a smooth satin finish. The fly clips are stainless steel. The transparent plastic covers for each dry-fly compartment are held in place with delicate stainless springs and clip latches. It is easy to understand how anglers have been enchanted with these Wheatley boxes since the Halford era on the chalkstreams.

Wheatley boxes come in a large number of designs. Some have a foam pad in the lid for drying flies, while others provide a numbered index table to identify their contents. Such tables are fine for those lazy-minded fishermen who never seem to remember the names of their fly patterns, let alone the insects they imitate. Their forgetfulness means that the contents file occupies lid space that could hold more wet-fly clips.

The Silver Seal models that I prefer and carry are the clip-style that carry wets and nymphs in both bottoms and covers. For dry flies I use the compartment-type boxes with wet-fly clips in their lids. The following designs are my favorites in the exquisite Wheatley line:

F224–6   The most simple wet-fly box, measuring five-eighths by three and a half by six inches, holding 140 flies in its bottom and lid.

F231–6   The slightly larger swing-leaf wet-fly box is an inch thick and adds a thin middle leaf of aluminum. Its capacity is 280 wet flies and nymphs.

F234–6   This one-inch-thick fly box has a swing-leaf and stainless clips for 140 larger wet flies and nymphs.

F251–6   This one-and-a-half-inch-thick box has spring-lid compartments in both lids, totaling thirty-two sections. It is the premium trout-fly model.

F251C–6   This model comes in either ten or sixteen snap-lid compartments, and measures one by three and a half by six inches, with fifty-eight wet-fly clips in the cover. The sixteen-compartment box is designed for smaller flies, and the ten-compartment version comes with six compartments of one and three-eighths by one and five-eighths inches, for larger dry flies.

F251C–4¾   This model also comes in two types, both having forty-one wet-fly clips in the lid. One provides twelve spring-lid compartments, and the other has only eight, since four are of the larger dry-fly size. These designs are perfectly suited to the intermediate size pockets found on many of the new wading vests.

F251C–3½   The tiny compartment box measures only three-quarters by two and three-eighths by three and a half inches, and has six spring-lid compartments with clips for twenty-one wet flies and nymphs. It is small enough for a shirt pocket and ideally suited for minute dry flies or hot weather.

F299A   This fly box measures only one-half by two and three-quarters by three and a half inches with tiny clips for fifty-one wet flies and nymphs.

F298   Also designed for wet flies and nymphs in a shirt-pocket size, and fitted with a swing leaf. It is a one by two and three-quarters by three-and-a-half-inch design holding 102 fly patterns.

Wheatley has also introduced some new Black Seal fly-box designs that hold the flies in stainless coil springs. The F273–1 has ten springs mounted across the width of both the bottom and lid. It will hold any type of fly, of course, but it will hold delicate no-hackle and trimmed spent-wing spinners and long-tailed drakes better than anything else. Such flies are tied with delicate tail fibers, and their wings and hackles should lie absolutely flat in the surface film. The coil-spring clips should hold such flies by their hook bends and protect their delicate dressings. Some nymphs are tied with flat bodies that will not lie properly in a standard clip box, or have legs tied to project laterally from the thorax. Such nymphs should perhaps also be stored in the coil-spring boxes.

The Wheatley fly boxes complete my observations on fly-fishing tackle and clothing, except for a precision device recently perfected in Switzerland for Orvis. It is a remarkable new wristwatch that Orvis has appropriately called the solunagraph.

The watch naturally records standard solar time and has a sweep second hand, but it has a number of other unusual features. The stop-watch chronograph dials record duration time of a trip, given compass heading in poor visibility, and elapsed time for fuel capacity or scuba-tank oxygen. The bezel indicates the hour in the time zone of your departure while the watch itself displays the time at your destination. The watch can tolerate diving operations well below three hundred feet, so it is clearly waterproof enough for a fly-fisherman. But the unique feature of the Solunagraph is a lunar dial that records the phases of the moon, tidal actions, and the solunar feeding periods of the fish.

It was the late Samuel Jennings who first argued for combining the hatching calendars in *Matching the Hatch* with the solunar theory. Jennings had also worked out his own Catskill version of Howitt's *Book of the Seasons*, combining it with charts on the entomology of his favorite rivers and the solunar tables. His chronography equated the early stoneflies and Gordon Quills with the first budding leaves, Red Quills and Hendricksons with flowering shadbush, and the first hatching of the fluttering olive-bodied sedges with the dogwoods.

My time in life means old tweeds fit my character, Jennings explained wryly before his death. *Complicated theories give me comfort, and I like intellectual crutches in difficult currents and difficult times. Hardy makes a bamboo wading staff for a fisherman like me, and just any old stick won't do!*

Samuel Jennings is gone now, part of those eternal cycles he observed and loved on the storied Catskill streams, but I have never forgotten that fly-dressing night years ago at the Fraunces Tavern quarters of the Anglers' Club of New York.

Howitt understood the clues in the seasons, Jennings ended his soliloquy. *He called them the silent language of the Deity.*

Jennings intrigued me with his observations, and I started to study the relationships between the solunar cycles and the fly hatches that started the fish working. Local weather conditions sometimes cancelled them out, along with factors like excessive water temperatures and turbidity, but it was surprising how often the fly hatches and heavy rises of trout coincided rather well with the solunar theories.

There was an unusual example this last year on my home mileage of the Brodheads in Pennsylvania. It was a cold April morning with a raw wind when we reached the stream, and I did not feel much like fishing. My father had not yet fished that spring, and he was eager to get started in spite of the slightly milky current. It started to rain when I opened the trunk of the Mercedes, hard and straight down into the river, and it erased the last of my own urge to fish that morning.

You going to try it? my father asked.

No. I shook my head. *It's too wet and cold, and look at the river—it's like strong coffee and getting worse!*

What'll you do? he asked.

Don't know, I said. *Maybe I'll tie flies in the car.*

Think I'll try fishing, he said.

The rain settled into a steady rhythm on the roof of the car, and I sat in the feather-littered seat with the vise attached to the glove compartment. There was a row of dark little Blue Quills sitting beside the vise, and I suddenly realized I was hungry. The picnic basket was still in the trunk, and the rain had stopped when I carried it toward the weathered table two hundred yards below the bridge. The river looked less milky.

Strange, I thought, *with all the rain.*

The sandwiches tasted good with the hot coffee from the thermos, and I sipped it slowly, studying the river beyond the trees. It looked different in some unexplained change of mood, and a warm wind eddied downstream. Fly hatches usually come between noon and three o'clock that week in April, and I glanced at my solunagraph. It was now almost four, but the moon clock predicted a major period of activity. The river flowed smooth and silent under the buttonwood trees, and suddenly, tight along the willows upstream I saw the first trout rise.

The fish came up again several seconds later, and then I saw a tiny *Paraleptophlebia* mayfly coming off the current. Two others flew downstream, working toward the wet foliage, and several fish were rising steadily now. It was clearly a hatch, and I quickly shouldered into my fishing gear.

The little Blue Quills lying on the glove compartment door were a perfect imitation, and I coaxed them into a fly box carefully. I clinch-knotted one to the leader and sprayed it lightly with silicone. The fish were working greedily in the run along the willows upstream, and when I dropped my little fly above the fish that had been the first to rise, it took quickly. It was the best hatch I saw the entire spring and I took twenty-odd fish in the next two hours. It was simply a matter of getting a decent float over a fish, landing and releasing it quickly, and getting the fly in shape to float again. Slowly the rhythms of the hatch ebbed and died, and I waded happily back to the car.

My father was already breaking down his tackle, and he was smiling broadly. *You tried it after all. How'd you do on this pool?*

Pretty well the last two hours, I said.

Fish started coming about four-thirty at the Slide Pool. My father capped his rod case. *Took a small Blue Quill for an hour.*

That's right, I said.

What were those little flies? he asked.

Paraleptophlebia adoptiva, I replied. *They usually hatch in late morning and early afternoon this time of year.*

How do you explain their hatching so late?

My solunagraph said it was a major period, I laughed.

Your solunagraph was right! he said.

Orvis has recently developed an unusual fishing tool. Its accuracy is remarkable, and that episode on the Brodheads has been repeated many times on trout and salmon rivers in several countries. My solunagraph is a regular companion these days.

Several years ago Ed Zern observed that my book *Matching the Hatch* was outrageously expensive when its cost-per-pound was considered. Zern has since decided, fixing me with a level eye, that somebody like Orvis should design a tiny chest-pack computer with the data of both *Nymphs* and *Matching the Hatch* in its memory bank. The fisherman could then take temperature readings of both the water and the atmosphere, determine the barometric conditions, check the current for alkalinity and dissolved oxygen, describe the fly hatches of the preceding days from insects trapped in the cobwebs between bridge struts, record pertinent data about cloudiness and precipitation and water clarity, and feed in the solunar data. Zern concluded his poker-face dissertation with the observation that a fisherman could finally press the read-out button on his computer and it would tell him exactly what tippet and fly to use.

But they had to abandon it, he mused sadly.

Why? Somebody delivered the straight line like a hatchery brookie taking a Mickey Finn. *Why give it up?*

Cybernetic science has its limits, Zern continued. *They don't build those old trusswork bridges any more, so the spiders can't spin cobwebs that catch yesterday's fly hatches, and we had trouble with the computer prototypes.*

What kind of trouble? I asked.

Maybe it lacked enough circuits or transistors or something. Zern added more sour mash whiskey to his glass and sat philosophically admiring its slowly mingling colors. *But even with its memory bank stuffed with entomology and solunar theory, it always came up with the same answer.*

What was that? I laughed guardedly.

Worms, he smiled.

For recent developments in streamside accouterment, see Appendix: Notes on New Equipment.

5. Observations on the Modern Fly Reel

I t was surprisingly warm that evening on the Alta, almost a dozen years ago, when I had been invited to fish the river in a party that included the Duke of Roxburghe. It is a legendary river among fly-fishermen, lying deep in the forest barrens of arctic Norway. The writings of Charles Ritz had first introduced me to the Alta legend in his charming *Fly Fisher's Life,* and the anticipation of fishing it made me restless. After dinner in the charming old Jøraholmen farmstead, I wandered out to the ghillies hut while the other anglers gathered their tackle for the night's fishing.

It never really gets dark during midsummer on the Alta, almost a thousand miles north of Oslo, and the sun was still warm on the rough-sawed walls of the ghillies' hut. The boards were brightly painted with a primitive mixture of iron oxides and milk, the ancestor of thousands of red outbuildings and barns from arctic Lapland westward to Oregon and British Columbia.

Carved larchwood hooks held a dozen fly rods under the protective eaves of the moss-grown roof. Most of the rods were the two-handed type, of English and Scottish manufacture, with a single Castle Connell Greenheart from Ireland, and there were two or three American rods only slightly smaller—exquisite Paynes with their richly perfect finish, Leonards with their pale bamboo, and a newer two-handed Orvis.

The reels were primarily English, like the four- and five-inch Hardy Perfects with the patina of a fine double shotgun. The Paynes and Leonards carried elegant Vom Hofe and Walker reels, and the solitary Orvis was fitted with a finely machined Bogdan.

It was a rich display of beautiful salmon tackle, but three of the rods were mounted with unfamiliar aluminum reels that I had never seen before. These huge reels were almost eight inches in diameter, elegantly machined and perforated, with the look of highly skilled hand labor. The aluminum already had the gleaming quality of time, the character usually found in antique rifles or pistols from the American frontier, and they were engraved with the name Roxburghe. Finally, the Duke of Roxburghe came down to the ghillies' hut to check his equipment.

Those are remarkable reels, I said. *I've never seen anything like them.*

The Duke smiled faintly. *They're quite old,* he explained. *Hardy built them for my grandfather almost a century ago.* He took his rods down and passed them carefully to his boatmen.

But they look like aluminum! I said.

They are. Roxburghe nodded.

But modern aluminum processing didn't start until 1886, I said, *and the famous Conroy aluminum reels first appeared in 1878—that makes these even older!*

Yes, Roxburghe shook his head. *Hardy made each reel specially by hand to my grandfather's specifications—he was fascinated with aluminum and he wanted reels with enough diameter that each turn retrieved considerably more line.*

Reels? I asked. *How many were there?*

Twelve, Roxburghe replied. *Each was engraved with his name and its identifying number.*

And these are numbers six and nine, I said.

Yes, Roxburghe nodded.

It's remarkable that you're still fishing them almost a century later. I shook my head in disbelief. *They're probably the first examples of aluminum reels.*

Perhaps they are, Roxburghe agreed.

Although our early chapters demonstrate that fishing reels first evolved in China before the twelfth century and that Thomas Barker apparently introduced reels to British literature in his *Art of Angling* five hundred years later, the modern fly reel is surprisingly recent.

Primitive reels were probably fashioned of wood. Black walnut reels were still manufactured and popular as late as 1930, and British makers like Foster and Hardy regularly featured them in their catalogues. But reels of brass and German silver and aluminum had begun to dominate fly-fishing toward the close of the nineteenth century. Since few trout fishermen had much experience with fish large enough to make reel-wearing runs deep into the backing, and our fine modern nylons were not introduced until after midcentury, most fishing writers paid surprisingly little attention to reels.

Bergman is a good example. His classic book *Trout* devotes surprisingly little space to fly reels, except to comment on line capacity for steelhead fishing and his preference for left-hand reeling. Other well-known writers seem to concur in the observation that reels are meant merely to store line and backing, and are both the least expensive and least important item in one's tackle boxes.

It is time to terminate such mythology. Our lack of concern for the importance of the fly reel and its performance undoubtedly results from two factors. Our major fishing writers were British or American experts with little experience with big fish and really big water. When *Trout* was written, Bergman had had only a brief exposure to steelhead and salmon, and to the grinding stresses such fish can place on our tackle. Our trout were far less crowd-shy in those years, and a .008 silkworm-gut tippet was considered fishing really fine. Modern limp nylons with their delicate .003 to .005 diameters were not available then, so the smooth-running qualities of a precision reel in surrendering line to a bolting fish were much less critical. The lessons of our big western rivers, with their sea-armored steelheads and cartwheeling rainbows, have taught us that line capacity, fine machining, and firm drag systems are extremely important. Twenty years of experience at the opposite end of the spectrum, with fragile tippets on highly selective trout, have also demonstrated the unmistakable importance of delicate click-and-drag mechanisms that will not shear .003 nylon on a running fish. Fine reels must contend with both kinds of problems.

Webster is correct in defining a reel as a diminutive windlass fitted to the butt of the rod, its principal function to surrender and retrieve line in fishing—but a truly modern fly reel is much more. It should provide sufficient weight to balance the rod and complement its casting dynamics, it must provide sufficient capacity for both fly line and backing, its precision and drag system must be smooth enough to fish relatively fine leader tippets without shearing them, and its ability to surrender line grudgingly and retrieve it swiftly are also important qualities in playing a fish once it is hooked and fighting.

Past ratios of rod-and-reel balance recommended that a reel should weigh approximately fifty percent more than the rod. Application of such ratios means that a four-ounce rod would call for a fly reel weighing six ounces. However, these ratios evolved during the years when split-bamboo rods ruled the fishing world, and reels were principally made of aluminum and German silver.

Modern materials have upset such traditional thinking, in both the construction of rods and fly reels. The conventional ratio dictating a reel weighing fifty percent more than the rod should not be applied too literally. Reels are being made of remarkable new alloys of surprising weight reductions and strength. English fly reels of conventional aluminum weighed about three and a half ounces in a three-inch diameter model, but aerospace metallurgy has made it possible to fabricate reels of that size weighing only three ounces. In converting from German silver to modern aluminum alloys, the superbly crafted Walker trout reels have become a full three ounces lighter in the three-inch model. Similar reductions in weight first came with the hollow-built Winston and Powell rods on the Pacific Coast, which reduced the weight of eight- to nine-foot rods as much as ten to fifteen percent. Such developments in cane construction made the usual line- and reel-weight recommendations obsolete. Fiberglass rods caused even more radical changes. Rods balanced with eight-weight lines weighed about four and three-quarter ounces in bamboo to only three and three-quarter ounces in the new synthetic materials. Such changes mean that a weight ratio of two-to-one for reel and rod is possible—and a three-ounce fiberglass rod is perfect with a six-ounce reel.

Recent field experience on the Pacific Coast steelhead rivers with an experimental tubular rod of carbon graphite clearly proves that our formulas for matching our rod-and-reel weights are totally outmoded. Both high-modulus graphite and boron fiber fly rods are so light, relative to their stiffness and power, that a rod designed for an eight-weight line in these synthetic materials can weigh much less than three ounces. Such graphite and boron construction will undoubtedly make a six-ounce reel a viable match for rods weighing as little as two and one half ounces.

Capacity can also dictate similar rod-and-reel weight ratios, particularly when we are fishing tackle somewhat lighter than usual for the water. Perhaps fishing big rainbows with light gear yet needing the capacity for more than one hundred yards of backing to handle their tail-walking runs is typical of situations where the reel might be twice the weight of the fly rod. Steelhead fishing offers even more exaggerated examples: a field-testing session in California once found me fishing a graphite rod weighing just over three ounces with a ten-weight forward taper line and two hundred yards of backing on a British reel weighing eight ounces.

Such fishing also means relatively long casting, and with average line lengths beyond sixty feet, the old ratios of rod-and-reel balance no longer matter. The length of line load brings an extra heavy reel into perfect equilibrium. Obviously there are no immutable rules-of-thumb for balancing fly rods and reels. It should be decided by your strength, your casting skills, and what feels right in covering the kind of water you usually fish; adding lead weights or lengths of solder inside your reel frame to meet theoretical ratios of weight is merely an inertial preoccupation with obsolete theories of balance.

Reel specifications and design are important too.

Obviously, basic reel design lies between the polarities of the most line capacity at the lightest weight. The larger the line capacity the greater the stresses on reel frame and spool and parts, yet maximum reduction in weight pares away at the thickness of each component. Big fish can actually rack the reel frame of a lightweight design, and the dynamic loading of thin backing can even distort a delicate reel-spool alloy, causing it to bind and freeze. Reel frames that are cast or brazed into a single piece are superior to reels assembled with set screws, since the screws both add weight and tend to work loose. Some anglers modify such reels by setting the screws in a locking compound, but this makes dismantling for repairs difficult.

Precisely machined tolerances in the gears and ratchets are important too, along with the fit of the drag springs and pawls. Poor springs are a serious problem. Sometimes fishermen forget to release their drag settings between fishing sessions, seriously fatiguing the temper of the springs. Metal fatigue can cause a drag spring to snap under the run of a heavy fish, and its metallic death rattle is a harsh and frightening sound.

Breaking a drag spring means the reel is free-spooling dangerously out of control, and it can easily overrun and snarl the line. Such a tangle can break off the running fish, and if the rod is held high to counter a really long run, its fragile tip is in danger too.

Line-guide design is also important. Early fly reels were not fitted with special line guides, and this resulted in excessive wear on the frames at the pillars. Some manufacturers responded with a primitive version of the rolling pillars now found on expensively made modern reels. The classic round line guide had its debut on the exquisitely made Hardy Perfect, its hand-polished agate guides fitted into a delicate German silver fitting seated into the frame with four tiny set screws. It was a beautifully designed reel of classic simplicity, and it still sells for as much as fifty to eighty dollars when a well-kept Perfect is available. But experience with round line guides on big fish points up a serious conceptual flaw in their performance, however beautiful their appearance. The round line guide inescapably concentrates the line in the center of the spool, reducing its capacity before the line accumulates and binds against the pillars. Line can also slip off the mounding layers in the center of the spool, tangling and jamming when a good fish starts to run and strip out line. Such reels are not recommended in the larger big-fish sizes. Reels fitted with semicircular line guides of heavy gauge steel wire are also troublesome, and the best designs are the simple U-shaped line guides of German silver, stainless steel, and specially hardened alloys fitted to the reel frame. Such guides allow the fisherman to distribute the line evenly and smoothly on the spool as he retrieves it from a good fish, and they effectively reduce wear when line is stripped off while casting. Rough places and nicks should be polished down with a fine file or abrasive cloth, should they form in a reel frame, and a damaged line guide should be replaced.

Performance in capacity and drag systems is easily attained in reels not required to have a click mechanism precise enough and smooth enough to fish .003 to .005 tippets, but only the finest reels are capable of both qualities. Such reels are not inexpensive, and a serious angler should not buy cheap copies. Such economy can cost you the biggest fish of your career if it makes a run strong enough to test a reel, and good fish hooked on light tippets will probably shear them by simply bolting against the click system. Even some light reels ostensibly designed for delicate rods have click mechanisms too balky and coarse for nylon finer than .005, and their intermediate price is money wasted on hard-fished trout.

Line capacity is also important. Obviously, sufficient backing is needed to handle big fish in heavy water, but the backing has another function. It has a silent role in playing every fish you hook, even if many are not large enough to take out much line. Such backing forms an arbor, magnifying spool diameter and the length of line recovered with each turn of the reel. Quick recovery of line is a major factor in playing a fish effectively, and the backing multiplies the rate at which line is returned to the spool.

Few trout will make runs that strip an entire fly line from the reel, except for big rainbows or steelheads fresh from salt water. However, a good reel should have the muscle to stand up under such pressure. Since there are trout large enough to make runs of more than 150 feet in many average-size streams—including the gentle brown-trout rivers of our eastern mountains—reels that cannot hold thirty yards of fly line with another fifty yards of backing are not workable tools. Some of the tiny reels designed for ultralight rods under two ounces provide only twenty yards of backing behind a three- or four-weight line. Although these reels are exquisitely machined, their limited line capacity rules them out on water holding really large trout with sufficient room to make a sustained run. It is wise to choose your tackle on the basis of the biggest fish that might be hooked on your favorite waters, not by the prevailing fashions in lighter and lighter equipment. Too little line could cost you the fish of a lifetime.

The quality of the drag system is critical in a reel intended for fishing big water. Few conditions call for leader tippets of more than twelve-pound breaking strain, except perhaps huge bucktails or marabous in high winds, and a drag system capable of exerting eight to ten pounds is more than adequate for the most demanding sea-run fish. Such systems vary widely in quality and design, and few trout reels are capable of drag settings much over three or four pounds. Few rivers will require heavier drag systems, and most small reels have drags designed primarily to prevent inertial overruns that can free-spool and tangle the line.

Drag systems are designed to operate only when the line is running out with a fish. Retrieving line is not wound against the drag setting, only the click mechanism is engaged. It should be remembered that drag systems are usually set when the reel is relatively full. Therefore, the effective moment arm forcing line from the spool equals the distance from the center of its spindle to the outermost layers of fly line. When line is stripped from the reel, this radius becomes shorter and shorter. With half of the line capacity expended, the distance is also reduced by fifty percent, and the force required to turn the spool must be doubled. The laws of physics mean that a three-pound drag set when the reel was filled will resist a six-pound pull when it is almost empty, and this strain is added to line friction in both the rod guides and the water. Drag settings must be used judiciously, because of the strain exerted by an emptying reel on the tippet diameter.

Cheap drag systems pose a more serious problem. The tension required to start the spool is heavier than the drag exerted once the reel is spinning. Such performance spells trouble. The starting tension might be set at three or four pounds, but while a fish is running, only one or two pounds are working. Such a run might last fifty yards into the backing, increasing the inertial drag steadily as the dwindling line decreases the moment arm between the axis of the spool and its pulling point. Such radical variations in drag are troublesome, but a fish that suddenly stops and bolts again is a disaster. The two- or three-pound drag of the turning reel drum ends abruptly, and a fresh run that starts the spool with most of the line gone can exert as much as six or seven pounds of drag. These radical changes in pressure can both break a leader or literally work the fly free. Such oscillating drag systems are unacceptable. Since the best drag mechanisms exert considerably more tension as the reel spool is emptied, the drag should never be set at more than forty percent of rated breaking strain for the leader. It is a lesson that must be learned.

Reel-spool design is also important. The workmanship must be precise, with a strongly made spindle and side plates. The drum should be as light as possible without distorting under the tension of a heavy fish. The drum plates should be smoothly tapered or slightly convex, so the width at the spindle is approximately forty to fifty percent less than the outer width of the spool. Such refinements mean the line layers more quickly near the spindle, where the mechanical advantage is least, and most of the line is concentrated near the circumference of the spool. Line can be controlled and recovered better there, and the reel will spin less rapidly while line is being surrendered to a running fish. Fine reels like the Hardy Lightweight series carry this convex spool feature one step farther, placing more exaggerated convexity on the ratchet face of the spool and the midpoint of its spindle off center, locating it approximately halfway between the weight of the gear system and backplate and the position of your fingers on the handle of the reel. It is such refinements, as well as exquisite workmanship, that make an expensive reel easily worth its price.

Automatic reels are designed with a tightly coiled spring system surrounding the spindle. The spring is tightened by turning the face cover of the reel or by stripping out line, and its tension recovers line with a slight finger pressure on their triggers. Although automatic reels are made of aluminum, and their manufacturers were among the pioneers in using that material, the working springs are steel and relatively heavy. Automatic reels lack the capacity to hold more line than the fly line itself, and their inability to provide backing is a serious fault. Automatic reels also weigh from eight to twelve ounces, without the extra weight of the fly line, an unacceptable weight-to-capacity ratio. The inadvertent triggering of the reel can shear a light tippet, and the spring is wound tighter and tighter as a fish takes line. Such tension can break a fine leader, and although some automatic reels can release their tension with a half-turn of the casing that encloses the spring, it is such a crude system that it can also shear a tippet or tear the fly free from a running fish. These shortcomings make automatic reels unsuitable for serious trout fishing, and the loss of a big rainbow on the Gunnison in my boyhood years convinced me that single-action reels were infinitely better.

The modern reel has an interesting history. Its evolution can certainly be traced to the simple brass and nickel-plated reels common before the Civil War, and the elegantly made German silver variations imported from British tackle makers. Thomas Conroy was selling fine fly reels with black rubber faceplates and spools, plate trim, and other fittings of German silver as early as 1873. Many of the best early reels were sold under the trademark of Dame, Stoddard & Kendall, the fine old tackle company in

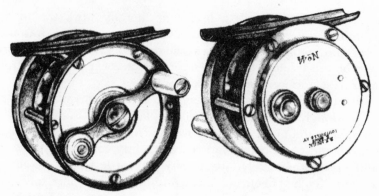

B. F. Meek Trout Reel
from the collection of G. H. Howells

Boston. Conroy also provided trout reels for the old Charles F. Orvis Company in Vermont, and featured two elegantly detailed designs. The inexpensive model was machined from nickel-plated brass and had a spool enclosed in hard-rubber end plates. It sold for less than two dollars in 1875, and its more expensive version ranged from four to five dollars and was fashioned from German silver with hard-rubber plates and German silver fittings. Thomas Conroy was one of the early giants of American tackle design and was selling his first reels about 1873. His craftsmen were working with hard-rubber end plates and aluminum only five years later, and his elegant raised-pillar designs ultimately evolved into the classic Leonard trout reels, which remained in production until only a few years ago at William Mills & Sons.

Orvis patented its unique perforated end plate and spool reel in 1874, and although it was machined from nickel-plated brass, it was a prelude to similar modern designs. The perforations were intended to reduce weight,

Dame, Stoddard & Kendall Reel

Orvis 1874 Patent Reel

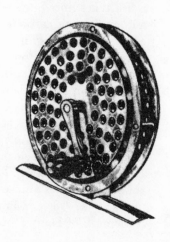

facilitate drying the fly line and backing, and help free the reel of dirt and sand. It was machined of fine brass alloys and heavily plated with nickel, so carefully finished that the examples I have examined have a beautiful patina and luster in their pewter-colored plating. The click system is simple and effective. The reel is exaggeratedly narrow, placing its center of gravity as far from the rod as possible. Such configuration also supplies a remarkable mechanical advantage for so small a reel, recovering an optimal amount of line on each turn of the spool. The reel was made in two sizes, with capacities of twenty and seventy yards of fly line, and is about the diameter of the original Hardy Lightweight. The handle was made detachable and fitted into a black walnut case beside the reel, with the unconscious elegance of the best nineteenth-century design.

Julius Vom Hofe also began building his own remarkable fly reels in these same years, and began experimenting with hard-rubber end plates in 1874, the year the Orvis reel was patented. Vom Hofe is a half-legendary name in the history of the fly reel. History is unclear on the genesis of the German silver and black rubber designs, since both Vom Hofe and Conroy were experimenting at about the same time. Some historians believe that Vom Hofe built the Conroy reels as well as his own. It is clear that Vom

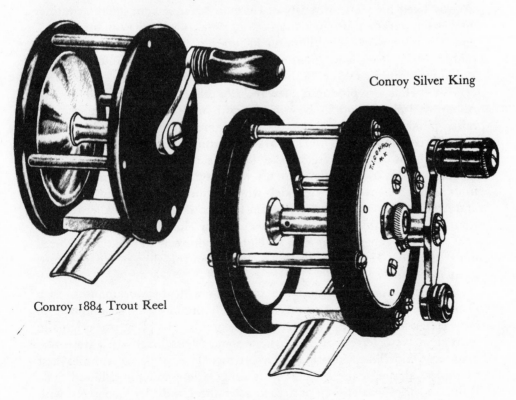

Conroy Silver King

Conroy 1884 Trout Reel

Vom Hofe Reel

Hofe built nothing but reels with black rubber end plates after 1881, while Conroy liked his reels primarily of German silver, except for the contract models his workmen produced for Orvis, Wilkinson, and William Mills & Son. Conroy's work for Wilkinson included a fine little reel with hard-rubber end plates, and Conroy also produced an aluminum reel for Wilkinson patterned after the Leonard raised-pillar design.

Vom Hofe also produced a few reels for other tackle sellers like the fine Abbey & Imbrie shop in New York, both under their trademark in a raised-pillar model and under his own name. Vom Hofe reels are still highly prized in the used tackle market, like the beautifully machined reels later built by Otto Zwarg, whose fly reels are among the finest ever designed. Otto Zwarg, who had his workshop in Brooklyn, never made trout reels, concentrating on models with specifications designed for tarpon and Atlantic salmon. Conroy and Vom Hofe both designed smaller reels for trout fishing. With the death of Edward Vom Hofe, the halcyon years of American reel building came to an end. Salmon reels were later produced under the Vom Hofe name in Philadelphia, but this shop never machined trout-size models.

Although his reels were never in a class with the workmanship in a Conroy or Vom Hofe, August Meisselbach produced large numbers of serviceable, inexpensive reels early in this century. His plant was originally located in New Jersey, although later some Meisselbach reels were also made in Ohio. The Meisselbach Expert models were perhaps the earliest examples, although the skeletal Featherlight designs soon followed. The Rainbow series was closely patterned after the Hardy Uniqua reels, with their crescent-shaped spool catches. The Symploreel was a similar design fabricated in Bakelite. Meisselbach was absorbed by the Bronson Reel Company in about 1932.

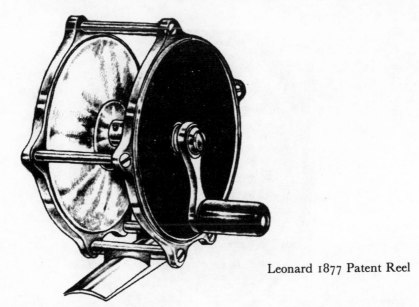

Leonard 1877 Patent Reel

The lovely Leonard fly reel is no longer made, although it also commands an excellent price in the used tackle market. It was a classic design of simple elegance. Its back and face plates are hard rubber, with raised pillars and frames of brightly polished duraluminum alloy. The raised-pillar design originally developed by Conroy slightly increased its line capacity. Its click system was both smooth and firm enough to prevent an overrun of its spinning drum. The reels were made in three sizes, from two and a half inches to three inches in diameter. Like all such reels, these Leonard types are relatively heavy, ranging from three and three-quarters to four and three-quarters ounces, for their line capacity. However, such reels are living artifacts of another time, like the Burberry fishing coats worn by Edward Ringwood Hewitt and George La Branche in old photographs taken on the Brodheads and Willowemoc and Neversink—their intricately wrapped rods fitted with elegant Leonard reels.

Hardy ultimately began building its prototypical aluminum trout reels late in the nineteenth century, although the custom-made Roxburghe designs had come almost twenty-five years earlier. Apparently the perforated-spool concepts in the Roxburghe were only used to reduce the weight in such large spools, and were not considered important in the smaller trout models. Some of the early types were the simple closed-drum Uniqua reels popular before the First World War, and subsequently recommended by writers like Eugene Connett and John Alden Knight.

The Hardy Perfect series also featured a closed spool and back plate, machined from three pieces of solid alloy, and it combined aluminum frame-and-drum specifications with ball bearings and the classic revolving line guide of agate. It also offered a superb compensating drag-and-click system. Earlier British reels had displayed a disturbing tendency to freeze at certain drag settings, and the Hardy Perfect solved this problem. The reel

Hardy Uniqua

pawl that engaged the spool gear was fastened under a steel bridge, secured to the back plate with four screws. The slotted pawl allowed its contact point to work freely among the gear teeth, as well as rising back against the drag spring in case of any malfunction. The drag-spring design is still used in the modern Hardy Lightweights, although the tension and pawl system is much simpler now. The regulator screw was fitted with a knurled head, and forced the tension arm to compress the spring. Elements of this system

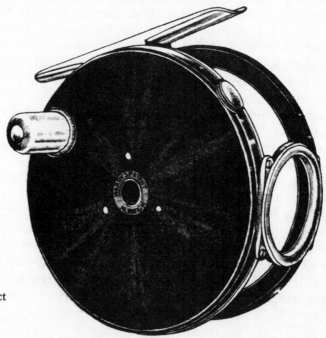

Hardy Perfect

Hardy Saint George

are found in most British-made reels more than fifty years later, although the perforated spools found in the Eureka and Silex coarse-fishing reels still had not influenced the trout-size models. However, the elegant Hardy Saint George was not long in coming, with its partially drilled drum and fitted agate line guide. The modifications cut a full ounce from the weight of the Hardy Perfect, dropping the three-and-three-eighths-inch model to only six and a half ounces. The Hardy Saint John reels also had a partially drilled spool, but did not offer the circular line guide, and were made only in a heavy-trout diameter and weight. The tiny Hardy Saint George of less than three inches, with its perfectly fitted line guide and fine machining, is one of my most prized possessions.

These reels are no longer manufactured in our time, although Hardy is considering reintroduction of the Perfect and the Saint John. The developments worked out in these reels fifty-odd years ago are still found in the modern Hardy Lightweight series, as well as in similar reels produced for Orvis and Scientific Anglers. Such reels are clearly the best large-production reels available to fishermen who want acceptable quality, line capacity at surprisingly light weight, and not too much cost.

The lightweight aluminum alloys available at midcentury led to the Hardy Lightweight series of reels. Their introduction fifteen-odd years ago resulted in unparalleled popularity, and the line was expanded to six models. The first design was three and three-sixteenths inches in diameter and weighed a surprisingly little three and three-quarters ounces, almost half the weight of a comparable Hardy Saint George, and a full four ounces lighter than the three-and-three-eighths-inch Hardy Perfect. It was named in honor of Laurence Robert Hardy.

Hardy Saint John

The startling potential of the new alloys and designs was soon apparent, and Hardy quickly introduced its Featherweight and Princess reels to the Lightweight line. The lovely little Featherweight measures slightly under three inches and weighs only three ounces, a fine design for four-weight lines and rods. The Princess was a larger model. Its diameter was three and three-sixteenths inches, slightly smaller than the largest Saint George, and it weighed only three and a half ounces. The Princess is a superb reel for a six-weight line, its assembly capable of handling tippets lighter than .005, as well as medium-size salmon and steelhead.

The dainty little Hardy Flyweight is virtually a toy, although it is still a practical fishing tool designed for rods weighing between one and two ounces. Its capacity is sufficient for a three-weight line and a limited amount of relatively light backing. The Flyweight is two inches in diameter and weighs two and one-eighth ounces, and is not fitted with an adjustable drag system. It is a handsome, jewellike object.

The success of these four lightweight models led Hardy to add two larger designs a half-dozen years after the first design was introduced. The Saint Aidan was intended as a heavy-trout and light-salmon type, measuring a full three and three-quarters inches and weighing only six ounces. It was designed for seven- and eight-weight lines, with capacity for as much as two hundred yards of backing. The Saint Aidan will strip smoothly enough for a .006 tippet with only one of its pawls engaged. The Saint Aidan is also workable for nine-weight lines, but Hardy also developed the still larger Saint Andrew model, which was rarely sold in the United States and has now been discontinued. While the reel frame of the Princess had been only an inch, the Saint Aidan frame was widened to one and three-sixteenths inches, and the Saint Andrew was a full one and five-eighths inches. The Saint Andrew was a generous four and one-eighth inches in diameter, and weighed seven ounces, but it carried a full eleven-weight line with 250 yards of thirty-pound backing. However, the Saint Aidan was about the limit of the lightweight design, and its springs often failed. The bigger Saint Andrew proved less workable. Although its drag bridge and screw were bigger, the larger springs were rather brittle, and the weight of the frame often worked it slightly loose from the reel-seat flange. It was not entirely successful, although it did carry an incredible amount of fly line and backing for its weight—the four-and-a-half-inch Hardy Perfect weighed almost a pound, more than twice the weight of the similar Saint Andrew.

Less than a half-dozen years ago Scientific Anglers convinced Hardy to build a similar reel for their series of lines and fiberglass rods, and the Lightweight series was discontinued. It was a major footnote to the law of qualitative obsolescence that fishing writer Ted Trueblood expressed unhappily some years ago.

When you find a piece of equipment you like, Trueblood argues wryly, *buy five or six—they'll soon stop making it if it's really good!*

However, this time Trueblood was wrong, and Hardy has happily started making its Lightweight series again. The reels are again available in all sizes from the Flyweight to the Saint Aidan. Their workmanship is still enviable, with a precision and hand-detailing that belies their production volumes. The fit between spool and frame is so finely machined that even a leader cannot easily slip between and tangle. Fine aluminum alloy is used for both spool and frame, and the German silver line guard is reversible. It can be turned around and the pawl reversed, to permit left-hand operation. The handles are smooth and nonfouling, and the reels come apart easily for maintenance or repairs, using the small spring-loaded latch that secures the spool to its spindle.

Scientific Anglers retained all of these features, and added several modifications of their own design. The most obvious is a rolled spool rim that laps the outside of the reel frame, and is intended as a manual brake

Hardy Lightweight Series

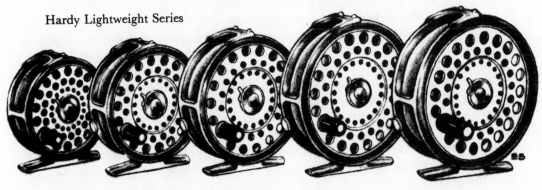

Flyweight   Featherweight   Lightweight   Princess   Saint Aidan

that can be palmed when a fish is stripping line. It is a feature better suited to salt-water species and hard-mouthed fish like steelhead and Pacific salmon. However, the rolled, external drum-flange can bind against waders or clothing in a salt-water lock position, with the butt of the rod in the stomach. Also, reel palming should seldom be tried with fine leaders and strong fish, and these reels employ an unusual drag system. Instead of the conventional Hardy spring mechanism, these reels use a circular spring encased in neoprene. There is a single, slotted pawl mounted on the back plate near the flange, and opposite its position is a twelve-notch eccentric that activates the drag tension. It is set with a nylon button on the back plate of the reel, and an extremely strong drag-setting is possible if the spool is removed, forcing the eccentric past its final notch. However, the spring should not be left at this heavy setting. It is a drag system that cannot be fouled with dirt or sand, although it does not exert a really firm pressure and has a tendency to fade on a really strong fish.

The spool is released from its spindle with a simple push-spring latch and is fitted with a line notch in its back flange to help keep the line clear of the reel frame when it is being reseated. The nylon housing over the spindle on the back plate seems less desirable than the aluminum fitting on the Hardy Lightweights, and the line guard is a much lighter nickel-plated fitting than the genuine German silver line guard on the original British prototypes. However, the larger models are fitted with corrosion-resistant components for fishing salt-water and sea-run trout.

These reels are also somewhat heavier than comparable models in the earlier Lightweight series. The two-and-three-quarters-inch System Four Reel weighs a full half-ounce more than the Hardy Featherweight, while the System Eight model weighs about the same as the similar three-and-three-quarters-inch Saint Aidan. The Lightweight and Princess reels are significantly lighter than the System Six and System Seven designs, so the difference in weight could be important in the smaller trout-size reels. The Scientific Anglers' specifications also provide the easy conversion to left-hand wind found in all Hardy-built reels, and even the smallest System Four provides the rolled flange for applying manual drag.

Hardy has also started making a Viscount Series of fly reels using somewhat less expensive components, but derived directly from the Scientific Anglers' designs. The frames and spools are pressure die-cast of high strength aluminum alloy, but unlike the more expensive systems, the reel foot and rim are cast integrally with the frame. The spool-handle pivot and cup are cast with the drum itself. The line guards are identical, but there is no rolled rim for manual braking with the palm. The drag systems are adequate and precise, with a full range of settings. The Hardy Viscount reels are made in three sizes, designed to accommodate four-weight, five-weight, and six-weight lines, the basic sizes for most trout fishing. Their price is moderate, about half the cost of the more expensive reels in the Hardy line.

Cheaper still are the several Japanese copies of the Hardy Lightweight

System 4

System 5

System 6

System 7

System 8

System 9

series being marketed by companies like Berkeley and Heddon. The Berkeley models are available in three sizes. The 530 is a size approximately equivalent to the Hardy Featherweight, with its two-and-a-half-inch spool diameter, but it weighs more than the Lightweight. The Berkeley 540 is virtually identical to the Hardy Lightweight in size and appearance, but it weighs almost as much as the larger Hardy Princess. The 550 reel is the largest of the Berkeley series, its diameter roughly equal to the Hardy Princess, yet it weighs almost as much as the bigger Saint Aidan. The metals are slightly heavier and less costly throughout than the English prototypes, but they do provide a single-piece frame, an easily removable spool, a heavily plated brass line guard, an acceptable drag with a slightly coarse click mechanism, and ready conversion to left-hand use. The Berkeley reels are about one-third the price of an original Hardy, and the Heddon copies of the Lightweights are even less expensive.

The Heddon imports are such accurate copies of the Hardy prototypes that the spools are interchangeable with the Featherweight and Lightweight models. Their appearance is virtually identical, although a knowledgeable eye can easily detect the differences in workmanship. The adjustable drag is smooth and positive, the frames are solid and well built, and the reels are reversible to left-hand operation. Skilled anglers who have fished them agree that for average fishing problems such Japanese copies are probably satisfactory, but that such facsimiles are not equal to the more costly British products for really difficult fishing conditions—big steeplechasing rainbows in heavy water or a reel that must surrender line smoothly enough to cushion a 7X tippet against a bolting fish.

Pflueger has built a single-action reel for many years that is widely used on American trout waters, and the company is more than a century old. The Medalist series has been undeniably popular. It includes six reel designs. The Pflueger 1492 is about the diameter of a Hardy Featherweight, and its thirteen-sixteenths of an inch spool will hold more line, but it weighs a full ounce more. It is without an adjustable drag, and its click mechanism

Pflueger Medalist

is a little too harsh for tippets finer than .005 nylon. The 1494 Medalist is slightly smaller than a Hardy Princess, although it weighs much more, and the next larger model is a little larger than the three-and-a-half-inch Hardy. However, it weighs a full six ounces, as much as the Hardy Saint Aidan. The 1498 reel has a four-inch diameter and is roughly equivalent to the Saint Aidan, although almost three ounces heavier. It is fitted with a reinforced back plate and spool, and a stronger drag system than the other Medalist reels.

These American-built reels are workhorse designs that will take more abuse than their more elegant British cousins. They are constructed of strong aluminum alloys with a machined-steel spindle. Although the spool cover for the spindle head is plastic, it houses a practical push lever securing the spool in the frame. The pillars, cross plates, and line guard are all finely tooled brass with a heavy nickel plating. The drag system is the oscillating type that can vary radically between stopped drag tension and the pressure on a spinning drum, but it is adequate for most fishing, and only fishermen skilled enough to fish the delicate tippets from .003 to .005 will find its click system harsh. Perhaps the two-part frame assembled with set screws seated in the pillars is the worst fault of the Medalist, since vibrations of fishing and travel and casting seem to work them slowly loose. Lost screws can cause the frame to rack and bind the spool, and I have had Medalist reels freeze with big rainbows in South America. However, the fisherman who prefers a serviceable fly reel manufactured in the United States will find the Pflueger practical and moderately priced.

Perhaps the most remarkable fly reel to evolve from the Hardy Lightweight series is the recently developed Orvis CFO. Although it was conceived and designed in the United States, it is machined and assembled by the British craftsmen at Hardy Brothers. Its development came in part from some experiments by the famous Stanley Bogdan, using highly sophisticated new alloys and some of the old Hardy Lightweight components. One of his experiments with a drilled inside spool and back plate that considerably reduced the weight of the standard Hardy-type reel is displayed at the Museum of American Fly Fishing in Vermont. But working with still more sophisticated alloys led to the exciting discovery that the outer rim of the reel frame could be jettisoned entirely, along with two of the three pillars, leaving only a single T-head pillar at the bottom of the reel. Its curved head was matched with a machined rail on the reel-seat flange mount, and a precisely tooled rim on the reel spool itself provided the circumferential track for the T-head pillar and flange mount.

The click-and-drag mechanism is a symmetrically loading echo of the tongue-activated, drag-spring system originally introduced before the First World War on the Hardy Perfect, but it incorporates more sophisticated metals. Instead of the screw-tightened yoke used in the Hardy Lightweights, paired springs are symmetrically placed inside the back plate and tightened with a pair of curving metal tongues. The tongues are adjusted with a smooth cam and turning button. The drilled back plate and spool are complemented with three additional perforations in the reel-seat flange, the center hole penetrating both the flange and its mounting bar. These drill patterns achieve a marked reduction in weight, as well as providing ventilation for a wet fly line and backing. The minimal frame results in a slight increase in line capacity, and the spool can be removed and reseated without pinching the line in the reel cage.

But these functional considerations, important as they are, seem less important than the esthetic and historical qualities of these reels. It should be remembered that although the Roxburghe aluminum reels built by Hardy for salmon fishing about 1875 were a remarkable design break-through using a sophisticated new metal, the fully perforated trout reel patented by Charles F. Orvis in 1874 was equally important. It did not employ advanced metallurgy, but it did introduce the fully drilled spool and back plate to fly-fishing. After a full century has passed, the new Orvis CFO reels have updated the concept with modern aerospace alloys and superb craftsmanship.

Orvis is also a firm with a sense of history. The conceptual debt these new reels owe to old Charles F. Orvis has been acknowledged by christening them in his memory, and the Orvis CFO series of reels promises to take its place in a long and honorable tradition. These CFO reels are elegantly designed and made, and fly-fishermen everywhere have come to appreciate their character and quality.

There are presently four models in the CFO series. Its smallest size is the CFO II, indicating that Orvis may have a smaller design in mind. At a jewel-tiny two and a half inches and two ounces, this diminutive reel is the same weight as the Hardy Flyweight, although it is a half inch bigger. The CFO III is a particular favorite of mine after seven seasons of light-tackle work. It is three inches in diameter and weighs three ounces. The CFO IV weighs three and one-quarter ounces with a diameter of three and one-quarter inches, much lighter than the comparable Hardy Lightweight. The largest model in the series, the four-inch CFO V, has sufficient capacity to hold a WF10F fly line and a full 150 yards of backing. It weighs only four ounces, two full ounces under the smaller Hardy Saint Aidan. Such weight reductions result in remarkable capacity-to-weight ratios, although the larger CFO reels have demonstrated some problems in racking and binding under the strain of recovering line from a particularly strong fish. Extreme pressure can distort the ultralight alloys enough to bind the rim groove of the spool on its contact points, and both must be kept well lubricated and absolutely clean. Such care has resulted in faultless performance from the CFO reels in my collection.

There is a three-inch CFO prototype that I particularly prize, since it is one of the first produced. Leigh Perkins of Orvis sent it to me for field testing before its back plate was engraved, and it is utterly without markings. However, its workmanship and design are so striking that it needs no trademark nor identification, like any classic piece of equipment that is instantly identifiable.

Orvis CFO Series

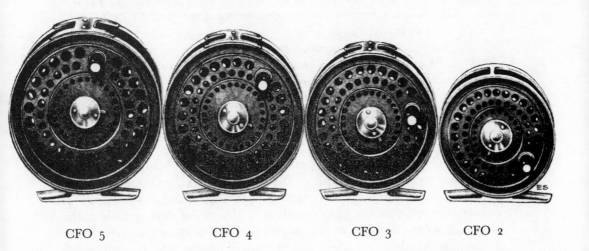

CFO 5   CFO 4   CFO 3   CFO 2

Orvis CFO 3

The best thing about that reel is its functional simplicity, I told Leigh Perkins after fishing it a few weeks. *It's exquisitely made and can speak for itself—and I hope it will not be marred with trademarks.*

The first reels are already engraved, he said.

Well, I said, *I hope the future reels are perfectly plain, like the prototype.*

Perhaps they will be, Perkins smiled.

Orvis also markets the Battenkill Ultralight reel manufactured for them by the J. S. Sharpe Company in Scotland. These little fly reels are not made from the fine aluminum found in the Hardy Lightweight series, or the ultralight alloys of the CFO reels designed at Orvis, but are still workable tools capable of yeomanlike performance. While their click systems are not quite as smooth as the Hardy mechanism, and can prove troublesome on leaders finer than a .005 calibration, their price is considerably less than the Hardy-built reels. There are three models in the Battenkill series. The Flyweight measures two and three-quarters inches and weighs slightly more than three and a half ounces. The Featherweight is a half-ounce heavier, with a diameter of three inches. The Lightweight model is three and one-quarter inches and weighs almost four and a half ounces, making it slightly less than an ounce heavier than the comparable Hardy Lightweight. The spool is perforated on both drum plates, and its inner rim is notched to hold the line during reassembly. The drag spring is activated with a cam and curved-tongue lever. Although the design and workmanship of these Battenkill Ultralight reels are not equal to the expensive British types, they are only slightly more than half their cost and offer the fisherman an alternative cost range between Pflueger and Hardy.

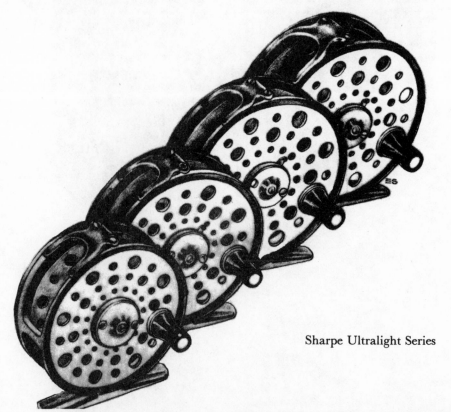

Sharpe Ultralight Series

The Morritt reels are also made in England and are quite popular there because of their reputation for durability at a moderate price. The Intrepid Rimfly series includes the Lightweight at three and three-eighths inches and four and three-eighths ounces, the Regular at three and a half inches and five and one-quarter ounces, and the King that measures three and five-eighths inches and weighs a full six ounces. Both cage and drum are made from aluminum alloys, with an exposed flange for exerting drag with the palm. There is no adjustable drag system. Morritt reels are sold through the Gladding Corporation in the United States.

The Sharpe's reels include the Cobra series, with models of three and one-quarter inches and six ounces, and three and a half inches and six and three-quarters ounces. The famous J. W. Young reels include the Beaulite model, which is made of ultralight magnesium alloys in a three-and-a-half-inch trout reel. It features an exposed rim for manual drag, a plated line guard, and adjustable tension. The Speedex is similarly fitted, but provides a geared multiplying system with an approximate two-to-one ratio. It is three and a half inches in diameter and weighs only five and a half ounces. Both are narrow frame trout reels with moderate capacity.

However, there are other reel builders who produce work of such quality that price is virtually no object. Their work is almost totally hand crafted, and in a time when there are few surviving artisans, there is still a small circle of dedicated fly-reel men.

The late Joe Brooks used to like the smaller Fin-Nor reels for fishing trout where a strong drag system was needed, although these reels were originally developed for fishing bonefish and tarpon on the salt-water flats

J. W. Young Speedex Reel

Tycoon Fin-Nor Reels

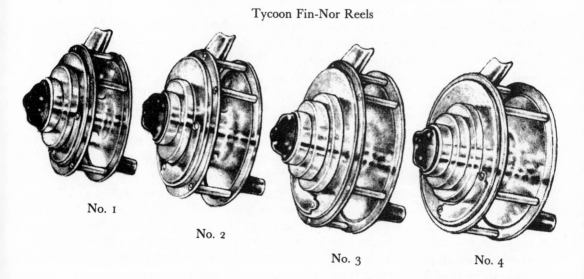

No. 1

No. 2

No. 3

No. 4

off Florida. The spool and back plate are machined from a solid dowel of costly high-density aluminum alloy and anodized to reduce corrosion. The drag system is set with a strong tightening knob and will deliver fourteen pounds of nonoscillating tension. The Fin-Nor One will hold a six-weight line with more than one hundred yards of twenty-pound backing, and it weighs about ten ounces. The Fin-Nor Two will carry a full WF9F fly line with almost two hundred yards of twenty-pound backing, and although it weighs slightly more than twelve ounces, it sometimes is found on big trout streams. The Fin-Nor Three is almost too much reel for trout. It has sufficient capacity for a ten-weight salt-water taper with almost 250 yards of twenty-pound backing filling out the spool. It weighs a full sixteen ounces, and like the Fin-Nor Two, it is available with an antireverse mechanism that protects a fisherman from a spinning handle when a trophy fish makes a wild run. Each of these reels has a full-circle-disc drag system that adjusts quickly from a delicate setting to tension stern enough to handle a sailfish or marlin. It is firm and will not fade. However, the Fin-Nor reels have a relatively delicate center spindle, anchored deep in the back-plate structure, and rough treatment can jar it out of alignment. When the spindle is not perfectly centered, the drum can bind against the frame of the reel cage. Although the Fin-Nor reels are expensive, their quality is exceptional, and an angler will have no problems with fading or erratic drag nor a spinning reel spool that will seize or bind.

Stanley Bogdan is justly famous for the quality of his trout and salmon reels, and their workmanship and design are excellent. Like the Fin-Nor, the Bogdan is machined from solid high-density aluminum stock. Both the reel frame and the spool are perfectly fitted, with no cross-frame pillars to work loose. Although I prefer more traditional German silver or aluminum fittings, the gold-anodized finish of the Bogdan reel is extremely effective against corrosion. Unlike the other fly reels, the Bogdan design has a multiplying gear system that delivers a two-to-one ratio. The drag employs a double brake-shoe system with seven settings, ranging from a tension barely stronger than the click mechanism to a full fifteen pounds. The click can be either audible or silent. Both left- and right-hand models are available. The end plates are hard rubber, returning to the traditional configuration that started with the flawless nineteenth-century work of Conroy and Vom Hofe.

The Bogdan reels are made in three sizes. The trout reel measures three and one-quarter inches in diameter and weighs eleven ounces, since lightweight design was not a requirement. It will hold a full eight-weight line with 250 yards of twenty-pound backing. The salmon model is three and three-quarters inches in diameter and weighs thirteen ounces, with a capacity of 250 yards behind a nine-weight forward taper. The salt-water reel is even larger. It has a slightly wider spool in the same three-and-three-quarters-inch diameter and weighs fourteen ounces. Its drum can accommodate a ten-weight salt-water taper with almost 300 yards of twenty-pound Dacron filling out the spool. Although these reels have a relatively heavy weight-to-capacity ratio, their flawless performance on really big fish and big water make them useful for heavy work. Cost was also no object when Stanley Bogdan worked out his reel designs, and the Bogdan series is even more expensive than the Fin-Nors. His experiments with sophisticated new alloys, which played a role in the evolution of the CFO reels for Orvis, have led Bogdan to add fully perforated side plates and spools to his trout-size reels—materially reducing weight and improving their performance for trout fishing.

Bogdan Reels

Although the Bogdan reel is clearly derived from the traditional Conroy, Vom Hofe, and Zwarg designs, with their solid frames and hard rubber end plates and counterweighted handles, the character and workmanship of those early masterpieces still lives virtually without modification in the matchless Walker series.

The Walker firm has been making exquisite reels on the Vom Hofe patterns since 1942, although modern materials have led to many internal modifications and refinements. The prototype reels designed by Conroy and Vom Hofe almost a century ago had simple click systems, employing a two-way dog, tension spring, and ratchet. Walker manufactured its reels with these same components until about 1959, when they began exploring other directions, hoping to evolve a fresh design that might trigger a renaissance in high-performance trout reels—reels of a quality they believe died with Edward Vom Hofe and the nineteenth-century patents worked out in his shop.

These old Vom Hofe trout reels were marvelous, Arch Walker gestures and rolls his eyes for emphasis. *They still function well in spite of the hairline cracks in their rubber end plates—like aristocratic ladies just starting to look their age!*

Their experiments in the past fifteen years have led the Walkers to conclude that a major problem with the old Vom Hofe patents lay in our modern trends toward light tackle on large, free-wheeling fish. Handling a six-pound rainbow in heavy water placed demands for high-speed running on reels that were originally designed for eastern brook-trout fishing. Such problems soon led to highly sophisticated alloys and steels in the drag system, spool, and frame and to a unique compound ratchet that separates the functions of running and retrieving.

The most recent Walker reels are based upon completely fresh patents granted in 1972 and employ the high-speed compound ratchet. The trout reels are supplied without an adjustable brake system, having a click only firm enough to prevent overrun and subtle enough to cushion a .005 nylon tippet. Current experiments are playing with a system delicate enough to surrender line with only a .003 point smoothly, for extreme light-tackle work with a reel as solidly built as the Walker. Such performance is beyond the fine leader capabilities of the Bogdan and Fin-Nor reels, and the Conroy and Vom Hofe prototypes as well. Medium-size Walker reels, lying between the trout and heavy-duty sizes, are fitted with a superb self-lubricating drag. It is adjustable and will not fade. These trout- and medium-size reels have performed well in my fishing, handling trout and Atlantic salmon and bonefish much larger than their performance specifications intended. Sturdily made, these reels could easily handle these larger fish, except for the obvious ceiling imposed by their line capacity. Two considerations were paramount in the modern Walker trout reels: optimal performance in high-speed running and longevity in reels that are literally intended to outlive their owners.

The heavy-duty Walker reels are like the classic Rolls Royce and look exactly like the old Vom Hofe patterns, although their internal specifications and components have been radically improved. The new waterproof drag can be adjusted to handle anything that swims, and it can be set so tightly that a sudden lunge from a big billfish could strip the guides from a rod like popcorn. Weight is not one of the performance criteria, and these big Walkers are not exactly lightweights.

How solid are they? Arnold Gingrich posed a rhetorical question over lunch in Manhattan. *Would you believe a silver-plated bulldozer?*

These reels are too heavy for trout fishing. Both single- and multiplying-action models are available. There are six types holding from 200 to 1,200 yards of thirty-pound Dacron backing, to satisfy anything from a bonefish flat in the Bahamas to the gargantuan billfish that come to the surface and feed on the calm mornings off the coast of Ecuador and Baja California and Panama. The salmon modifications have spools turned from solid barstock of high-density aluminum alloys, but the salt-water models feature spools of gleaming stainless steel, capable of backing-line pressures of 45,000 to 56,000 pounds per square inch. The edges of the hard rubber end plates on the salmon and salt-water models are encased in rings of delicate German silver, in exacting homage to the traditions started by Julius Vom Hofe in 1875.

The new series of exquisite Walker trout reels also continues firmly in the Vom Hofe traditions, although it has abandoned German silver for brightwork and spools of sophisticated new aluminum alloys. The result of these changes is a remarkable reduction in weight.

These reels are fully machined from solid high-density stock, completely without stamping or casting or synthetic components. Such attention to quality makes the Walker trout reel unique. The spindle is fashioned of corrosion-resistant steel, revolving in bronze bearings machined to tolerances as fine as .0002 inch. The reels are sold with a five-year warranty, and their appearance honors their Vom Hofe ancestry right down to the counterweighted, balance-type handle. Experience in servicing reels built by Conroy and Vom Hofe and Zwarg has led the Walkers to continue using their classic end plates of hard rubber.

Their hard-rubber fittings are still perfect after fifty years of fishing, Arthur Walker explains, his eyes twinkling behind his silver-rimmed glasses, *and we like them. Need a better reason?*

The Walker series of trout reels begins with the exquisite TR-1, which is the Midge at two and a half inches in diameter and weighing only three and three-quarters ounces. Such light weight is unusual in such a solidly made reel, and is possible only because of high-performance aluminum. It is intended for matching with superb fly rods under two ounces, and will hold 100 yards of ten-pound dacron behind a three-weight double taper. Like the other three trout-size reels, the Midge has a spool diameter of fifteen-sixteenths of an inch, and is adjusted to fish .005 tippets. Walker will modify its internal design to accommodate tippets as fine as .003 nylon, and unlike most fishing equipment, the smallest reel is the most expensive.

The TR-2 is the light trout model in the Walker series. It measures two and three-quarters inches in diameter and weighs slightly more than four and three-quarters ounces, and is intended for two- to three-ounce rods. Its capacity is a four-weight double taper ahead of 150 yards of ten-pound Dacron, although if large fish are a possibility, backing of heavier diameter is more practical to prevent biting and binding with a strong run.

The Walker TR-3 is the standard trout reel in the line. It has a full three-inch diameter and weighs just over five ounces. It is intended for fly rods of three to three and three-quarters ounces, and will hold almost 200 yards of ten-pound backing behind a four- or five-weight line. My own TR-3 reels are fitted with twenty-pound backing, although the Walker specifications are for light-tackle trout. The heavier backing was used to fish big rainbows on the Caleufu and Malleo in Argentina, where a good day can total twenty or thirty cartwheeling fish over twenty inches. Field-testing one of the first TR-3 prototypes on these strong rainbows caused some modifications of the click system, although it is unthinkable that normal trout fishing could give a reel that kind of beating. However, the Walker family is utterly dedicated to excellence, and they insisted on improving the unimprovable. The modified TR-3 was given the acid test on the Grimsá in Iceland, fishing it on fresh-run Atlantic salmon in spite of the limited backing possible with a twenty-pound test. It has since taken almost one hundred salmon between six and twenty-eight pounds, including eleven fish between six and eighteen pounds in a single morning, although its performance criteria were clearly never intended to accommodate the stresses of such fishing.

Well, Arch Walker beamed with pleasure, *you can kill an elephant with a little rifle—but a little muscle is wiser!*

The Walker TR-4 is the heavy-trout model. It has the identical precision click system with a setting designed to fish a .005 tippet, and finer settings can be specified. The TR-4 measures three and one-quarter inches in diameter and weighs just a fraction under six ounces. It works beautifully with rods weighing four to five ounces, and holds a five- or six-weight line

Walker Trout Reels

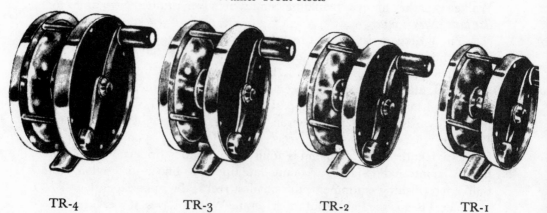

TR-4   TR-3   TR-2   TR-1

with almost 250 yards of ten-pound Dacron backing. Its capacity of twenty-pound backing makes it a workable reel for most trout fishing, although it still has a smooth click system set fine enough for 6X points. Its proportions are also visually attuned to the proportions of trout-rod grips and reel seats, while the smaller Walker reels look a little undersized with most fly rods.

The medium-size Walker reels with their adjustable brake systems and larger diameters have just become available. Several experimental ratchet and drag mechanisms are still being field-tested at this writing. These reels still feature a click system fine enough to fish .005 nylon with the drag disengaged, and are available in three models from three and one-eighth inches to three and five-eighths inches in diameter. They are designed to balance rods from four to six ounces, and lines from six- to eight-weight tapers, with enough backing for big sea-run rainbows on the Pacific Coast.

Walker fly reels are superbly conceived and made, worthy heirs to a virtually unbroken tradition in American craftsmanship and angling. It is often argued that lighter reels are more attuned to contemporary fishing, with its growing emphasis on light tippets and selective fish, and that a reel like the Walker is too well made for trout-fishing performance. The Walker family would probably agree with these arguments, except that they are artisans rather than mere craftsmen, passionately opposed to the slightest compromise in workmanship or quality. Their reels are dedicated to the proposition that precision and costly materials are essential in the full achievement of their art, and that price is secondary once the goal of absolute quality has been established. The firm continues to experiment with new patents and materials and models. It was Arnold Gingrich who described the Walker firm perfectly, and his recent book *The Joys of Trout* contains the following observations:

> The Walkers are clearly to reels as the late Jim Payne was to rods—sworn enemies of any least semblance of compromise, and passionate adherents to a standard of craftsmanship that in the old Vom Hofe days might have been taken for granted, but in this slapdash age seems downright eccentric, not to say fanatical.

It was also Arnold Gingrich, in his pleasurable book *The Well-Tempered Angler*, who observed that reels with a silent click system were certainly no improvement, and that only a poacher could find virtue in a reel that made no sound. Gingrich also noted that a temperament that could appreciate the matchless finish of fine violins or the whine of a superbly tuned Alfa Romeo would also find beauty in the shrilly protesting music of a fine fly reel. But that music has a practical side, too, which only experience in playing big fish can reveal: its tonality is another tool in knowing just what a strong fish is doing, and how quickly it is doing it. Such complex sensory clues are critical in trout fishing, but ultimately it is the complete poetry of a fine fly reel that really matters.

Several years ago I was fishing the Brodheads in Pennsylvania with Colin Pittendrigh. It was an April morning with a cool west wind, and weak sunlight between minor showers. The fish were surprisingly selective quite early in the season, and a good hatch of tiny *Paraleptophlebia* duns was coming down the current. There were some excellent fish working quietly, and when we coaxed them into taking, they often bolted and ran well down the shallow flat.

Our tippets were delicate, and we allowed the better fish to take line freely, enjoying the fragile melody of our reels. Pittendrigh was working over a particularly selective fish, and I waded out to give him a special little blue-winged dry fly dressed with a slender body of rust-colored quill. It worked on the second float along the alders, and the fish bolted along the shallows, stripping line melodically from the delicate reel.

Lovely! Pittendrigh sighed happily. *Isn't that reel making one of the sweetest sounds in the world?*

You're right, I replied.

For recent developments in fly reels, see Appendix: Notes on New Equipment.

Appendix:
Notes on New Equipment

S ince our first typesetting, which began in 1973, and proofreading
of the last galley sheets two years later, many changes and new
products have evolved throughout the fishing-tackle industry.
These notes on new equipment are intended to supplement the
chapters in the first edition of *Trout*, bringing the reader up to date.

Some Notes on the Modern Fly Line

Several developments have occurred in both the design and manufacture of lines, and some of these developments are quite important.

Our linemakers, particularly Scientific Anglers and Cortland, continue to experiment with tapers, densities, synthetic finishes, and hybrid
designs that combine sinking tips and full weight-forward bellies with half
bellies and running lines designed to float.

The improvements are excellent.

Anglers now have several sink-rate options in their bag of tricks,
including line densities that sink deeper and more quickly.

Floating-and-sinking hybrids are a remarkable development. Although I seldom fish sinking-tip lines, because their disparate finish
densities tend to hinge in casting, diminishing both delicacy and control to
some degree, they are useful in situations where subtlety and precision are
not critical. I tend to prefer weight-forward hybrids designed to sink the
entire shooting belly, with a light running line designed to float. The result
is startling. Long casts are often repetitive, particularly on big riffles and
pools, and older running lines sank quickly during a fly swing or retrieve.

Combining a full-sinking belly with a running line that floats is much better; it makes a long cast easier, stripping the running line from the surface with less energy than is needed to lift it through the water from the bottom, where it has often drifted around your ankles.

Modified line tapers also facilitate easier casting and greater distances with less effort. Although several anglers familiar with a wide range of manufacturers (including this writer some fifteen years ago) have speculated about longer shooting heads and weight-forward bellies, it was Lee Wulff who introduced a true long-belly design at Garcia. Better rod design and improved casting techniques have made it possible to keep greater amounts of line aloft in false casting; that means more line length and weight in the air; and more weight times line speed equals more distance: It is simple physics, if you have the casting skills to false-cast a longer line.

Line finishes are evolving too.

Some manufacturers have offered lines with oily finishes that are hard and lumpy. The theory holds that a smooth line continuously in contact with the rod guides while casting is subject to more friction. Such lumpy finishes hopscotch through less smoothly but experience less friction and shoot better. British makers first developed such lines.

Other makers are exploring line finishes that offer oily-smooth casting and a polyvinyl chemistry that repels water, riding still higher in the surface film. The floating qualities of such lines are obvious. Since they float higher, with less diameter in contact with the water, these lines mend deftly, pick up more easily at greater distances, and are less visible. Many experts find they shoot better.

Strike indicators and lead-core are recent concepts.

Cortland has introduced a full series of color-tip lines intended for nymph fishing. The concept seemingly originated with Dave Whitlock and his experiments with dead-drift nymph tactics on his Ozark rivers. Several years ago, Whitlock sent me a hand-built shooting head, with a hot orange strike indicator and a running line attached. It was a prototype worth studying.

However, the Cortland design added a buoyant bulb tip to their standard 444 floating line. Its bulb is a brightly intense orange. It is readily visible and, like the red-and-white bobbers of boyhood, it is used to detect a subtle nymphing take when it stops almost imperceptibly in the currents. It has proved popular on many waters, although its fat indicator bulb drops a little harshly for the shy fish of our spring creeks.

Both Sunset and Cortland have explored the potential of lead-core shooting heads. Pacific Coast fishermen have been experimenting with relatively primitive lead-core heads for more than fifteen years. Such homemade gear first evolved from saltwater tactics, fishing deep for striped bass and yellowtails, and was quickly adopted by the inventive chinook fishermen on salmon rivers like the Smith and Chetco.

These pioneers built their lead-core heads from ordinary lead-core trolling line, cutting off lengths and weighing them to match line-weight specifications.

Splicing the lead-core heads to light running lines, the California anglers used them to fish in extremely deep pools and tidal rips. Such tackle also worked on river tarpon in Costa Rica, and it worked so well in the bridge tides at Islamorada that it was banned from Gold Cup competition. Such lead-core designs cast and fished rather clumsily, requiring a hard double-haul stroke and a swift head-bobbing evasion.

Better duck! Hal Janssen explained during my baptism on big chinooks. *Tuck your head under your wing when you start it forward—or you could be guilty of your own mugging!*

The lead-core trolling line was thin and relatively rough. It almost clattered through the air and landed like a javelin. Both Cortland and Sunset set out to build lead-core shooting heads with polyvinyl chloride coatings. The prototypes looked and cast almost like big fly lines. We tried them first at several fishing expositions, and later I used a prototype in the deep brook-trout lagoons of the Argentine lakes with good results.

There are a surprising number of new line-density designs.

Cortland has added several to its line. Its peach-colored 444 is highly regarded among skilled dry-fly anglers everywhere, particularly in Europe. It offers a uniquely supple finish over a tubular, braided core, with a chemistry intended to protect its integrity under exposure to solar denigration and keep its smooth-casting qualities in cold weather. Taper specifications are at the heart of Cortland 444 quality, and hand inspection is part of its secret.

Cortland has also changed its old 333 series of lines, employing a coating formula to create the 333 HT floating lines. The 333 HT line is white, and its high-technology finish makes it a superb choice in the medium-priced range.

The 444 sinking lines now come in several variations for different fishing conditions. Both ten- and twenty-foot sinking tips are made. Thirty-foot sinking heads, and full-sinking lines are available in fast- and super-fast-sink densities. Super-sink shooting heads and lead-core heads complete the list, with a new .031 running line that floats high.

What will we call our lead-core head? Leon Chandler told me with a quiet smile in San Francisco. *Kerboom!*

The Cortland 444 intermediate lines are a new product introduced in 1983. They float awash if cleaned and dressed, but their specific gravity of 1.06 is slightly heavier than water, sinking them quite slowly for shallowly fished flies and nymphs. The lines are pale ice-blue.

Cortland has also introduced its new 444 SL floating lines recently. 444 SL lines have a specifically formulated coating that makes them relatively stiff. The stiffness is intended to reduce line sag between rod guides. The oily finish and stiffness make a 444 SL shoot effortlessly. These lines are a bright green, and come in a full range of tapers, although only the classic 444 is made in a three-weight.

The Wulff long-belly concept has recently been refined in the Rodon Borkast lines. Their specifications were designed to match the remarkable tip-speed performance of modern carbon-fiber and boron fly rods. Past tapers were first worked out in the nineteenth century, with bamboo and silkworm-gut leaders and lines of braided silk.

It was time to change, Ron Bensley explained at his plant outside New York. *Everything else had already changed.*

Graphite and boron accelerate so sharply into the casting stroke that a standard thirty-foot belly, with its light running line, was overpowered in flight. It worked with a choppy flutter. Line flutter kills both accuracy and distance, and it delivers a fly too hard. Short distances often resulted in sloppy, too open loops, and a strong distance stroke could collapse the loop into a tangle. Both graphite and boron are capable of sharp roll-casting delivery, but standard weight-forward tapers execute a roll cast poorly. The Borkast tapers were designed to solve these problems, and equal the potential of our modern rods.

Double-taper lines can roll-cast beautifully, and handle short- to medium-range problems. Our standard weight-forward tapers fluttered badly at long distance, and fished clumsily.

Ted Simroe is responsible for the graphite and boron rods at Rodon. *Line modification wasn't enough,* he explained on a trip to the Avco Boron Laboratories in Massachusetts. *We're starting out fresh.*

His first step was to change the front tapers. Such designs were still echoing silk prototypes from the nineteenth century. The forward level section was eliminated, and Simroe shortened the standard front-taper specifications. The result was a tighter loop and clean power transfer to the leader. His next decision lengthened the forward-taper belly to more than thirty feet, and extended its rear taper to eighteen feet. His new taper totalled fifty-two feet, *before* the light running line started.

It's working beautifully! Simroe said.

The new weight-forward designs were complemented with a smooth, oily finish conceived to float. The first Borkast lines were light gray, and their popularity led Rodon to expand its series.

Sink-tip and extra-fast sinking models were quickly added. These lines were slate colored. Long-haul shooting heads followed, responding to the remarkable capacity of our synthetic rod fibers, which can carry as much as fifty feet of shooting head easily. Both floating and extra-fast sinking heads are now available. Simroe also designed a buoyant running line for his floating and sinking tapers, with .030 and .035 diameters.

Lee Wulff continues to experiment with line specifications, after seventy-odd years of fishing. His early long-belly designs have been further refined in his new Triangle tapers. Like the Rodon designs, and his earlier Garcia lines, the weight-forward belly is considerably lengthened in the new Wulff concept.

We're excited about it, Wulff told me recently at dinner in New York. *Give them a try!*

His four- and five-weight tapers start at .030 and increase continuously to .055 inches. The medium six- and seven-weight specifications start tapering at .032, progressively increasing to measure .060 inches at forty feet. The diameter drops sharply to the .032 running line, which completes the full ninety-foot design.

It's designed for trout fishing, Wulff explains, *and it's perfect for such problems.*

The unbroken Triangle taper steadily transmits casting power from its .055 and .060 butts into the leader. It places its finest diameters near the fish, keeping its heaviest belly weight well back. The constant taper roll casts excellently. With the entire forty-foot belly outside the rod, like the overhang of a shooting head, the Triangle taper outperforms a conventional weight-forward line.

It is a promising concept.

The oily, rough-finish specifications first worked out in the United Kingdom are being explored further at Sunset and Berkeley.

Such lines feel almost brittle when new, and require several days of fishing before they cast smoothly. Modern tapers are combined with a supple self-lubricating finish. The relatively lumpy, polyvinyl coating is a surprising concept designed to bounce through the guides, reducing line friction. Stiffness mitigates against line slap between the guides, which further reduces line velocity and distance. Such oil-impregnated coatings are combined with a microscopic roughness that seems to steeplechase through the guides, and experience confirms the theory.

Sunset has started manufacturing such lines as its Ultimate Formula series, and they are finished in a medium Oxford gray. Berkeley Specialist lines are pale yellow, offering similar technology with the visual character of earlier British silk.

Scientific Anglers first developed our modern polyvinyl chloride lines, and the firm continues its history of leadership.

It offers almost two hundred choices of line weights and tapers today, and more than a hundred in its floating-line models alone. It continues its Aircel and Aircel Supreme floating lines, and it has expanded the famous Wetcel series. Its Wetcel I has a sink rate of 1.75 to 2.50 inches per second, and parallels its designs for the first sinking lines at mid-century. Wetcel II offers a sink rate between 2.00 and 3.00 inches per second, and the Wetcel HI-D performs between 3.25 and 4.25 inches per second. The Hi-Speed HI-D sinks like an anchor at 3.75 to 6.50 inches per second. The Wetcel I and Wetcel II are available in double-taper, weight-forward, and shooting-head designs. The HI-D and Hi-Speed HI-D are manufactured only in weight-forward and shooting tapers.

Scientific also offers a full series of sink-tip lines with sink rates matching the performance of its Wetcel I and Wetcel II densities. Its Wet Belly HI-D has a full twenty feet of sinking line rated at 3.25 to 4.25 inches per second. Its Wet Head HI-D offers the same sink-rate density, with its entire thirty-foot shooting belly designed to sink. Like its other sink-tip designs, the running line is designed to float, while the tips and bellies sink at controlled rates.

The Scientific inventory also has lines in weight-forward tapers with sink rates between 1.25 to 1.75 inches per second. Its Deep Water Express series includes three shooting tapers with sink rates between 7.00 and 10.00 inches per second, which make bottom fish in high lakes, reservoirs, and unusually deep channels catchable.

But its new Ultra series of floating and sink-tip lines is the result of continuing research and development, and its marriage to a larger corporation, with a broad spectrum of technology in other fields.

Ultra series lines still use the patented microsphere process to control the specific gravity necessary in a floating line, but have combined that technology with a new chemical formulation that repels the surface film. The line sits so high on the meniscus that less line diameter is actually in contact with the water, unlike earlier floating lines, which ride slightly awash. Such performance means easier and longer pickups, easier mending during fly swing and drift, and better line control. The total chemistry of these lines also includes better durability and shooting qualities. The finish steadily oils itself from its unique internal compounds, and its mix includes the ability to resist ultraviolet radiation, the principal cause of fading and finish cracking in modern lines.

Quick popularity is testimony that Ultra lines are a step forward in line technology. Some experts have called them a breakthrough that parallels the polyvinylchloride lines themselves, with their weight-controlling admixtures of microspheres.

These lines are remarkable evidence of the peripheral impacts of recent technology. Modern fishermen have a mind-boggling palette of lines and line-performance specifications that would have dazed a generation limited to a single type—the floating double-taper design of British silk, which required drying each night on a teakwood rack and a fresh dressing of red-stag fat each morning.

PROBLEMS IN LEADERS, KNOTS, AND BACKING

Since the completion of this chapter, several important developments have taken place in both leader material and backing. Perhaps the most remarkable evolution has occurred in polyamide tippet material and knotless tapers. Such nylons share superb breaking-strain performance with surprising limpness and knot-resisting qualities, although their knotting qualities make them somewhat different from earlier leader materials, and their suppleness poses both advantages and problems.

Cortland has introduced its flat Cobra monofilament and its pale Micron as backing material. Cobra is a highly effective line behind big-water shooting heads, and is available in breaking strains of fifteen, twenty, and thirty pounds. Micron displays very little stretching under tension and comes in twelve, twenty, and thirty pounds. Gudesbrod Dacron is similar, although it is slightly larger in diameter for comparable breaking-strain performance. Although its diameter will mean less capacity on a given reel, its available spools, in fifteen, twenty, and thirty pounds, are less likely to bite and bind into the backing when a big trout bolts suddenly.

Sunset recently introduced its Amnesia-type monofilament for its shooting-head running lines. Amnesia is available in two-hundred-yard spools, and in breaking strengths of fifteen, twenty, twenty-five, thirty, and forty pounds. It stretches less than other nylons and is relatively memory-free, having less tendency to tangle and coil.

My first experience with the new polyamide tippet materials came with Racine Tortue in the Yellowstone country and Racine Water Queen on the Henry's Fork of the Snake. Both materials displayed similar knotting and fishing qualities, and virtually identical breaking strains in the same diameters. Water Queen appears slightly more limp, and offers the following specifications:

SIZE	TIPPET DIAMETER (INCHES)	BREAKING STRAIN (POUNDS)
8X	.003	1.2
7X	.004	1.9
6X	.005	2.4
5X	.006	3.3
4X	.007	3.7
3X	.008	4.2
2X	.009	5.1
1X	.010	6.2
0X	.011	8.4

Pezon & Michel soon introduced Kroic, which is a favorite tippet material of my good friend Jack Hemingway. His experience with Kroic at Sun Valley leads Hemingway to extol its knotting, casting, and fishing properties. Pezon & Michel markets its new tippet material in the following specifications and spools:

SIZE	TIPPET DIAMETER (INCHES)	BREAKING STRAIN (POUNDS)
8X	.003	1.1
7X	.004	1.4
6X	.005	1.8
5X	.006	2.2
4X	.007	3.0
3X	.008	4.0
2X	.009	5.0
1X	.010	6.0
0X	.011	7.0

Cortland found its supple Nylorfi was a remarkable advance in breaking-strain performance. Its knotting properties were so striking that casting knots scarcely reduced its strength, although its slippery finish and limpness made blood knots critical, and fly knots demanded both discipline and care. Some skilled fishermen have seemingly found it slightly brittle in cold weather, but several of the new nylons display similar symptoms. Nylorfi has developed some fierce partisans since its introduction, and is available as follows:

SIZE	TIPPET DIAMETER (INCHES)	BREAKING STRAIN (POUNDS)
8X	.003	1.3
7X	.004	1.7
6X	.005	2.4
5X	.006	4.0
4X	.007	4.8
3X	.008	6.0
2X	.009	8.0
1X	.010	8.5
0X	.011	10.2

André Puyans has developed perhaps the strongest polyamide nylon yet introduced to fly-fishing. His remarkable Creative Sports Enterprises material is quite limp, has superb knotting performance, and offers the demanding angler unique breaking-strain properties. Its limpness and stretch mean that its fine diameters must be constantly replaced after casting and playing fish. It is spooled and sold as follows:

SIZE	TIPPET DIAMETER (INCHES)	BREAKING STRAIN (POUNDS)
8X	.003	2.0
7X	.004	3.0
6X	.005	4.0
5X	.006	5.0
4X	.007	6.0
3X	.008	7.0
2X	.009	8.0
1X	.010	9.0
0X	.011	10.0

Several factors should be kept in mind when using these new polyamide nylons. Their tensile strength and knotting properties can cause some problems when combined with other types of nylon, and their limpness and supple finishes presage knotting complications, too. When joining a series of supple tippets to older middle- and butt-section materials, or adding a single tippet of the new nylons to a conventional leader, it has proved wise to make this hybrid connection of same-diameter line. The result is a more secure knot and the elimination of a hinging knot which can diminish the smooth progression of casting energy from the line to the fly. It is possible to test a leader without casting it, simply by holding it a few inches on either side of the critical blood knot and bending the leader through the knot. The power transfer will prove optimal if the knot lies in a smooth curve from tippet to tippet; but if there is a sharp parabola formed with the knot at its apex, there is too abrupt a change in either diameter or relative suppleness from material to material.

It is also critical to remember that the combination of suppleness and strength in these new nylons can mean that your present knotting techniques do not deliver enough internal friction to hold. It may prove necessary to experiment with more turns in your knots to achieve adequate strength and performance. Symmetry in your blood knots is also more critical in the ultrafine diameters now available. It is important to count the exact number of turns in each part of any symmetrical knot to insure proper friction and knotting properties. Other significant factors include tightening your knots slowly and wetting the partially formed knots with saliva to avoid thermal stress buildup, which could damage the molecular integrity of the nylon. Long periods of casting or playing large fish can expend the elasticity of fine nylon. Serious tangling and coiling can occur then, and the nylon can lose too much stiffness to deliver even tiny flies. Breaking strain is also radically diminished when the stretch factor is reduced, so such tippets should be replaced more often than conventional nylons to insure dependable strength in fine diameters.

Since Puyans first introduced his remarkably strong polyamide nylon leader material under the Creative Sports label, similar products have evolved in Japan.

Aeon is a worthy competitor. Some experts feel that its slightly lower breaking-strain ratings are less important than its other superb qualities, and Aeon is still twice as strong as earlier American nylon in its critical diameters under 4X.

Its supporters point to excellent knotting properties, a controlled limpness that cushions stress and still turns over well, less stretch than some polyamide material, and rigorously accurate calibrations. It also has surprisingly little memory, a doubtful quality shared by many synthetic materials, in which a leader stubbornly remains in its packaging coils. Aeon uncoils with remarkable straightness, and mere hand friction is sufficient to straighten its coils in fishing. The following specifications obtain:

SIZE	TIPPET DIAMETER (INCHES)	BREAKING STRAIN (POUNDS)
8X	.003	1
7X	.004	2
6X	.005	3
5X	.006	4
4X	.007	5
3X	.008	6
2X	.009	7
1X	.010	9
0X	.011	11

Since writing the early chapters of *Trout* more than ten to fifteen years ago, I have had extensive experience with these polyamide materials on large fish, particularly on the Henry's Fork of the Snake.

Its lessons have been important.

The leader specifications and tapers found in *Trout* remain quite useful, but big selective fish are a demanding yardstick. The tapers found in the two pages of diagrams on leader design are sound. The Smutting Tapers and Light Nymphing Tapers have proved themselves, along with the Standard Tapers to 5X and 6X, but I would add a critical footnote to their design today: The tippets might be lengthened to a full thirty-six inches in 7X and 8X diameters, and extended a full forty to forty-eight inches in 6X and 5X points.

This footnote is quite useful. Such long tippets demand good casting, but they are not intended to straighten out cleanly on the current. Their loose coils are part of a subtle difficult-fish strategy. The slack creates a longer float that is drag-free over a selective trout. The limp character of polyamide nylon contributes too, and its limp stretchiness is like a delicate shock tippet. Even cobwebs stretch long before they break, and there is sufficient elasticity in a thirty-six- to forty-eight-inch tippet that it provides a safety factor on big fish. Subtleties are critical in delicate tippets.

Our forefathers would shake their heads in envy at such fine-tippet breaking strains. Modern technology has given us 6X tippets that surpass the performance of 0x silkworm gut, and there are rumors of still more surprises in nylon performance.

Plus a final caveat for fishing the 7X and 8X diameters: Cut the tippet off and replace it after taking a fish, just as you should reknot the fly with salmon or steelhead, when you are fishing such cobwebs.

Such disciplines pay.

RANDOM THOUGHTS ON WADERS, CLOTHING, AND
OTHER EQUIPMENT

The past three years have also seen considerable evolution in wading gear, clothing, and fly-fishing accessories. Wader designs have been introduced and subsequently discarded by several manufacturers, principally because their hybrid construction of exotic fabrics and adhesives failed to perform as anticipated. Such failure seems related to poor quality control and workmanship as much as to hybrid laminates of excellent materials that did not work together properly.

Marathon experienced some difficulties with its waders in the past five years, and the company has continued to improve its products. Its current boot-foot designs include both insulated and conventional models with a choice of felt or cleated rubber soles. Marathon has also introduced an improved nylon-and-rubber stocking-foot wader for use with separate brogues. These improved designs are lighter and tougher. The lamination of industrial nylon fabric to the neoprene lining has been perfected, providing unusual puncture and abrasion resistance. Insulation is available in the boot-foot models only, and all Marathon waders have a pale olive coloring. Custom sizes are still provided on order.

Converse makes a more expensive line of boot-foot waders in both insulated and conventional types. Their construction is based upon a more typical rubber-coated, cloth-lined specification. The insulated models employ a wool-lining sandwich to capture and retain body heat. Like Marathon, Converse also manufactures a complete line of hip boots, and its best wading equipment is olive drab. Its Wadewell line offers both cleated and felt soles in a series of khaki-colored waders. Converse also imports a series of less expensive nylon waders and hip boots employing two layers of rubber-coated cloth. The Hampshire nylon waders are similar to the Converse 13955 designs, except that they are of fully insulated construction and are manufactured in cleated boot-foot models only. Converse is an old company with an established reputation.

Fritz von Schlegel has started to make nylon-laminated chest waders and hip boots with polypropylene soles. His rubberlike cloth has proved itself durable and puncture resistant. Von Schlegel and his products have attracted a surprising number of partisans.

André Puyans has been working with a well-known maker of wet suits used by divers. Waterproof nylon cloth is specified for both surfaces of a thin layer of closed-cell flexible sponge. Both the waterproof fabrics and their sponge core are capable of 360-degree stretch, and are easily repaired after a puncture. Five body sizes are available and can be matched with any foot size; custom sizes can also be provided. The spongelike layer provides both insulation and buoyancy, and these unusual new waders are rapidly gaining popularity.

Orvis, which experienced considerable trouble with its waders in recent years, has returned with a completely new line of lightweight designs. Waterproof nylon cloth layers surround a core of rubber, and both cleated feet and woven-felt soles are made. Hexagonal aluminum studs are also available on both waders and hip boots from Orvis. The company has introduced a second line of waders using nylon satin cloth laminated around a rubber shell. Leg chafe guards and seams are fully vulcanized. Steel arch shanks and semihard toes protect the feet, and rubber cleats, felt, and fully studded soles are available.

During the absence of conventional stocking-foot waders, which I prefer because of the foot-and-ankle protection provided by leather wading brogues, many anglers came to like Sealdri products. Fabricated of pure latex rubber in one-piece construction, these stocking-foot waders have no seams. The rubber is easily repaired after tears or punctures, and Sealdri waders are much less fragile than the earlier prototypes. The latex is both flexible and warm. Extra-thick Sealdri waders are available too, providing fifty percent thicker latex construction. The result is better puncture and tear resistance. Sealdri waders fold into a compact roll for travelling, making it easy to pack two pairs in a duffel bag, and I have used them happily.

Red Ball has recently offered two new lines of waders. Their Master series includes both chest-high waders and hip boots. The fabric is a supple and durable three-ply nylon and nitrile rubber, and it has proved resistant to reasonable wear, abrasion, ripping, and punctures. The boot feet are reinforced with a steel shank, a hard safety-type toe, and a cushion insole. Metal fittings are rustproof. The boots are fitted with heavy woven-nylon felt soles and heels. There is no internal inseam to chafe or leak seepage, and the knees are reinforced. Belt loops, chest pocket, and reinforced suspender buttons are standard, and Red Ball waders are dark mahogany brown.

Red Ball hippers are fabricated to the same specifications. The harness fittings are rustproof and reinforced, and there are internal holding straps to make low-position wear possible.

Red Ball also introduced its unusually light flyweight stocking-foot waders in recent years. These waders quickly became popular, although fishermen experienced some problems in the field. They were lightweight and packed tightly, but they offered little protection in cold water and winds, and some anglers found them brittle or easily torn. Red Ball has worked on its problems, and subsequently introduced its Master Flyweight ST series.

The new flyweight fabric is a full two ounces heavier now, and the ST series is even more popular. The fabric is a remarkably strong 220 denier polyurethane-coated nylon. The seams are painstakingly heat sealed. There is a built-in inflatable chamber just above the waist, and the carrying bag snaps inside to form the stomach-high pocket. The stocking feet are shaped of heavier nylon, to reduce abrasion and chafing. The suspender fittings are rustproofed and reinforced, and the entire chest-high wader weighs only fourteen ounces.

Feather River has just introduced its light stocking-foot hippers, using the same polyurethane-coated fabric as the Red Ball Flyweights. The hippers weigh only twelve ounces. They have strong, adjustable belt straps, and Velcro water cinches at the thighs. Like the Flyweight ST series, these stocking-foot hippers are dark brown.

Anglers who like these flyweight waders and Feather River hippers find they hug the legs and body closely. With less bulk and weight, wading becomes easy and sure, particularly in swift currents. Walking is less difficult, too, and climbing through fences is less clumsy. There is little protection against cold, but there is less perspiration and heat when out of the water. Both waders and hippers are so light, and fold so compactly, that they can easily be stowed in the rain-jacket pocket of a fishing vest. Fishermen are purchasing both waders and hippers to have the flexibility of a complete wading system, compact and light, using the same wading brogues.

However, such lightweight wading gear must still be combined with leg-warming clothes and socks, like the acrylic-lined Sokkets. But common sense and care are still required; if you avoid thorn trees and berry thickets and barbed wire, such lightweight fabrics will last.

The O'Neill neoprene waders first tested by André Puyans are no longer unique. Such equipment is now made by Scott and Imperial.

Scott neoprene wading gear is made in both chest- and waist-high designs. They are tough, and have almost two hundred percent elasticity to facilitate walking, sitting, and wading. The Scott waders consist of closed-cell neoprene insulation sandwiched between chocolate-colored nylon facings. The material has proved itself surprisingly snag resistant and punctureproof. Adjustable suspenders are attached, and feature quick-release buckles. The neoprene insulation keeps you both warm and cool, and there is even a special cuff attached just above the ankle. It is designed to fold down over the wading socks as a built-in gaiter, keeping out sand and pea gravel.

Imperial Polar Bear waders are slightly more expensive, offer similar rugged specifications and performance, and weigh slightly more than three pounds. They offer both buoyancy—a tight enough fit at the waist and hips to exclude water should you fall down—and comfort in both cold and warm weather. Some steelhead fishermen swear by these neoprene waders, and they fish in weather that would discourage a mindless duck hunter used to February storms.

O'Neill, Scott, and Imperial neoprene waders have developed fierce partisans, and although I dislike float-tube fishing, such wading gear is perfect for tubing lakes and reservoirs.

Ranger has attempted to manufacture hip boots and waders like the equipment common in my boyhood years. Such designs were warm, quite durable, and were often rented daily by fishing shops, season after season. Fifty years ago, our waders combined an outer layer of tough cotton tenting material with an inner layer of rubber. These layers were tightly bonded.

The new Ranger wader offers such specifications to contemporary anglers. Brass suspender fittings are resistant to corrosion. There are wide belt loops and a stomach pocket. The inner seams are reinforced with smooth chafing strips, which are also fitted into the crotch. The rubber boot feet offer hard toes and heels, steel shanks, and cushion insoles. Suspenders are not included, although the hip boots have belt loops attached. Both chest-high waders and hippers have thick felt soles of the old type, and although these cotton-fabric waders are more expensive than we remember them in the Depression years, they are quite welcome.

Two firms are offering cold-weather bib pants for wading comfort. The Polar Fleece design has zippers at both ankles and crotch, for easy access over clothing. It is made of a synthetic Celanese fiber that is washable, breathes, is relatively quick drying, and allows perspiration to evaporate. There is a rear pocket. The bib buckles are quick-release.

Mark Pile bib trousers are a little less costly than the Polar Fleece design. Their properties are well known in duck blinds and goose pits. The wicking-pile keeps you completely warm and dry, and the trousers are surprisingly light.

Last season I was fishing on Upper Tularik, on the north shore of Lake Iliamna, with André Puyans. October had turned wintry in Alaska. The chill north wind was freezing our reels and guides, but the big rainbows were still taking well.

You going to fish or freeze? Puyans laughed.

We built a fire on the brushy island in the upper lagoon, but the water was so cold it took only a few minutes before our toes ached. When they stopped aching it was time to stop fishing too, and retreat to the fire. Puyans was wearing bib trousers under his waders that afternoon, along with a pair of neoprene boot-socks, and he was the only angler who fished steadily in spite of the cold. He took several eight-pound rainbows.

Although his shop was more than 2,000 miles south at San Francisco, Puyans filled several orders for his cold-weather trousers at supper.

Scott neoprene footgear includes three designs that are perfect cold-weather equipment. Their neoprene boot-socks include a zippered ankle-length model, a calf-length model that simply pulls on, and their original neoprene boot-sock with a fold-down gaiter to keep out river gravel.

Simms makes a similar neoprene boot-sock. It is designed to cover a woolen wading sock, providing both insulation and a cover to keep out grime and aquatic weeds. Simms also makes a tight-fitting gaiter of stretch nylon, to fold down over wading brogues and keep out gravel and other aggregates. Another intriguing Simms product is called a spool tender, a thick nylon ring with a finger tab. Its fit keeps a spare reel spool from unwinding.

Stream Designs has also developed a laced spat-type gaiter that fits over brogues and wading socks. Its product is less simple to wear, but it is better at excluding river aggregates.

Although I still use English brogues, and the fine wading shoes made by Russell are also favorites, I have come to prefer the elegant brogues designed by André Puyans at Creative Sports. Reinforced toes and side leather protect the feet well, although I would prefer a thicker sole in difficult wading. The polyfelt soles provide excellent traction. Speed-lace eyelets are combined with conventional eyes. The ankles are cut a bit too low to prevent accumulation of small pebbles and fine aggregates along the Achilles tendon, but I use these handsome Puyans brogues on most trips now.

Puyans has also started to manufacture an improved brogue, partially based on my comments in the first edition of *Trout*. His more expensive designs include a higher ankle cut, cushioned with a padded roll that closes tightly when the brogues are properly laced. The cushioned roll may prove a little fragile, but it has solved the pea-gravel problem.

Other manufacturers have also started to make workable brogues for stocking-foot waders.

Weinbrenner is marketing a wading shoe designed by Gary Borger, a young fisherman who is among our best American writers. His brogues are fabricated of synthetic materials that look, feel, and perform like leather, except that they do not absorb water and will not shrink or rot. They are not stiff and impossible to pull on after drying out. Their durability has amazed the fishermen who have tried them, and they dry quickly at room temperature. Their lacing offers a good toe-to-ankle fit, with an internal ankle padding that keeps out gravel. Both toes and heels are rigidly reinforced to protect the feet. The arches are also reinforced at midsole. The soles are cut from a tough nylon-and-polyester felt. Although it is less than elegant, the Borger shoe is moderately priced and its durability is unsurpassed.

The Danner Corporation has added a lightweight wading shoe to its line of outdoor footwear. Its high-cut ankle keeps out stones, like its fully gusseted tongue. Its polyester felt sole is bonded to a neoprene cushion. Both toe caps and heels are reinforced split-grain leather backed with neoprene. Leather and neoprene enclose the ankle, and the shoe has a pattern of side drains. Its uppers are a dark brown bulletproof mesh of nylon, which makes a lightweight brogue that drains off water and dries out quickly.

The difficult wading conditions on the Umpqua in Oregon evolved the effective Korker sandals. Heavy rubber soles are laced to the brogues with parachute cord, and the soles are fully studded with twenty-five to thirty ice studs originally developed for winter tires. Korkers provide unmatched footing.

Stream Cleats are not new, having been made popular by the late Dan Bailey, but I had not actually used them until a recent trip on the Deschutes with Jock Fewel. The cleats are a simple concept. Aluminum zigzag cleating is riveted to ordinary rubber overshoes. It is a relatively cheap solution that slips on over the wading shoes. The cleats are ugly, but they work well on slippery bottom conditions.

Muncie wading grids are the Rolls-Royce of aluminum systems. Their design features an interlocking gridwork that bends to place the gridding under the ball of the foot, and just under the arch. The heel is left free, and a roller is fitted at the toes. Wire frames lock back over the toe and at each side of the shoe, and are secured by strong T-straps. Muncie grids are widely considered the best wading-grid system available.

Fishing vests continue to evolve and improve. The Stream Designs products introduced in Colorado five years ago were the result of a collaboration between Leon and Linda Sagaloff. Their fishing vests were first conceived while they were managing a tackle shop at Fort Collins, where the Cache la Poudre leaves the mountains, spilling into the High Plains.

Their first model was excellent, well designed, and superbly made. Quality and fit and first-rate fabric were obvious, although such quality is always expensive. Many experts predicted that such expensive vests were too costly, and predicted failure.

The experts were quickly proved wrong.

The original Stream Designs vests proved so popular that their makers were forced to abandon their tackle business and concentrate on fishing clothes. The first design was a full-length vest with twenty-five pockets and a waist-length cut. Its specifications included twelve fly-box pockets, thermometer and sunglasses pockets, leader spool pockets, a fly-dressing pocket, leader pouch, and a zippered rain-gear pocket and game pouch.

The Spring Creek and short deep-wading models soon followed. They offered sixteen pockets and, like the first prototype, included front snaps, zippers, rod snap holders and loop, fleece patch, forceps holster, rear-mounted net ring, and two front D-rings. The first prototypes placed the forceps holster outside the vest, but that detail was changed after I pointed out that double-haul casting often fouled slack line on the forceps when mounted there. Other changes were considered, but Stream Designs was sold to a large clothing manufacturer before those changes were fully worked out.

Quality declined quickly, but the fledgling company has been recently sold again, acquired this time by a firm justly respected for its rod fittings and boron rod designs.

We liked their vests from the start, Ron Bensley explained his plans for Stream Designs. *We're committed to making them best again—their wide-shoulder cut and concealed yoke panel were unique.*

Orvis has surpassed the conceptual excellence and quality of the Stream Designs prototypes with its Super Tac-L-Pak series. Their designs offer more pockets than a magician's tuxedo. Orvis has specified a heavy-duty poplin of thirty-five percent cotton and sixty-five percent polyester, with a 7.7-ounce rating. The waist-length standard design offers thirty-five pockets, excluding the zippered rain-gear pouch. There are six fully zippered pockets in front, plus two zippered rear pouches for extra reels and spools. There are inside holsters for sunglasses and thermometers, plus Velcro mini-pouches for tippet spools. All seams are extra stitched and bar-tack reinforced at corners and flaps, a hallmark of quality at Stream Designs too. There is a rear net ring at the neck, and oversize Velcro tabs on the smaller pockets. The Super Tac-L-Pak is excellent.

There is also a short Super Wading Tac-L-Pak in the Orvis line. It is seventeen inches long, almost four inches shorter than the standard design, but it has an incredible twenty-nine pockets. Its nine fully zippered pockets still include two rear pouches for extra reels and spools. The Super Wading model allows an angler to wade almost four inches deeper without shipping water into his sheepskin fly books and Wheatley boxes. Soggy flies and rusty hooks are troublesome.

Although these new Orvis vests are expensive, they are worth the price. Both the standard and deep-wading designs offer features still not available on other vests today.

Although the Wheatley and Hardy reel cases of yesteryear are gone, Thomas & Thomas has recently introduced a similar hard-leather design for travel protection. The reel seat sits flat in the bottom of the case, while the lid rolls and locks tightly around the frame. The handsome case, fully lined with felt, is available in three sizes. Hardy Brothers has also begun to sell its highly practical round cases, formerly provided only with Hardy reels. These cases are fabricated of heavy vinyl and open with a peripheral zipper. Sponge lining covered with acrylic velvet protects the reel from impact in shipment.

The simple landing nets designed originally by Joseph Swaluk are still produced by John Gayewski at Guyrich. The frames are made of laminated white ash, and the handles are formed around a core of select black walnut. The mesh bag is exquisitely conceived and woven, with all of the features of the original design.

Several other makers now supply wood-frame nets of simple beauty and functional design. Orvis produces a beautiful design with a cherrywood handle and frame, as well as a less expensive net fashioned of white ash and mahogany which is made in two sizes, fitted with bag depths of seventeen and nineteen inches.

French clips have dominated net connection systems for years, but an improved quick-release design is now available. Some anglers have begun to use a swivel snap with a push release, and the net is readily separated from its connection to the vest.

Since the equipment chapter was written, photosensitive lenses have created a revolution in sunglasses. These are lenses that change color from quite smoky to almost window-glass-clear in response to changing intensities of light. Such qualities make these new sunglasses quite useful at low levels of illumination in both morning and evening. Some fishermen argue that the new glasses do not darken sufficiently to compensate for extreme intensities or glare. However, I find that I suffer less eye fatigue after a day's fishing with photosensitive glasses. These glasses must be "seasoned" according to the manufacturer's instructions.

Other optical devices can prove useful. Orvis is supplying the familiar eyeglass loupe, a tiny lens which attaches to any eyeglass frame and swings into position in front of your glasses on a slender arm. The loupe provides threefold magnification, a great help in delicate work along the stream.

Unlike the conventional loupe, which must be permanently attached to your eyeglass frames, the new Optipak is a remarkably imaginative device for three-power magnification. It is a lens mounted on a ball joint, and folds into its own matchbox-size case. The case itself functions as a stand for scanning charts and diagrams, and will also clip onto eyeglass frames, fishing-hat brim, fly vise, vest pocket, or your thumb for checking insect identification or threading a tippet to a tiny dry fly. The case even includes a foldout scale in millimeters for contour maps or fly-hatch specimens. Since the lens is mounted in a strong lightweight plastic, the Optipak is available at a surprisingly low price.

Since recommending monoculars in my earlier work, I have learned from Jack Hemingway that a fine pair of binoculars is useful in fishing big water. It is possible to study a broad expanse of river for rises, or spot the soft dimples of bank feeders at considerable distances. Sometimes a fisherman can identify the hatch with binoculars. The character of rise forms can be studied. Binoculars are obviously better than a monocular, and have better light-gathering qualities in morning and evening. It is important to steady binoculars by standing in quiet currents, resting against trees or boulders, or leaning across a vehicle. Several times in recent years we have studied the far sides of streams like the upper Madison or the Henry's Fork, able to spot big bank-feeders at a hundred yards. The binoculars saved considerable time once spent hiking and wading in search of fish, particularly in glassing places like the Slow Bend in the Yellowstone.

Orvis catalogs a fogging stick designed to prevent condensation on camera and eyeglass lenses. The product is quite useful in combating the temperature changes typical of trout country.

Several years ago I discussed the white-panel aquatic collecting nets and their tendency to frighten fast-swimming nymphs and pupae. Cascade has now designed a plain mesh net with handles of hardwood dowels that neatly solves the problem. Larval forceps with flexible pincers are now available for handling insect specimens gently.

Cascade also manufactures a wallet protector of bright orange vinyl with a Velcro closure. The wisdom of such an item will be obvious to anyone who has drowned his clothing thoroughly. George Gehrke is the developer of a fine dry-fly dressing, but he has also perfected a two-finger stripping glove to protect the hands from cold water and chapping. The stripping gloves provide an alternative short of full-finger gloves.

The quality of the Hardy scissor pliers has declined in recent months but other similar tools are now available. The Fisherman's Pal is a six-inch scissor with plier points, file, screwdriver, and lead-shot crimper. Sunrise is also producing a long-nose scissor plier of a better design than the Hardy original, and I am using a pair at present. The large surgical hemostats that we have all carried for years have been supplanted by a smaller version that is less cumbersome.

Hank Roberts is still offering his famous stream knife, poetically called Walton's Thumb. It is made of surgical-quality steel, and it boasts a

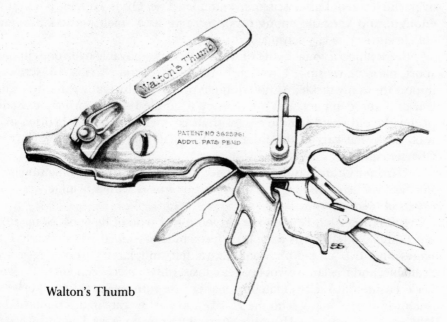

Walton's Thumb

startling array of features: It has clippers, tiny scissors, shot crimpers, fittings for widening and reusing shot, a stiletto point, and a knot-making tool. Walton's Thumb is a fishing cousin of the Swiss Army knife.

Orvis has recently introduced a similar product that folds compactly and is elegantly simple, like a man's cuticle knife from Tiffany. It has a small file, knife blade, and scissors. Its opposite end has retractable

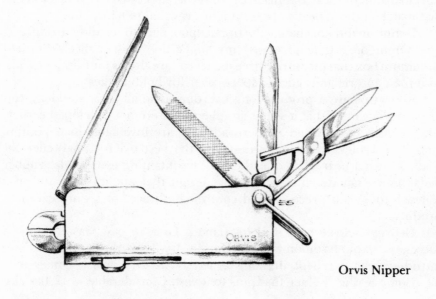

Orvis Nipper

clippers with a slim lever. The clippers retract and lock, closing the lever over the folded knife, scissors, and file. The Orvis Nipper is elegant enough, and versatile enough too, to serve as a small pocketknife and cuticle cutter in a city setting.

Since an occasional bottle of wine offers us enjoyable overtones in our sport, particularly since I lived in Europe for several years, a corkscrew is important to my tackle. Although the type carried by many wine stewards is useful and compact, and operates on a simple fulcrum principle, I still prefer the old wood-handle type with its corkscrew firmly embedded in a used cork that carries the faint bouquet of a fine Beaujolais or Corton Charlemagne.

Gardner Grant has the best advice on wines for trout-fishing lunches. *Vintages with screw-on caps or finger-holes,* he insists with a twinkle, *are poor choices in trout country!*

Bill Hunter has revived the old loose-leaf type of fly book. Some fine old things die hard. His dark brown cowhide loose-leaf has six white felt pages and two of lamb's wool. Extra felt and lamb's wool pages are available, and the lamb's wool pages consist of two pieces cemented back to back. Hunter also sells a matching leader case with six parchment pockets. Such wonderful items echo the Hardy and Farlow catalogues published a half century ago, and Hunter's charming shop in New Hampshire has many unique items—including some of the most elegant flies.

Randall Kaufmann offers a similar cowhide leader case, evolved from the Wheatley pigskin leader wallets of the past.

Dennison has designed an interesting new leader dispenser. It eliminates carrying six full tippet spools inside a four-inch case. Each leader pack provides a stainless cutter tip and is moulded from buoyant plastic. When the first edition of *Trout* appeared, I was critical of the color and workmanship of these Dennison cases. It was suggested that a silver Mylar that matched the Wheatley boxes might prove more handsome.

Dennison did not change the tippet-spool pack, but it did introduce its new Omni box. It leapfrogged my suggestion with a nicely finished aluminum box that measures three inches square. It has four tippet spools, with foam inserts in its lid and spool cover for holding flies.

Rod grips are a product long overdue. Like all first-rate ideas, rod grips are so simple that it seems strange they were not developed earlier. They consist of textured rubber pads that are invaluable in separating jammed ferrules. Laggies has designed the best nylon straightener for leaders, with a pear-shaped leather cover containing two circular rubber pads. The straightener is a pleasing design that applies pressure on a coiled leader with precision and control. Both accessories are excellent products.

George Gehrke perfected his famous Gink in past seasons, and its success is ample testimony to its value in dry-fly work. Laggies has also introduced its excellent dressing called Hi & Dry, which comes in a handsome leather holder that pins to a vest. Considerable work has also been done with leader sinks. Laggies' Fast-Sink is intended for application in advance of fishing, and must be allowed to dry an entire twenty-four hours. Seidel's 800 sink is another reliable product. However, many anglers believe that the new Gehrke's Xink is the finest streamside fly- and leader-sink yet formulated. It may yet convince a generation of old-time fishermen to forget about bentonite, marl, laundry soap, detergents, and a handful of alder leaves.

I dislike wading staffs, because I firmly believe that a staff can impart a false sense of security, leading an unwary angler to attempt currents and crossings he should not try. Too, most wading staffs are cumbersome when not in use. However, the new Folstaf circumvents the latter problem. It folds into twelve-inch sections of lightweight black-anodized aluminum, and is fitted with a cork grip. The staff unfolds and snaps instantly into its locked position, using the principles of post-tensioned structures. Such a wading staff can be carried in its belt holster or tucked into the bellows pocket in the back of a fishing vest.

Orvis has introduced some elegant leather-bound fly books with sheepskin linings. The fly books are available in two sizes: a small version for nymphs and pupal imitations and a larger size designed for big nymphs and streamers.

Since completing the chapter on equipment and accessories, I have acquired two 32-compartment Wheatley fly boxes. The elegant F1609 Wheatley is available again. Mine are filled with a rich assortment of no-hackle patterns dressed by René Harrop, and a full spectrum of sedges I tied myself. The boxes are so beautiful that I enjoy simply looking at their spring-lid compartments.

Carrying rods on long trips has become a little easier these days. Wray cases are merely designed to protect rods and reels in use, and are padded holsters intended for carrying tackle in a car or van. These cases are fabricated of ballistic nylon layers that sandwich a thin neoprene padding between their tough covering.

River Systems is making a similar rod jacket, using a strong nylon shell outside, a middle cushioning layer of urethane foam, and an inner layer of smooth tricot. These rod covers are not holster-shaped.

Artful Angler is selling two recent systems of protecting tackle in travel. Their zippered case is sheathed in eight-ounce parapac synthetic, a high-density plastic stiffener, a cushioning filler of polyfoam, and a liner of four-ounce coated nylon. It holds aluminum rod cases in webbing loops, has nylon web handles, and a nylon coil-zipper system. The Mark Pack system is completely different. It offers an obviously strong design, although sad experience tells me it is unwise to suggest that any system is airline-proof. The Mark Pack consists of paired two-inch tubes wrapped together in eleven-ounce Cordura nylon. The system will take four rods in their cloth sacks, or two standard aluminum cases. The Mark Pack is completed with a carrying strap, nylon webbing handle, and a lock-and-key closure system.

Thomas & Thomas makes a rod-carry system for six aluminum cases. It is constructed of heavy-duty marine canvas reinforced with leather at the corners. It is water repellent. The shoulder strap and handle make transporting it quite easy, and the rugged nylon-zipper closure offers a locking-ring capability.

Orvis makes a combination rod blanket and caddy that is excellent too. Its blanket holds eight two-piece rods in their sacks, and it may also be used with rods in their cases. The blanket is intended to cushion the rods inside a rod caddy, but inside their cases, it can be used with the Orvis traveller bag. It is made of dark brown urethane Cordura. It is water repellent, stainproof, and resistant to ripping and fraying. Locking zippers are provided the full length of the Orvis travel caddy and its pouches.

Orvis has stopped making its earlier canvas rod caddies. They were trimmed with leather and had an ingenious combination of case pouches, rod loops, and a continuous flap. The caddy was tightly rolled and secured with three leather straps, and the design was completed with a handle and full-length carrying strap. It was Ted Trueblood who jokingly observed that you should buy any product you really liked, because they would stop making anything really good. My favorite rod caddy is copied from the original Orvis design. It is made of thick, softly tanned cowhide and was specially made in Buenos Aires.

But the best rod caddy I ever saw belonged to my good tarpon-fishing friend Rip McIntosh of Palm Beach, and was custom-made in Costa Rica. It was constructed around a six-inch lightweight pipe of polyvinylchloride. The core was quite rigid and strong. Its outer shell was saddle leather, with a cap and carrying strap system. The leather cap could be locked. The big case was a gargantuan version of the leather scabbard cases first made by Orvis for its little Rocky Mountain bamboo rods.

It was the best that I have seen. *It was beautiful, all right,* McIntosh explained wryly one night at Iliamna, *it was so beautiful somebody stole it!*

There is a lesson in that story.

Small gadgets continue to emerge from the tackle industry. Some quickly disappear, but others survive and prosper. Russ Peak has developed a new line dressing that repels water so effectively that a line rides demonstrably higher in the surface film. It conditions the finish and restores its fresh suppleness, and it lubricates the line too. The Peak formula is excellent, and makes pickups and shooting easier, as well as floating the line high.

Thomas & Thomas recommends the new Schmidt high-speed line conditioner. Unlike paste cleaners, this product comes in liquid form. It leaves a smooth high-speed finish that adds distance to any caster, and prolongs the fishing life of modern lines.

We were skeptical, Tom Dorsey explains, *but it really works!*

Maxima has also expanded beyond its nylon leader material line with a new polyvinyl conditioner called Mono Slik. It cleans and lubricates our modern plastic finishes, adds to fly-line life, and is highly recommended among anglers.

Although weighting leaders is not exactly a favorite fishing technique, it is a deadly method under some conditions. Weighted leaders quickly prove themselves in extremely fast, broken currents. Early season finds fish lying deep in high water, its chill making them dour and listless. Big Alaskan rainbows have become caviar addicts by September, after a summer of gorging themselves on freshly spawned salmon eggs. No salmon ova ever drifted anywhere except in the bottom currents, and such eggs arrive dead drift over the gravelly shallows. Weighting the leader slightly is a perfect solution to these problems, and anglers have long used split shot and lead-strip Twistons.

Although they obviously work effectively, split shot and thin lead strips are a bit crude. Using progressively smaller shot, with finer sizes stepping down toward the tippet, is a simple refinement. Using shorter and shorter lengths of lead strips can accomplish the same thing. But there are better methods today. The popular, reusable shot have little tabs that permit them to reopen, but they are asymmetrically weighted, and tend to create eccentric patterns of drift and flutter.

Thomas & Thomas offers a rotary assortment of tiny French split shot. Such minute shot are not used for fly fishing in Europe, but are designed for fishing coarse species like roach and tench and chub. It is a world of slender Calcutta rods and fine nylons and quill bobbers.

The largest shot is still smaller than regular BB-shot, Len Codella told me recently, *and the tiny ones are like skeet loads—small enough for 6X and 7X tippets.*

Fly-Rite Sleeves and Shape-A-Wate are two fresh concepts in leader weighting. The lead sleeves are soft little tubes that are slipped on the leader above its barrel knots. They come in four weights and diameters and are conveniently packaged in a rotary pack, but the sleeves involve building leader knots on the stream.

Shape-A-Wate is completely new. It consists of a malleable lead putty that can be molded on the leader with the fingers. It can be increased after trial and error, or decreased with the fingernails, pinching the lead and stripping it off.

However, my favorite method of weighting a leader involves familiar materials: lead wire in fly-tying diameters and clear head cement. Such fly-weighting wire is available in diameters of .015, .025, .035, .045, and .055 inches, which offer a subtle progression in weight. Leaders can be butt-weighted just above the barrel knots, using fewer turns and finer diameters to balance them for sink rate, drift behavior, and ease of casting. Such leaders can be created and modified in the field, but they are best made up ahead of time, with the precisely coiled lead wire seated carefully in fly-head lacquer.

Dermot Wilson introduced the Aymidge extractor several years ago in southern England. It was simply a rudimentary stomach pump, intended to extract the insects from a living trout's stomach. Several modifications have evolved since. One doctor friend was concerned enough about damaging a trout's alimentary tract, and the clumsy introduction of air into its stomach, that he redesigned the concept. His design was more complex and six times as costly to fabricate. Thomas & Thomas offers a simple, new stomach analysis pump in its catalogue. It is similar to the first Aymidge design, with a slim polyvinyl tube and a finger bulb. It should be used with skill and care.

Monocle-type loupe magnifiers are available for anglers today. Such loupes offer two-and-a-half-power magnification; unlike loupe glasses, they are not permanently attached to our glasses frames. The loupe monocle frees both hands, and is carried in a fishing vest.

It turns midges into Wulffs, Len Codella laughs.

Thomas & Thomas also stocks a ten-power glass for studying insects and knot problems afield. It folds compactly into its own nickel-plated case. It is inexpensive and workable, and it can be attached to a pin-on lanyard cord inside a tackle vest.

Field entomology and fly-tying will both benefit from a stainless scale that offers graduations in both inches and millimeters.

Fishing clothes are changing too.

Cold-weather garments, rain gear, and other equipment are steadily improving. Even fishing gloves have changed. British Millar Mitts have long been available to anglers and duck hunters. They are hand-crocheted to fit snugly, and are eighty-five percent wool, keeping the fingers warm even when the wool is soaking wet. The fingertips are left free, offering good cold-weather dexterity.

Orvis Poly Mitts are woven from warm nonabsorbent polypropylene, and fit even more snugly than Millar gloves. When they are wet, you merely wring them out and they feel dry almost immediately. The cuffs are elastic and fit tightly. Poly Mitts leave the fingertips free, like the British designs, but they lack the scratchiness of wool.

Down-filled garments have achieved widespread popularity in recent years. Many have proved excellent. Designs that are fully quilted are better than those designs with tubular down-filled sections, because full quilting holds the down in place.

Tubular sections permit the down insulation to gravitate into lumps, leaving other areas relatively unprotected. Feathers are obviously less effective than down itself. Pale colors and bright chromatic hues are clearly ill-suited for fishing, and the bright yellow slicker is a laughable choice for the pursuit of trout. Camouflage is recommended, although it has echoes of the war-surplus stores, and it is not useful everywhere. Every season we see fishermen wearing camouflage clothing on western meadow streams, obviously secure in the belief that they are hidden from the trout. Contrast is the key factor, and in the late meadows the color of a newly made broom, camouflage is visible for miles.

Orvis produces a superb piece of cold-weather equipment in its Three-in-One jacket. It consists of a Gore-Tex windbreaker shell with four pockets that sheds rain well. The Gore-Tex shell has a superb quilted-down liner that zips out and fastens at the neck and cuffs. Although it is pocketless, it is a fine jacket in its own right. There is also a Gore-Tex down-filled rain hood that clips on the collar securely. The jacket gets its name from its wearers' options: the windbreaker rain jacket, the down jacket worn separately, and the rain shell and down liner worn together. It has served me well in mountain country and fishing the arctic latitudes of Iceland and Norway and Alaska.

However, the Orvis Three-in-One has fallen a partial victim to the Trueblood Factor. It was originally made in khaki and camouflage, but so many waterfowlers bought it that the khaki option was dropped. It is such a versatile garment that perhaps Orvis will elect to make its less-military design available again.

Orvis offers several fishing hats today. Its perennial favorite, the Irish wool tweed hat, which seems to have an alchemy capable of changing its owner's personality, is still available on its Vermont shelves. Irish fishing hats are stocked in olive Donegal, gray, and houndstooth tweeds. The Orvis Longbill hat is highly popular with guides in the Florida Keys, and offers a green underbrim to control glare. The Longbill shades the eyes quite well. Its rear brim folds down to protect the ears and neck from a searing sun, and also sheds rain outside the collar. Although it looks a little strange on trout streams, it is an excellent item of fishing gear. Orvis also makes a soft, folding helmet of tan poplin with a green brim liner to reduce glare. It is a fine hot-weather fishing hat with hooded air vents on its sides. Orvis recently introduced its folding black-fly headnet hat. Its design consists of a rain-shedding skullcap with a mesh hood that includes a circular stiffener just above the shoulders. It can be worn both with and without a regular hat. Fishermen who have suffered the summer mosquitoes of our western high country and Alaska, or have fought the fierce black flies of the Labrador, will welcome an Orvis headnet so light and compact it can be folded and stowed in a fishing vest.

Orvis makes several pieces of outstanding rain gear too. Its hooded wading jacket is designed for wearing over waders and a fishing vest. It has two wide-flap outside pockets for temporary storage of the flies and other gadgets you are using in the rain. Such details eliminate the fussing to get inside your rain gear to replace a tippet or fly, and then button up against the weather again. Its hood and cuffs have drawstrings.

Gore-Tex is a remarkable fabric.

It is completely waterproof, yet it inhibits perspiration, the *bête noire* of other foul-weather clothing. Gore-Tex consists of a film sandwiched between fabrics that breathe. Its waterproof film is a technical breakthrough that literally offers billions of microscopic pores. The pores are too small to pass water molecules in their liquid state, but water vapor and air pass through freely.

Testing has demonstrated that a vigorously exercising person produces as much as 2,500 grams of perspiration per square meter of skin.

Government studies determined that Gore-Tex is capable of transpiring up to 4,800 grams of moisture per square meter when it is laminated to fabrics that breathe too. It has quickly proved itself in the field.

The Orvis rainsuit includes both a hooded jacket and rain pants. Its fabric sandwiches the Gore-Tex film to a poplin composed of eighty-seven percent polyester and thirteen percent cotton. The jacket is thirty inches long and is fitted with a nylon zipper. Its zipper is covered with a Velcro-sealed storm flap. There are two small bellows pockets with large Velcro flaps too. Behind the cargo pockets are side-vent pocket hand warmers. The jacket has a raglan cut to facilitate active sports, and it has adjustable gusseted cuffs with Velcro tabs. Seams are waterproofed with tape and sealed. The matching rain pants offer similar construction, suspender buttons, and a drawstring waist. There are snap adjustment tabs at the ankles. Both jacket and trousers are fully lined.

Orvis also makes a crusher hat in a matching fabric and construction. It has introduced a Gore-Tex Longbill fishing hat too, designed for rain and wind, which keeps raindrops off your sunglasses and rainwater dripping outside your collar.

Old things are often worth keeping, and both silk and cotton are in this category. Leigh Perkins at Orvis understands such truths.

Silk and cotton are superb.

Silk is still the lightest, warmest insulation worn against the skin. Its qualities have long been understood in skiing circles. Orvis still offers undergarments cut from the finest Chinese silk, in both men's and women's sizes. Silk long johns are matched with long-sleeved T-shirts, and these silk garments are excellent.

Orvis has included cotton knit shirts in its recent catalogues. Both T-shirts and turtlenecks are listed. The cotton knit is relatively light and is a handsome olive khaki. These light cotton shirts are intended for layering under other garments, but can also be worn by themselves.

Marathon is still making conventional fishing slickers and rain jackets, which are considerably less expensive than Gore-Tex.

The Marathon slicker is made of lightweight vulcanized rubber over a seventy-denier nylon. It has a seamless raglan-style shoulder to facilitate casting. There is an attached drawstring hood, cuff snaps, and a back shoulder-vent design to reduce perspiration. Its fingertip length will cover hip-boot tops. It weighs only fourteen ounces.

The Marathon rain jacket weighs only six ounces and is cut from the same seventy-denier nylon coated with rubber. It also has an attached hood and elastic wrist cuffs. Like the slicker, the jacket has a fully zippered front covered with a storm fly, and two front pockets.

Marathon has also introduced a quilted rain parka at the top of its line. It consists of a rubber coating over a seventy-denier shell, and it has a drawstring hood, elastic wrists, a full-length zipper, and a storm fly. It is fingertip length and dark green. Unlike the slicker and wading-jacket designs, the rain parka has an insulative lining of nylon quilting. It is highly recommended for Alaska, Iceland, and the Labrador.

The matching rain hat is a crushable design of rubber-coated nylon. It is fully lined with cotton. The generous brim protects face, glasses, and neck, and there are concealed fold-out earflaps.

Polyester pile has recently been introduced to many sporting garments, and it has quickly acquired fierce partisans.

Polypropylene absorbs surprisingly little moisture, and in pile insulation, it wicks dampness away from the body so its warmth can evaporate it. When polyester pile is wet, wringing it out carefully will restore almost its full insulating qualities. It offers twice the insulation of wool at only half its weight. Like wool, synthetic pile retains its loft when wet, trapping air to sustain its insulation. No down-filled garment can match the performance of polypropylene and wool when it is soaked through. Perhaps the best-known fabric of this polypropylene specification is Patagonia cloth.

Patagonia makes a lightweight zip-front jacket with Velcro-cuff closure. There is a chest pocket of nylon, and the design includes two hand-warming pockets. The matching pile trousers feature a drawstring top and a single hip pocket. Both are dark navy blue.

Patagonia also produces a polypropylene underwear it calls expedition weight. It was designed for bitter conditions. Its fabric is a tight rib-knit type with a thickly brushed insulation. The tops are a three-button design with long sleeves; bottoms are completed wtih a spandex waistband, ankle cuffs, and fly. Both are also dark navy.

Fishing glasses have evolved quickly in these past months, adding polarization to the exquisite technology of photochromatic lenses. Such lenses are quite new. Their high-quality, optically ground glass is virtually distortion-free, and its lamination is guaranteed. Polarization extensively reduces glare and allows a fisherman to see fish more clearly. Their photosensitive glass also responds to varying levels of light, darkening at midday and becoming clear at nightfall. Such performance can mean substantially less eye fatigue in fishing.

The new sunglasses have handsome pilot-type frames, and come in tints of amber and gray. It is also possible to have these lenses in both single and bifocal prescriptions, although such technology is expensive. Amber lenses are like the familiar shooting glasses, which magnify lower levels of light on cloudy days, evenings, and early in the morning. Gray photochromatic lenses offer minimal color distortion, which is important in matching hatches. Both lenses are abrasion resistant and tempered, offering good protection to the eyes while fishing.

Several new wrinkles have also been added to survival equipment in the past five years.

Cutter insect repellent is still a leader in its field, and although it is expensive, it contains such a concentrated formula that a little works quite well. It has excellent skin life, does not smell noxious, and is not greasy.

Another product more recently introduced is called After Bite, and it contains an analgesic and subtle anesthetic that quickly relieves bites and stings. Both products really work.

Thomas & Thomas sells a pocket mini-screwdriver with its own protective cap and lanyard ring. It is about two inches in length, and has a one-sixteenth-inch screwdriver blade. The mini-driver is perfectly suited to repairing sunglasses and reels.

Another intriguing gadget from Thomas & Thomas is a magnesium tool for starting fires. Skillful use of this simple device triggers sparks of 5,400 degrees, sufficient to ignite even damp combustibles. The tool is only three inches long, but it ignites tinder quickly with its unique sparking insert, and it might save a life in the back country.

Thomas & Thomas also lists the old-fashioned infantry can openers, along with an ingenious pocket saw. The saw is a strong, abrasive wire with steel rings at opposite ends. It cuts firewood easily, and can be simply held taut between the hands, or fitted with a bowed handle of bent willow. Such a willow handle is easily rigged in the field, using either heavy leader material or fishing line.

Randall Kaufmann offers another unique item in his survival straw. It is a pocket water purifier that meets federal standards, and works instantly while water is sipped through its core system. It works without waiting, unlike boiling or the tablets issued in army kits, and it works on stagnant pools, turbid lakes, and streams, and water with high coliform counts. The water-purifying straw is intriguing.

Ever want a drink with cow-pies lying everywhere along the water? Kaufmann asks teasingly. *Carry the straw and you can!*

The perfect survival item for the collector of fine gadgetry is the Austrian flare pistol. It is a tiny nickel-plated pistol sold with a set of flares no larger than firecrackers. The Austrian mini-pistol fires a flare high enough to be spotted by rescue craft. It seems like an elegant toy, but it might save lives in a wilderness emergency.

Another recent experiment with a survival gadget was a laughable failure, but its testing did not occur at a critical moment of truth. Last year, when I was getting my equipment together for a trip into the Katmai wilderness of Alaska, a neighbor invited me for a drink. It was a welcome relief from packing. My hostess keeps several pets, has a surprisingly well-stocked aviary, and pampers a large herd of whitetail deer on the grounds of her estate.

She was worried about our trip. *It's the bears!* she blurted finally. *I'm worried about the bears!*

The Katmai has no shortage of bears, and it is not unusual to encounter them along its shallow rivers when the sockeyes are running. Sometimes we see a dozen bears in a day's fishing. My neighbor gave me a combination flashlight and tiny siren. It was designed for a woman's purse, and its batteries triggered a noise that was startlingly shrill.

It's for muggers, she explained.

Finishing my whisky, I promised to test her theory that its shrill warning would frighten the salmon-fishing bears. The gadget proved a complete failure in its field test, but my neighbor found that difficult to believe.

You really tried it? she challenged.

I tried it so many times on the Brooks, I told her puckishly, *that its batteries went dead the first day—and the bears never looked up!*

OBSERVATIONS ON THE MODERN FLY REEL

The developments in fly reels over the past few years have been both surprising and extensive. Changes have included the revival of old classics, which happily are back in production, and fresh examples of unusual new technologies.

Berkeley and Cortland were the first to explore recently developed materials. Their reels employ modern nylon and carbon-fiber materials in their frames and spools.

Berkeley introduced its reels first.

Its Specialist 2 and Berkeley 556 were the prototypes. Their spools were nylon and the backplates and frames were aluminum. Both designs display an unusual spindle technology, using a heavy tubular concept that has influenced later reels. The Specialist 2 easily converted to left- or right-hand wind, offered three drag settings, and incorporated a smooth-acting thumb brake.

The still newer Berkeley 500 has enlarged on these concepts, has corrected some of the spool problems first encountered with using nylon, and the aluminum reel frame is a single casting. Both are finished in a handsome nonglare black. Left- and right-hand wind is possible, and there are still three drag settings. Berkeley 500 reels include the 554 model, which weighs 2⅞ ounces and is designed for four- to five-weight lines. The 556 weighs only 3⅝ ounces and carries five- to seven-weight tapers. The 558 weighs a surprisingly little 3¾ ounces, and its capacity will handle eight- to ten-weight forward tapers. These hybrid reels of nylon and aluminum offer superb capacity-to-weight ratios, and at a surprisingly reasonable cost.

Cortland was the innovative firm that first experimented with carbon-fiber reels. Its exclusive CG series of reels is unique.

Graphite reels are a remarkable thirty percent lighter than aluminum reels of comparable size. Such lightness makes it possible to achieve the old bamboo rod-to-reel weight ratios with light synthetic rods of boron and graphite. These prototypes were almost unbreakable and self-lubricating. The entire reel, including its internal ratchets and drag-system fittings, is fashioned of carbon-fiber fabric. There are three sizes in this series: its little CG I is a 2⅛-inch reel weighing a surprising 2½ ounces, the CG II measures 3½ inches and weighs 2¾ ounces, and the CG III is a 4-inch reel weighing 3 ounces. Line capacity is comparable to conventional reels of such diameters. The Cortland CG reels come in a doeskin vinyl bag, are relatively inexpensive, and offer a unique capacity-to-weight ratio.

Except for the esthetically arbitrary ventilation pattern in their spools, the CG reels are quite handsome. The ventilation pattern is found close to the spindle, where it is critical if long casts and runs have occurred. There is no ventilation of the outer spool, where a fly line is most often wet.

Other reel news is less happy.

The Hart reels introduced a few years ago, and the Thomas & Thomas series based on the same prototypes, are no longer available. Sometimes mere excellence is not enough.

The elegant Walker reels are another tragic example. Like the Hart designs, the Walkers were the heirs to the patents and prestige of earlier makers like Conroy, Vom Hofe, and Zwarg. Their excellence echoes other jewellike machines bearing marques like Lagonda, Lamborghini, and Daimler-Benz. The reels still featured the closed-frame designs first patented in 1896, with their black side plates and German silver rims, and their elegant counterweighted handles.

The beautiful Walker reels are gone too, and the fishing world is less. *Some things should live*, my old friend Jim Rikhoff argues bitterly. *Sometimes I hate change!*

George Gehrke is a tacklemaker from southern Colorado, and is familiar with the big-fish water on the lower Arkansas. His country has been a crossroads in the history of the southern Rockies. Gehrke lives in the place the Spanish horse soldiers christened Salida, because it was their exit from the Sangre de Cristo basin into the heart of the Colorado high country farther north.

It's the roof of America. The old-timers in the Arkansas headwaters sat talking and whittling outside the Vendôme hotel in Leadville. *There ain't no rivers running into this country—they're born here!*

George Gehrke has long been known for his excellent dry-fly ointment called Gink, and in recent years he introduced a fine fly-wetting solution he wryly christened Xink. Gehrke is restless and peripatetic, and now he has turned his curiosity to reels.

His first reels were machined in Japan and were named in honor of George Selwyn Marryat, perhaps the finest British trout fisherman of the nineteenth century.

There were five Marryat reels in the original series. The basic concept of the Marryat series was similar to the Bogdan prototypes for Orvis, which evolved into the famous CFO line. The backplate and spindle are part of the reel frame. But other than its reel-shoe mounting and T-head spacer, the Marryat had no reel cage enclosing its spool. It was a brightly anodized gold. The reels were quite light for their line capacity, almost seeming fragile, and had a clumsy Victorian-looking medallion attached to the backplate. Some of the Marryat prototypes were imperfectly finished, and the spool-locking mechanism seemed too vulnerable to river silts and abrasives. It featured a deep-locking pin that seemed unlikely to self-drain well, and some expert fishermen complained about the bright finish and its visibility to skittish trout.

However, its internal improvements over other lightweight trout reels were less obvious. The reel shoe is not attached to the frame with rivets, which can work loose in time, but with tiny Phillips Screws. The ratchet and drag were unique, and proved better than the spring-and-pawl system found in the Hardy lightweight series and its several cousins.

The Gehrke design offered a surprising drag-setting capability in a light trout reel, and a solidly machined new concept.

His first Marryat reels had exposed-rim spools that were spool-drilled on their handle faces. The drag mechanisms were based upon a ratchet dish set on the spindle post. Both were machined from corrosion-resistant steel, and the spindle bearings were bronze. The cover plate was a bronze ratchet wheel. Spring-loaded pawls were pinned inside the ratchet dish. The assembly was solid and smooth.

The drag yoke is a fresh concept. It functions without moving parts, except for a cam-actuated setting centered on a Phillips-head screw. The yoke is shaped like a wishbone. Its drag shoes are fitted into notches at its tips, and an increased drag setting simply forces the yoke tips down more tightly into the ratchet-dish rim.

It is surprisingly simple and reliable.

The first drag shoes worried me, and I challenged Gehrke about their composition. *Don't worry,* he telephoned from Colorado, *I've already changed them—sent you a new yoke this morning!*

Gehrke is restless and quixotic.

His restlessness soon abandoned the first Marryat series, and I later found a dark chocolate-colored Marryat in the mail. It was a wide-frame Marryat MR-9. The prototype MR-8 designs had featured a $1\frac{1}{8}$-inch spool-and-frame assembly. The MR-9 had a $1\frac{5}{8}$-inch spool-and-frame width. Both the MR-8 and MR-9 were $3\frac{1}{8}$ inches in diameter. The reel-foot alloy and machining were obviously improved, the drag settings simplified, and Gehrke had wisely removed the ornate medallion from its backplate. The wide spool was counterweighted to reduce its wobble, a necessary modification that worked. But its monogrammed brass trapezoid was poorly designed, making one wonder why a simple dome-shaped weight was not tried instead, like the spool counterweights of older Victorian designs.

Gehrke has since changed his mind again.

His Marryat has been transformed into his Centurion II series. It is no longer manufactured in Japan, but is now machined here. It still has its smooth spool flange, which can be rim controlled with either fingertips or palms. With a drag-free setting, the reel still cannot overspin when a strong fish bolts. The drag yoke offers a full two pounds of drag, a setting that is unique in such a light fly reel. Centurion reels have passed some difficult tests. Prototypes have been immersed in a fifteen percent saltwater solution for twenty-five days without sign of corrosion. The reels have also been tested at 6,000 revolutions per minute, and passed those ordeals without wear on their stainless shafts and bronze bearings, with virtually no wobble.

Len Codella at Thomas & Thomas is quite excited about the Centurion reels. *Those reels have beaten tarpon better than a hundred pounds*, he said, *and you know about their reel-eating runs!*

Machined from solid aluminum bar stock, the Centurion series includes five models. The GR 70 is designed for four-weight lines and 150 yards of twelve-pound backing. The GR 75 takes a five-weight and 200 yards of backing, while the GR 80 holds a six-weight ahead of 250 yards. The GR 85 holds either seven- or eight-weight lines and 200 yards of twenty-pound backing line. The biggest Gehrke reel is the GR 90, which holds a ten- to eleven-weight line, with as much as 300 yards of Dacron.

The scope of recent innovation in fly-reel technology is quite unusual, considering that when compared to other sports, like skiing and golf, the fly-fishing market is virtually a cottage industry.

Hardy has been quite active too.

My earlier chapter on reels reported that the British makers were considering the return of old favorites like the Saint John, Saint George, and Perfect.

Those revivals subsequently took place.

The Saint John is still made only in the 3⅞-inch heavy trout size, weighing a full 8½ ounces. The elegant Saint George still has its beautiful drilled-spool design and agate line guard, which is mounted in a circle of German silver. It is also made only in a relatively large size, the 3½-inch model that weighs 7¾ ounces. Other popular models remain buried in the archives.

The Hardy Perfect has its own iconography. Our reverence for the Perfect has gathered religious intensity since its introduction in 1891. Its current incarnation is machined from more modern aluminum alloys. Our modern Perfects are slightly lighter in weight than the nineteenth-century prototypes. The small, truncated cone that secures the pedestal to the revolving handle plate is a concession to contemporary metalworking. The Perfects are machined to remarkably fine tolerances. The spindle is fitted with a circle of self-lubricating bronze alloy bearings, to produce its unusually smooth character and life-span. Perfects have three basic components: the perforated backplate and cage, the lightweight spool, and the solid reel-handle plate. The Perfects are made only in right-hand wind, and are not reversible. The 3⅛-inch model weighs 7½ ounces, and the intermediate 3⅜-inch Perfect weighs 8 ounces. The 3⅝-inch design is 8½ ounces. The Perfect series is revered for its solidity and its smooth running, rather than its lightness.

There are many anglers, myself included, who regret that the exquisite small Saint George reels have not been resurrected. There is still a single original in my collection.

Scientific Anglers has stopped selling its British-made reels, but Hardy found sufficient demand for these exposed-rim designs to keep making them at their Northumberland factory.

The reels have been given a new name, but the Hardy Marquis is essentially the old System series first introduced by Scientific Anglers. The reel cages of the Marquis are slightly lighter than the machining of the Hardy Lightweights. The spools are slightly heavier, between the exposed flange and a much heavier ratchet. The Marquis features a single pawl, and a unique circular spring encased in neoprene. It is a superb design, and American anglers are grateful to Harrich for keeping it available.

It's such a fine reel, Ted Rowe explained in his offices outside Boston. *We had no choice when 3M stopped selling them—keep making them!*

Hardy is still making the System models available before, from the 2³/₄-inch Marquis Four to the 3³/₄-inch Marquis Ten. The British market has caused Hardy to add a pair of larger models too, since Hardy is no longer making its salmon-sized Saint Andrews in the Lightweight series, and its drag-spring system had proved itself brittle on salmon. The Marquis Series has two recent models: its 3⁷/₈-inch spool sized to take 200 yards of backing behind a WF-10-F line, and a completely new 4¹/₈-inch reel that can hold 250 yards of backing with a WF-11-F saltwater taper. Western trout fishermen have adopted these big Marquis models happily in their autumn quests after big browns. The reels offer enough backing to make them feel secure on the alligator-size hookbills they find at Fontenelle dam on the Green, on the Big Horn in its arid Indian country, and between reservoirs in the Missouri Breaks.

Cortland continues to introduce new reels. Its Crown II series offers three sizes, with vented spools and rim-control flanges. The internal drag system is adjustable. There are no screws, the reel frame is a single aluminum casting, and the reels are reversible for either right- or left-hand winds. The small 3¹/₄-inch model is designed for four- and five-weight lines, and the 3¹/₂-inch Cortland takes six- to eight-weight tapers. The 3⁵/₈-inch design is intended for eight- and nine-weight lines, and 150 yards of backing on big-trout rivers.

We're proud of the Crown series, Leon Chandler told me at Boxborough this winter, *proud of both its quality and its price.*

Cortland has also introduced its new Graphite LTD series this past year. Like its Cortland Crown II reels, the LTD series offers three sizes. The spools are perforated to ventilate the line. The line guard is a two-way agate design, the spools are reversible for both right- and left-hand wind, and unlike the earlier Cortland graphites, its spool also offers rim-control drag. The reels are practically unbreakable, and are smooth running, with an excellent system of internal drag.

Sage has surprised fishermen with its recent introduction of a reel series, matching the superb glass and graphite rods they introduced at several western expositions in 1979.

We were excited by these rods at the show casting pools, but I did not actually fish one until I tried a six-weight on the Kulik, during an Alaskan trip the following year. It belonged to Les Eichorn, who was one of the founding officers at Sage. *We make a pretty rod that casts like crazy,* Eichorn told me over dinner in Sacramento. *We should make a reel to match it!*

Sage introduced those reels recently, and they are just as Eichorn promised that night, even to a richly anodized finish in a dark brown that matches the chocolate color of Sage graphite rods.

The British craftsmanship is obvious. The reels have the strength of a full-cage frame and are machined from a single billet of high-strength aluminum bar stock. The rolled-flange spool is intended for finger and palm work, and is mounted on a precise carbon-steel spindle. The adjustable drag-and-click system echoes the Hardy Lightweights. The drag setting, handle, spindle, cap, line guard, drag-spring studs, regulator screw and cover plate, pawl studs, and reel-foot rivets are entirely nickel silver. The click mechanism and drag system convert from left- to right-hand wind. The fittings and specifications are first-rate, and the final touch of elegance is the registered serial number on each Sage reel.

The Sage 505 is designed for light trout fishing. It measures $3\frac{3}{16}$ inches and is sized for four- and five-weight lines. The 506 is a medium-size reel of $3\frac{1}{2}$ inches that takes five- and six-weight tapers with a workable backing capacity. The 509 reel is the workhouse model in the Sage line, since it is $3\frac{3}{4}$ inches in diameter, weighs $8\frac{1}{2}$ ounces, and will store 240 yards of Dacron behind a WF-9-F line. Sage reels are handsomely made, richly colored, and worth their slightly higher price.

Fenwick has also surprised the fishing world with its new series of fly reels, although a firm that developed the first graphite rods should be expected to explore fresh ground.

Jim Green is responsible for these innovations, in both rod tapers and reels, and is among the finest tournament casters who ever lived. The new World Class reel series is the result of his collaboration with a circle of exceptionally talented engineers in Seattle, a center of high-technology aircraft firms. It was such proximity that led Fenwick to develop the first fly rods made of carbon graphite, when that material was still an aerospace oddity.

The Class 2 Fenwick is a light-trout design. It offers a strong cage of solid aluminum bar stock that has a handsome gold finish. Its perforated spool is anodized in a matte-black finish, with a gold spindle-cam cover. It is designed for trout fishing, and except for its coloring, it looks much like other expensive reels; but its important differences lie between its spool and backplate.

Our drag system is unique, Green argues.

The system has two separately adjustable controls: One monitors its click tension, and the other controls drag itself. Since these controls are separate, the Fenwick can be converted to either right- or left-hand wind without removing its spool. There are no pawls to change or install backwards. Each control button adjusts the setting between its prestressed spring and its separate pawl. The result is a wider spectrum of drag settings than other reels. Its minimum is capable of damping spool overrun, and its maximum setting is a fivefold increase. It is a superb system for most trout fishing.

The Class 4 Fenwick, along with the Class 6 and Class 8 Heavy-Duty models, features a completely different drag concept.

It offers a multiple-disk clutch system that poses carbon-steel plates against shoes of oil-impregnated bronze alloy. Fenwick believes that these materials offer significant advantages over other reels, which usually offer drag shoes of cork, leather, or mica. Metal to metal offers excellent dissipation of heat and will wear longer. And such older drag shoes cannot lubricate themselves like alloys of oil-impregnated bronze. The Fenwick alloys also resist deformation during long fights with big fish, or when a drag setting is fully tightened.

Its drag mechanism is different as well. Other reels exhibit a direct relationship between drag settings and rewind resistance. The Fenwick is free of such parallels. Its drag-loading system is completely independent of its spool, and it turns easily regardless of its drag.

The drag system is really tough, Jim Green describes it with quiet pride. *We've stripped four hundred yards off our bigger reels at thirty miles an hour—and there was no binding or fading.*

The Class 4 Fenwick is a direct-drive reel ideally suited to big water and large trout. It has a solid-plate spool that is counterweighted to damp its wobble at high rates of spin. The Class 6 model is of identical size, but has an exposed drag-setting disk and has antireverse drive. The Class 8 Fenwick is a big reel too muscular for trout fishing—it has been designed for billfish and tarpon.

It's a little more than you need for trout, Green comments quietly and smiles.

Orvis has busily added new reels to its catalogues in recent years. Its Battenkill series may not appear unusual, but these reels conceal some remarkable new technology behind their solemn façades, and at a surprisingly low price.

The Battenkill Mark series is alone in offering elegant trout reels cast from modern magnesium alloys. Their strength and lightness, relative to their line capacity, is unique. The one-piece frame (the reel foot is an integral part of the casting) and the spool are both cast from high-technology alloys. Like the more expensive CFO series, there is no reel cage to enclose the spool, and the wide spool flange permits finger drag and palming. The drag system employs a single-pawl spring. Conversion from right- to left-hand wind is easy, and the chromium line guard is switched with a common screwdriver. Unlike many reels, the backplates of the Battenkill series are fully drilled and ventilated.

We're excited about them, Leigh Perkins explains excitedly, *and our new Catinos are exciting too!*

The Catino reels now offered at Orvis were originally designed for salt water, but like the smaller Bogdans and Fin-Nors, they have started to attract some big-trout partisans.

Catino reels are elegant trucks, and if the delicate CFO is a finely tuned Jaguar, the Catino is a Kenworth or Peterbilt. Both its spool and its cage are machined from costly H-18 5056 aluminum bar stock, with heavy spacers and reel-foot designs. The bottom spacer is unusually wide, to provide a bearing surface for palming the spool that protects the hand from wildly spinning loops of line. There is no reel cage, but the spindle is machined from a highly tempered alloy of magnesium-chrome steel, rooted in the strong 5056 backplate. Other components and fittings are either corrosion-resistant steel or hard-anodized aluminum. The spools are a gunmetal finish, with polished bronze spindle caps and counter-weights that reduce high-speed wobble. The Catino Bonefish is a 3½-inch reel weighing 6¼ ounces, with a capacity of 200 yards of twenty-pound backing behind a WF-8-F taper. It has grown popular with anglers who fish big rainbows on our western rivers. Its big brother has a heavy gold-finished backplate, and is called the Catino Tarpon. It measures 4⅜ inches in diameter, weighs 12 ounces, and carries 400 yards of thirty-pound backing behind a WF-12-F saltwater taper. It is too much reel for trout fishing, but it is better looking than its salty competitors—other well-made trucks like the Fin-Nor and Seamaster and Pate.

The elegantly machined Ross is another recent entry in the reel market. It is the child of Ross Hauck, an engineer from northern California, in the watersheds of the Smith and Trinity and Klamath.

We thought about bad jokes like "reel beauty," Hauck admits wryly, *but we thought better of it—when a guy pays hard money for an expensive reel, he deserves more than cute—it's just the Ross!*

His reels are machined from three-pound billets of solid aluminum bar stock. After the precision machinework, the spool and frame weigh between three to four ounces, depending on model and capacity. But there are several other reels machined from solid H-18 stock, and it is the drag system that is unique.

It has no leaf springs, no sinter-steel pawls, and no ratchets. There is only a single button which tightens a Delrin drag button against the cam-plate assembly on the interior face of the spool. Delrin is a new synthetic material with properties beyond the Teflon drag systems tried on other reels. There are merely a tubular spool shaft that receives a large set screw, the spool itself with its cylindrical spindle, the reel frame and foot, and its linear set-screw drag. There is no ratchet-click system. Without conven-tional back pressure, the reel simply free-spools against its Delrin button. The Delrin drag button provides both drag when the spool is surrender-ing line and antireverse tension when retrieving. The Ross is simplicity itself.

And it's really tough, says Randall Kaufmann, a staunch supporter. *Hauck ran over his with a jeep, and the only thing hurt was the handle!*

The smooth action is also achieved with hard-tempered stainless bearings. Hauck is a painstaking technician, and his bench testing of the Ross prototypes involved some torture. He rigged the test reel to a belt drive system, tightened his Delrin drag button down full, and ran it at 2,450 revolutions per minute. His torture test lasted twenty-four hours, totalling more than eight million revolutions.

There was no measurable thermal effect, in spite of the obvious friction, and the crown of the Delrin drag button had deformed less than .003 inch. No other discernible wear had obtained.

Hauck builds three trout reels. The Ross One is slightly less than three inches in diameter and weighs 3.14 ounces. It can hold a DT-4-F floating line and thirty yards of backing. The Ross Two measures 3⅛ inches, weighs 3.38 ounces, and can accommodate a DT-5-F with twenty-five yards of backing. The Ross Three is 3⅜ inches in diameter. It weighs just a whisper over 4 ounces, and can carry a DT-6-F double taper ahead of seventy-five yards.

Ross RR-3 Reel

My only criticism of the Ross designs lies in their ventilated spools. Victorian flywheels used almost floral curves, with some of the sensuality of Art Deco esthetics, in their spokes. Although some of these early machines were designed with such ornamentality in mind, there were functional reasons too. The curvilinear spokes grew thickly from their drive-shaft housings, where stress transfer is greatest, and grew elegantly thin where they joined the flywheel itself. Their floral curves were not just esthetic decisions; they also understood that tangential load transfer placed less stress at the connecting points of such flywheels.

The flower-petal spokes of the Ross design are merely esthetic devices, totally unrelated to the function of stress transfer in machines. Mere prettiness, with little basis in technology or function, is a kind of florid thinking that has no place in modern engineering and design—giving the Ross spool some visual echoes of past die-cut cheapness.

Hauck has subsequently introduced his Ross Three-Five reel. It measures 3⅜ inches in diameter and weighs 4.2 ounces. Unlike its earlier cousins, the Three-Five has a solid, nonventilated spool. Its face still has the flower-petal pattern, but in a subtle *bas-relief* effect. It is counter-weighted to reduce wobble. The entire reel is anodized in a gunmetal color, including its foot assembly, and its concentric ornament and trademark are a handsome silver. The owner may have his own name engraved in silver at extra cost. The Ross Three-Five will hold a WF-8-F forward taper and 250 yards of backing.

These Ross designs are exquisitely made, in a family production line that includes soft reel bags sewn by Hauck's wife. There is even a special polishing cloth developed for anodized aluminum finishes, and each reel is sold in a hand-finished Ponderosa box from the valley itself.

Based on their quality, and their line-to-weight ratios, the Ross series of reels is likely to join the ranks of first-rate tackle.

They're great! Randall Kaufmann told me recently. *Who else would give his customers a lifetime guarantee?*

INDEX